PROFESSIONAL FLORISTRY TECHNIQUES

Professional Floristry Techniques

MALCOLM ASHWELL
SALLY PEARSON

The Crowood Press

First published in 1995 by Farming Press

This edition published by
The Crowood Press Ltd
Ramsbury, Marlborough
Wiltshire SN8 2HR

www.crowood.com

This impression 2004

British Library Cataloguing-in-Publication Data
A catalogue record for this book is available from the British Library.

ISBN 0 85236 570 5

All cover and text photographs by John Blyth except for pages 131, 133, 140, 143 and 30 (top).

Colour section photographs by Nigel Blythe

Cover design by Carol Jarvis

Typeset by Galleon Typesetting

Layout design by Liz Whatling

Printed and bound in Singapore by Craft Print International

Contents

Acknowledgements

We would like to thank John Blyth for his excellent photographs. All work was made up by the authors except for pieces by Christine Harbutt NDSF, FSF and Eileen Ward NDSF, FSF.

We would also like to thank Paul Norman NDSF, FSF, AIFD for his guidance with the chapter on continental design, and Sharon Austin and Ros Blyth for their help with the typing.

Introduction

It would be difficult, not to say foolhardy, to try to produce a definitive set of rules for the right way to make a piece of floristry work. So much depends on personal choice and preference, whether it be for a certain colour, flower or style. This must invariably influence a person's perception and appreciation of something as ephemeral as a display of flowers. Scent and even certain combinations of flowers can trigger emotional responses or memories which also affect a person's reaction to a particular piece of work.

Practical guidelines, however, are needed on construction techniques, whether it be something as simple as a buttonhole flower or the decoration of a church or marquee with many large displays. This nuts and bolts knowledge is invaluable as a starting point. Many good cooks use a recipe to begin with and then adapt and modify it to their own ideas, making it much more personal and individual. The opportunity to express personal style and individuality within floristry work makes it such an enjoyable and challenging field to work in. As with any learning process, however, the basic fundamental knowledge must be fully assimilated before experimentation can take place.

Floristry students embarking on a course of training face an ongoing conflict of opinions. On the one hand they are keen to try out their own ideas on pieces of work, but at the same time they must adhere to a clear set of criteria in order for their work to be assessed. It is only after the basic rules are understood and can easily be put into practice that experimentation can effectively take place.

Professional florists are often asked to make a piece of work which is very different from or opposite to their own taste. This can be difficult to deal with as most practical floristry work relies heavily on the individual's own skills and abilities, which in turn are based on their own definite ideas and preferences. Guidance and advice should be offered, but it is the customer's request which must always be interpreted in a considerate and thoughtful way.

Floristry and its associated subjects form a vast area of study. Many new plant varieties, techniques and sundries are constantly being introduced, which enable the florist to experiment and develop skills and techniques all the time. Nobody can say, 'I know all there is to know,' as we are learning all the time at whatever level of skill we have achieved.

This book sets out to explain the widely recognised and practised basic techniques and styles of floristry work. It should be thought of as a beginner's guide to how to make a wide range of commercial floristry items which are acceptable within the trade and within teaching and training establishments today.

Above all, personal development and individuality should always be encouraged. In a world which seems to demand uniformity and mediocrity in nearly everything we do, floristry or working with flowers and plants provides us with an ideal opportunity to be different and to create something individual and unique!

Malcolm Ashwell
Sally Pearson
May 2001

CHAPTER 1

Buying, Care and Conditioning and Storage of Fresh Plant Material

BUYING

All flowers purchased should be in first-class condition and as fresh as possible. There are many ways of sourcing flower material nowadays and it is a good idea for the florist to deal with at least four suppliers, as this gives the opportunity for choice. If one supplier can't get a particular order, others may be able to. It is important to have a local grower if possible amongst the suppliers – invaluable when the shop is running short of material. It is very difficult to predict sales on a daily basis.

It is ideal if the florist can go to a market regularly, as there is the flexibility of being able to choose and also negotiate the price. Alternatively it is possible to get to know the wholesalers from whom flowers can be purchased by telephone and sent by parcel rail, but it is not a good idea doing this if the wholesaler is not known to the florist as poor-quality flowers may often be included.

Some florists would say there is more choice buying from wholesalers who will call at the shop on a regular basis. It is all a question of what suits the individual. There are many suppliers who travel to Holland two or three times a week from the UK. They have a regular clientele and will take orders before they buy.

Some wholesalers are locally based and buy in from many sources, ordering direct from the Dutch markets, Guernsey flowers or Carmel, to name a few. There are quite a number of markets across the country, New Covent Garden being the biggest. They then distribute the flowers to their customers on a regular basis. Contrary to popular belief, there are a lot of English growers and the quality is excellent.

The Dutch flower markets not only sell Dutch-grown flowers but source from all over the world: Israel, Colombia, Italy, South Africa, Spain and the UK. So there is a vast choice of flower and plant material. All florists should make sure they visit the Dutch flower auctions and see the magnificent array of flowers available.

Buying flowers is a skill which is acquired through experience, but some fundamental knowledge is essential. Flowers are mostly sold in bunches of 5, 10, 20 or 25 or by weight and they are graded according to EU standards. The bunching and grading will vary depending on the type, stem length, colour and number and size of the flower heads per stem, but generally quantities within a flower type are standard in all wholesale outlets.

The following list gives the usual number of stems per bunch or the way sold for some of the more popular flower varieties available commercially:

Variety	*No. of stems per bunch*
Roses (standard)	20
Roses (spray)	10
Carnations (standard)	20 or 25
Carnations (spray)	5 or 10
Gerbera (standard)	box of 50
Mini gerbera	box of 50
Gladioli	5 or 10
Lilies	10
Freesias (specific colour)	10
Freesias (mixed)	5 or 10
Tulips	10
Bouvardia	10
Alstroemeria	10
Anemones	10
Chrysanthemums (single spray)	5
Chrysanthemums (double spray)	10
Chrysanthemum blooms	box of 30
Daffodils and narcissi	10
Irises	10

(cont.)

Cymbidium orchids	per bloom or per stem
Phalaenopsis orchids	per stem
Singapore orchids	5
Dahlias	10
Solidago	5
Aconitum	5
Liatris	10
Trachelium	5
Gypsophila Limonium }	bunches of about 5 stems or bundles of 5 bunches (always sold by weight)

The cost depends on the availability and demand worldwide. Various booklets give information on this. Many flowers are on the market the whole year round nowadays, as they are grown all over the world, enabling us to purchase flowers which were only available seasonally in the past.

It is unusual for any commercial cut flowers or foliage to be sold without some form of protective wrapping. The most widely used is clear cellophane paper, usually as a protective 'sleeve' which safeguards the flower heads from damage. For certain types of flowers such as roses there is also a protective inner wrapping of corrugated paper to avoid bruising and to prevent the flowers from opening too soon. Anemones are completely covered with dark tissue to stop the flower developing.

It is a good idea to keep the protective wraps on the flowers until they can be properly conditioned but note that if the weather is hot or the flowers are exposed to direct sunlight, condensation can occur on the inside of the wraps and discolour or mark the flowers.

When removing the wrapping, always cut the paper free rather than pulling it down the stems. This will avoid snapping off any flower heads which catch or snag against the plastic. Lilies and spray chrysanthemums are particularly prone to this.

Nowadays the aqua-pack is commonly used by growers and wholesalers. This is a packaging method whereby the flowers are packed in bunches, often wrapped in cellophane and placed in a bucket containing a small amount of water, which is then packed into an upright box. Although in water, the flowers will still need to be unpacked on arrival at the shop and conditioned correctly according to their specific requirements. It is not enough just to put them in the cold store as they are.

There are certain basic points and procedures to follow when receiving flowers into the shop:

- The flowers should appear firm and have good colour in the petals.
- Look for any broken or damaged heads.
- Look for any discoloration or petals dropping. This indicates disease or it could be that the flowers are old.
- The leaves on the stem should be green and not show any yellowing.
- Look for signs on the bottom of the stems of yellowing or a smell. These indicate that the flowers have been stored for some time.
- The calyx should be green and firm; yellowing on the calyx means that the flowers are old.
- Brown or yellow marks on the calyx indicate that the flowers are old or may have botrytis (a fungal disease).
- During warm humid weather flowers tend to sweat and overheat, leading to botrytis forming amongst the petals. This is particularly evident in roses which are closely packed. Apparently good-quality flowers may well have damaged petals so always check carefully after opening the pack.
- Flowers such as lilies, spray carnations and bulbs should have some colour showing in the buds; if they are too green they will not develop. On the other hand, if they are too open they will have a much shorter vase life.
- Look for strong, straight stems. Cheaper carnations often have very weak stems.
- Sometimes during very cold weather flowers suffer from the effects of the cold temperature during transit, and this may not be obvious at first. If they do not recover after conditioning, then they should be returned and credit given. Most suppliers have a code to follow whereby the florist should inform them within a certain time if the purchase is not up to standard.
- If carnation petals are shrivelled and marked at the edges, this indicates ethylene gas damage and the flowers will not open.

Tip

If using lilies in wedding work, think ahead and buy in a week before they are required, as they are always sold very tightly in bud and must open to give maximum impact.

When purchasing foliage similar rules apply. Never buy foliage which has smelly stems or yellowing, damaged leaves. Old foliage will usually have yellowing lower leaves and the leaves at the top will be curled at the edges.

These are only a few of the basic guidelines when purchasing flowers and foliage. There are many points to look for which are peculiar to individual varieties, but this knowledge will come with experience of handling a wide range of material.

A golden rule is that if in doubt, don't accept the purchase. Quality is the most important factor when purchasing flowers. Bad buying can ruin a business, as can a reputation for selling old flowers.

CARE AND CONDITIONING

All fresh materials need some initial conditioning treatment before being used in floristry work. Conditioning is essential for commercially purchased as well as locally harvested materials.

The main reason for carrying out this work is to ensure that the cut materials are able to absorb as much water as possible through the stem prior to use. As soon as a stem is cut from the parent plant, the cut surface begins to dry, forming a seal to prevent the loss of valuable water. The existing moisture within the stem continues to be lost through the remaining surface area of the flower or leaf, and if no available replacement is absorbed from the base, the flower quickly becomes dehydrated and wilts.

This process cannot be avoided when harvesting flowers but can easily be corrected provided the flower does not dry out for too long a period. There is a point at which serious damage can be caused to the internal cell structure due to total water loss and even with subsequent treatment the flower will not revive. Therefore, as a general rule of conditioning, all cut plant material should be placed in water as soon as possible after it has been harvested. Some plants have a greater resistance to wilting than others due to the greater amount of stored water in their leaves or flowers. Materials which have thicker fleshy leaves and petals such as tulips and orchids are better able to withstand prolonged water loss than flowers with thinner papery petals like roses or lisianthus.

It is important to minimise the rate of bacterial growth in the water, which is caused by decomposing plant material and results in the water turning green. This in turn reduces the amount of water the flower is able to absorb through the stem and shortens its vase life. Flower food is useful in dealing with this problem and should always be used. One of its main ingredients is an antibacterial agent, which keeps the water clean and by preventing bacterial growth and providing soluble nutrients can almost double a flower's vase life. Buckets and vases used for storing or displaying cut flowers should always be cleaned regularly with hot water and bleach to prevent a build-up of sediment and bacteria. The water should be changed every few days in any long-term displays or storage.

Another result of plant decomposition is the production of ethylene gas. It is odourless, and even relatively small amounts of it can dramatically shorten the life of a flower. Some species of flower are more susceptible to it than others, in particular roses and carnations. Ethylene causes limpness and general wilting in flowers which are otherwise well conditioned. Stored fruit also produces ethylene and even a bowl of fruit near a vase of flowers can make a considerable difference to its life. Good ventilation to disperse the gas is thus necessary. This is particularly important when flowers are stored commercially for a period of time in either a cool room or cold store.

Water temperature can affect the way some flowers respond to conditioning. Ice cold water is not recommended. Room temperature is the general rule, although lukewarm water will aid water uptake because it contains less air than cold water.

Before discussing specific conditioning methods, it is worth giving a checklist of easy commonsense things to do to ensure the freshness and longevity of cut material.

- Before placing a stem in water, always re-cut the end at an angle with a sharp knife to remove the damaged and dry cells.
- Remove any leaves which would be submerged and foul the water. With very leafy materials it is a good idea to remove some of the existing foliage to reduce water loss.
- Add flower food to the water.
- Stand buckets of flowers or leaves in a cool, shaded place to allow the flower to drink for at least two or three hours before use. Some material will need even longer.
- Do not overcrowd buckets or storage vases with material. Allow enough space for air to circulate between the stems and blooms.

- Whenever possible, stand flowers in tepid or room temperature water. Tepid water will also hasten bud opening, which is particularly useful during the winter months when many commercial flowers are in tight bud.
- Always choose flowers just before their peak of maturity. These will continue to develop after cutting and remain in better condition than a flower which has reached or passed full maturity.

Conditioning Flowers

The method of conditioning a plant depends on its stem structure: soft, hard, hollow or woody. Each type requires different treatment. Many bulb flowers such as tulips, irises and nerines have soft, fleshy stems, whilst harder stems range in thickness from those of carnations and roses to the large woody branches of lilac and protea. Many of the so-called summer garden flowers like lupins and delphiniums have hollow stems, whilst bleeding stems or those which exude large amounts of sap when cut include euphorbia, poppies and daffodils.

Woody stems

A great deal of woody-stemmed material is now commercially available. Shrubby flowers such as forsythia, prunus, viburnum and lilac are grown to provide early blossom. This type of branching material is extemely useful for large displays or as a distinctive or unusual addition to the more familiar florists' flowers.

The stems of these flowers are all generally hard, woody branches, which can have difficulty in absorbing water. Previously it was widely held that the base of the stems should be crushed with a hammer; however, this idea has now been challenged. Although the basic principle of splitting the stem is correct, excessive crushing can cause more harm than good, as crushed stems are not able to absorb water and so when submerged quickly begin to decompose. It is now thought to be more effective if the stem is split with a knife. A cross-cut of about 3.5 cm in depth at the base of the stem is sufficient.

Another problem associated with certain types of shrubbery flowers is wilting foliage. Even with correct conditioning the foliage will still wilt whilst the flowers remain firm. Possibly this is because the combined demands for water from both the flowers and the leaves is too much for the cut branch to sustain. This is particularly noticeable with lilac and prunus. Removal of some or all of the foliage not only allows the blossoms to receive more water but also enables them to be seen to much greater advantage.

Woody-stemmed flowers

Forsythia	Philadelphus
Prunus	Malus
Lilac	Rhododendron
Azalea	Viburnum
Trachelium	Daphne
Salix	Spiraea
Escallonia	Larger roses
Chrysanthemum blooms	Stocks

Hollow stems

Many of the so-called old-fashioned or garden flowers such as delphiniums and lupins have hollow stems. Most of these have the taller spiked shape which is so useful for adding height to a design.

As soon as the stem is cut from the parent plant, air enters the open stem and is trapped inside when the stem is placed in water. As the flower tries to absorb the water, the air is forced up the stem until it reaches a point at which it cannot escape, usually just below the neck of the flower, and thus effectively reduces or blocks the water supply to the bloom.

This can be prevented by holding the flower upside down and carefully filling the stem with water, which forces out the air. Then place your thumb over the end of the flower and put it in a bucket of water to drink normally.

When the flowers have to be taken out of water before arranging, a plug of cotton wool or tissue paper is also useful to prevent air from entering the stem again. Another popular remedy is to pass a fine pin through the stem just below the flower to allow the air to escape.

Hollow-stemmed flowers

Delphiniums	Gerbera
Lupins	Larkspur
Some types of spray chrysanthemum	Narcissi/daffodils (see next section)
Eremurus	Kniphofia
Hollyhocks	Alliums

Bleeding stems

A few types of flower and plant material lose a great deal of stem sap when cut. In some instances this loss is so acute that liquid drips from the end of the stem almost as soon as it is cut. This continues until the cut surface dries and forms a natural callus, by which time the flower will have lost valuable moisture. Unfortunate side effects of this problem are that in many cases the sap is poisonous to other flowers sharing the same water and the sap can also cause severe irritation on the handler's unprotected skin.

The treatment for this problem is perhaps the most dramatic form of conditioning. The base of the stem is passed through a flame (match or candle) for a few seconds to seal or cauterise the wound. This stops the flow of sap but does not prevent the flower from drinking. The flower can then be placed in water as with normal conditioning and safely mixed with other flowers. If the stem is cut again prior to arranging, the process will have to be repeated.

Boiling water can be used as an alternative to a flame to seal the ends of stems. Place just the tips of the stalks in the water for a few seconds and take care to protect the flowers and foliage from the steam.

When picking and conditioning flowers of this type it is a good idea to wear protective rubber gloves and to avoid any contact with the mouth or eyes. Many types of plant sap can cause allergic reactions such as skin rashes, itching, blistering and burn-like symptoms. People have different physical reactions to various plants and flowers but particular care should be taken when handling any plant material which bleeds a white milky latex sap, which is common in most types of euphorbia. The helleborus group also has an especially irritating sap, which causes a burning sensation.

Daffodils and narcissi, although hollow-stemmed, are best treated in this group of flowers, as when cut they exude a clear sticky sap that can poison other flowers if they are mixed with them immediately after picking. Because of their very soft stem structure, they cannot be burnt to seal the stem ends. The most effective treatment is to stand them in water on their own immediately after cutting to allow the flow of sap to stop. After a couple of hours they can be mixed and arranged with other flowers.

Bleeding-stemmed flowers

Most types of euphorbia
Poppies (oriental and annual)
All types of ficus

Some Specific Conditioning Techniques

Gerbera

This often arrives from market very limp. Stems should be cut and placed in water, and the flower heads can be supported by either chicken wire or the packing material from the box in which they were purchased. This will straighten the stems.

Bouvardia

Sometimes this does not take water easily and needs frequent re-cutting of the stem and removal of most of the foliage. The addition of flower food will encourage water uptake.

Carnations

Always cut the stem between the nodes, as the stem will not take water if cut on the node. Keep away from any damaged flowers or fruit, as carnations are very sensitive to ethylene gas.

Euphorbia

Seal the bleeding stems by passing through a flame or dipping the ends into boiling water for a few seconds. Then place into cool water. Remove the foliage as this tends to droop very easily.

Irises

Remove the white stem at the base as this does not take up water easily. Cut stems frequently.

Lilac

Remove all foliage and soften the woody stem by dipping the end in boiling water before placing in cool water.

Lilies

Handle very carefully as the flowers are very susceptible to bruising. They can be held in cold store to slow down the maturing process.

Lily of the valley

Forced lily of the valley is sold on the root and may be stored thus for up to two weeks in cool conditions. When the roots are cut, the flowers should be placed in water immediately.

Ranunculus

If they are limp, cut the stems, wrap tightly in tissue or waxed paper tightly and place in water.

Roses
Remove lower leaves carefully and de-thorn without damaging the bark. Wrap tightly in tissue, cut the stems and place in cool water. If the head is wilted and bent, re-cut the stem and place it in boiling water for a few seconds (this encourages the flow of water) and then place in cool water.

Stocks
This flower will last well if the water is changed daily and flower food added. Remove all the lower foliage and the white root.

Violets
These flowers are sold dry-packed in bunches in boxes. They should be cut and immersed in a bowl of water for a few hours. On display they should be sprayed regularly.

Conditioning Foliage

Conditioning of foliage often consists of no more than re-cutting the base of the stems and standing in water. With a little extra care, however, leaves and foliage can be prepared so as to extend their vase life quite considerably.

Commercially grown foliage tends to be evergreen or at least quite hardy and tough species. It is this quality which has made them so popular, requiring as they do so little in the way of specialised treatment. The main necessity upon delivery is to re-cut the base of the stems, loosen the bunches to allow air through the foliage, remove any foliage which may be below the water level and stand loosely in buckets of shallow water. It is only some of the more unusual garden types of leaves which need particular methods of treatment.

Wherever possible, choose mature foliage, as it responds much better to being used in an arrangement than very soft young growth. However some leaves, such as lime and birch, are particularly beautiful in their juvenile stage. To ensure these young leaves last when used in a mixed display, they should be allowed to drink and harden up for a couple of days before use. Any problems or wilting will become apparent before they are put in an arrangement. Young individual leaves can be conditioned in this way too, in particular hosta, bergenia and ivy. Any foliage, especially young leaves, should be placed in water as soon as possible after being picked. If allowed to dehydrate for too long, they might not recover at all.

Some leaves benefit from being completely submerged for one or two hours before use or normal conditioning. Again, larger leaves such as hosta and bergenia respond to this treatment but should not be left under water for too long. The leaf surface of very soft or young foliage will become transparent if left too long. Ideally water should be at room temperature, as if it is too cold, discoloration will result.

Foliage which has a greyish 'bloom' over the leaf surface like *Hosta sieboldiana* or grey or silver leaves such as senecio or stachys should not be submerged at any time. This removes or damages the coloration.

As with all conditioning treatments, the water and containers used for storing should be as clean as possible. Flower food can be used to prolong foliage but it is really only the antibacterial agents in the solution rather than the plant nutrients which will have any effect. A cheaper alternative is to add a few drops of bleach to the water to keep it clean.

USE OF COLD STORE AND STOCK ROTATION

It is very important to ensure a good method of stock rotation. Flowers on display in the shop should be checked daily to ensure they are at their very best, as well as flowers being used for make-up work. The flowers on display should be placed away from draughts, sunlight and areas where they may be knocked or damaged. The containers used for flowers must be absolutely clean to avoid a build-up of bacteria which will cause decay and in turn damage the flowers. It should be emphasised that the water should be changed daily and commercial flower food added.

A cold store enables the florist to buy in bulk and prepare work ahead. A big advantage in having a cold store is that work may be made in advance and stored. This is very useful when there is more than one wedding at a time. It must be stressed that the cold store should be maintained correctly in order to get maximum benefit from it.

- The store should be absolutely clean. Any dirt will cause a build-up of bacteria and botrytis will develop. Botrytis is a fungus which grows on flowers and is usually visible by the appearance of yellowing leaves or brown spots on buds or petals. Carnations often have evidence of botrytis on the calyx, which appears yellow; roses are also very susceptible and so great care should be taken when buying, particularly during the summer months when the warm air temperature combines with high humidity to create the conditions in which botrytis will thrive.

- The store should be well ventilated and flowers stored with plenty of space to allow air to circulate. This will allow the water produced by transpiration to evaporate.
- Old decaying flowers should not be kept in a cold store. One forgotten bucket in the corner can do a lot of damage.
- The temperature should be checked regularly to ensure there are no drastic changes. It is a good idea to have a thermometer which is easily visible. The recommended temperature for most flowers is around 3–5°C (36–41°F).
- Do not keep flowers in the cold store for too long. Old flowers may look fresh when taken out from the cold store but on meeting warmer air will deteriorate very quickly.

Some tropical flowers do not respond well to the usual treatment of a spell in a cool room or chiller. In their natural environment they are accustomed to a high temperature and humidity, and even a few hours in a cooler can result in discoloration and blackening of the petals, limpness and dehydration. Many of these flowers arrive with a small vial of water attached to the base of the stem. This should be removed, the stem re-cut and the flower stood in shallow water with some flower food added. The stored flowers should then be kept at a steady room temperature away from direct sunlight, heat sources and draughts. Occasional misting will help to maintain the humidity around the flowers. This should be done lightly so that excessive moisture droplets do not stain or mark the flowers.

Flowers best kept out of storage

Orchids	Strelitzia
Ornamental gingers	Anthuriums
Heliconia	Some tropical foliage

It is a good idea to keep flowers such as roses in the cold store and have just a small selection on display. The heads of correctly conditioned roses should be wrapped in paper to delay development. Roses should not be displayed in the shop by day and put back into cold store at night as constant temperature change causes the rose to blow very quickly.

Any flowers which have matured in the shop display should be removed and used for funeral work. This does not mean old flowers but flowers which have opened fully and are not suitable for cut flower sales.

Finally there should be a recognised code of practice within the shop routine to ensure good stock rotation. The reputation of the business is dependent on good-quality flowers which are long lasting and give value for money.

CHAPTER 2

Colour

Fundamental to any design made by the florist is the choice of colour. Colour is very emotive and affects so much of what we see. Feasts and festivals are associated with certain colours: for example, a traditional Christmas design will be red and green. Red is also associated with St Valentine's Day, Easter with yellows.

Sometimes requests are for specific orders such as an arrangement for a golden wedding made with yellow or gold flowers, possibly adding a gold bow. A funeral tribute for a grandmother would be made with pink or pale lilac tones, unless otherwise stated, but for a teenager a stronger colour harmony would be more suitable.

Colour can be vibrant and give a feeling of warmth and life; it can also be gentle and soft, producing a feeling of serenity and calm. Colour can interpret and relay a message. The red rose is used as a messenger of love, while a pink rose indicates young love. Each of us sees colour slightly differently but good colour choice is vital to the success of a design.

THE THEORY OF COLOUR

Recognised colour harmony is based on the twelve-colour wheel, made up of the following, which are referred to as true colours or hues:

Three **primary** colours	
Red Blue Yellow	cannot be made by mixing any colours

Three **secondary** colours	
Violet	made by mixing blue and red
Green	made by mixing blue and yellow
Orange	made by mixing yellow and red

Six **tertiary** colours	
Red-orange	made by mixing red and orange
Yellow-orange	made by mixing yellow and orange
Red-violet	made by mixing red and violet
Blue-violet	made by mixing blue and violet
Blue-green	made by mixing blue and green
Yellow-green	made by mixing yellow and green

Each of the twelve hues is altered by the addition of white, grey or black thus:

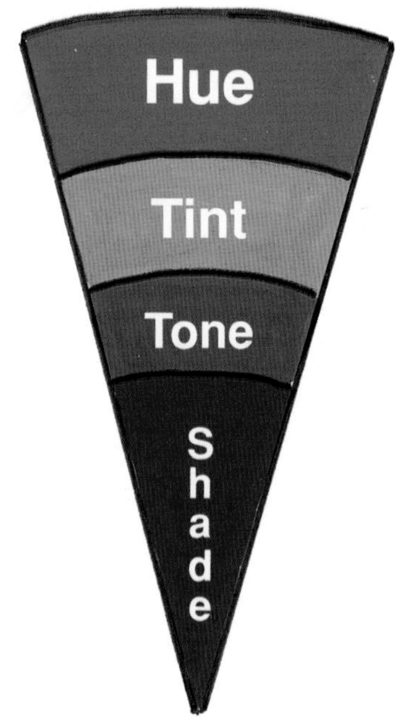

A very good exercise to develop your understanding of how colours are derived is to construct your own colour wheel using watercolour paints. You will need the three primary colours – red, blue and yellow – and also black, white and grey (black and white mixed).

Make a circle with white card and divide it into twelve segments; then make three circles dividing each segment into four sections to allow for the hue, tint, tone and shade of each colour. Mix the paints to give the correct colours in each segment.

Once the colour wheel is constructed, individual cut-outs can be made for each colour harmony and when the cut-out is placed over the wheel a colour harmony is instantly recognised.

Colour Wheel

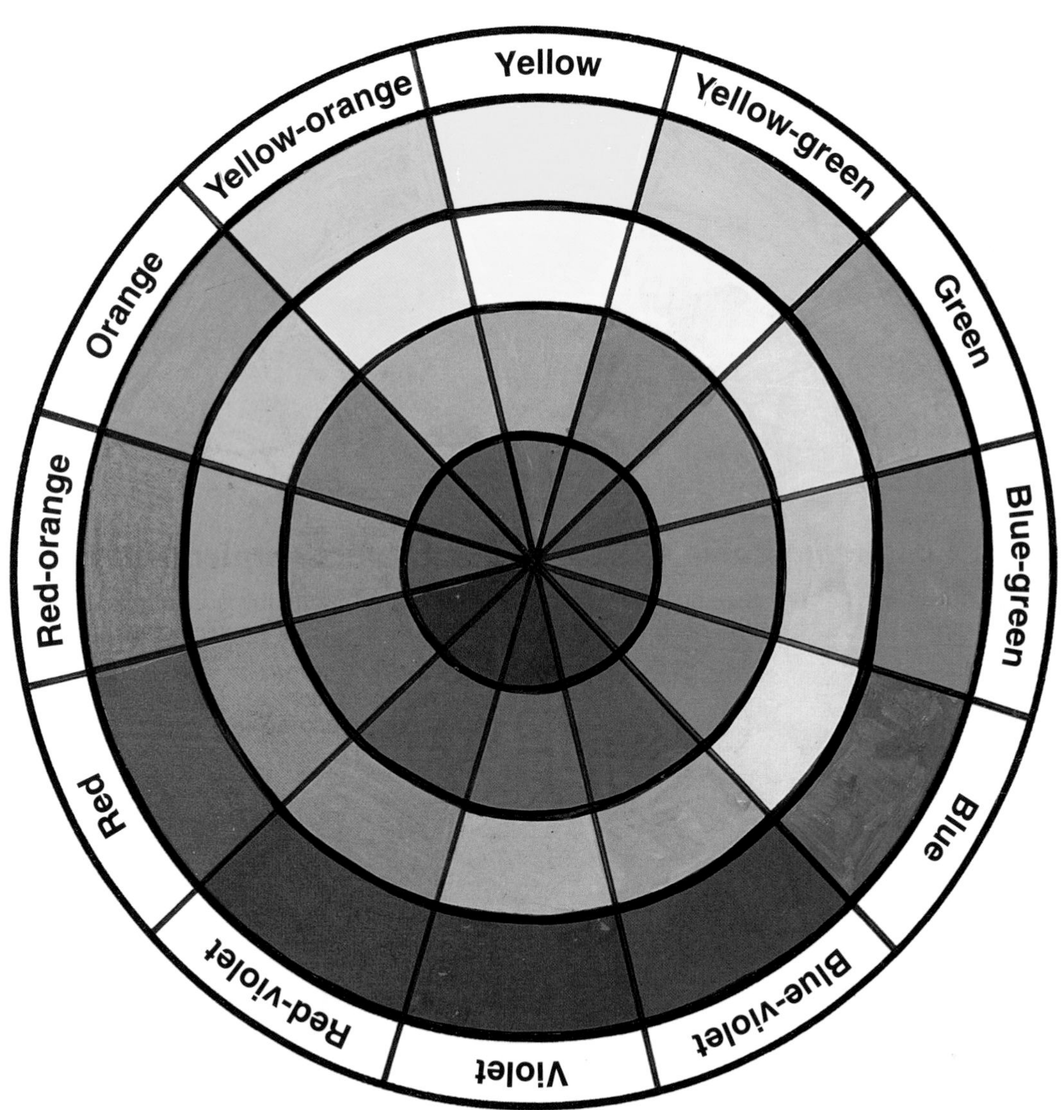

COLOUR HARMONIES

An understanding of basic colour schemes is very important, increasing the awareness of colour relationships. There are nine recognised colour harmonies, which are as follows.

Monochromatic

Mono means one, and this is the use of hues, tints, tones and shades taken from one segment of the colour wheel. The colours all tone together.

Red-orange, cinnamon, rust
Red-violet, pink-violet, purple
Blue, pale blue, airforce blue

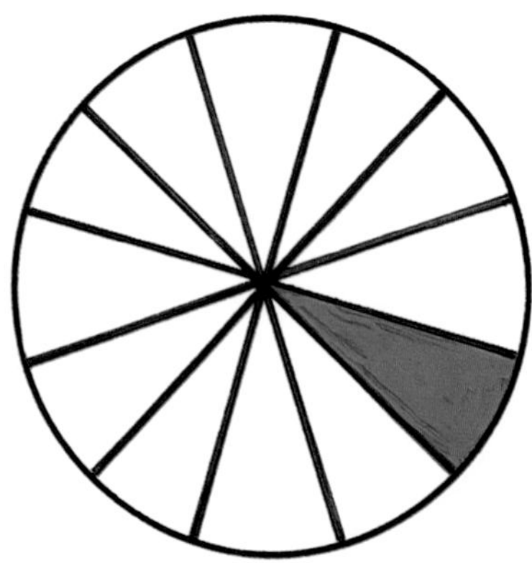

Split Complementary

This is made up of a colour on the colour wheel with the colours on either side of its complementary colour.

Red-violet opposite green and yellow
Yellow-green opposite red and violet

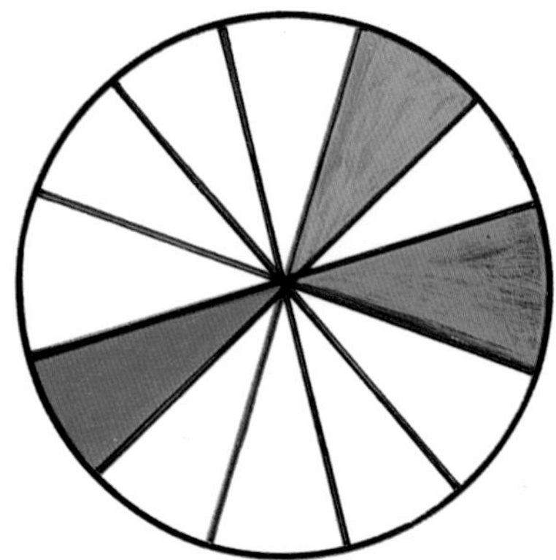

Complementary

This harmony is taken from two hues, tints or tones that appear directly opposite each other on the colour wheel.

Red and green
Red-violet and yellow-green
Blue and orange

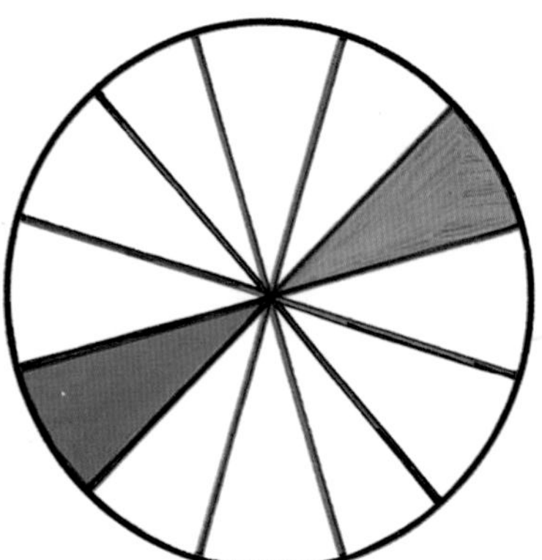

Near Complementary

This is formed by taking a colour and one of the two colours beside its complementary.

Red-violet and yellow
Red and blue-green
Yellow-orange and violet

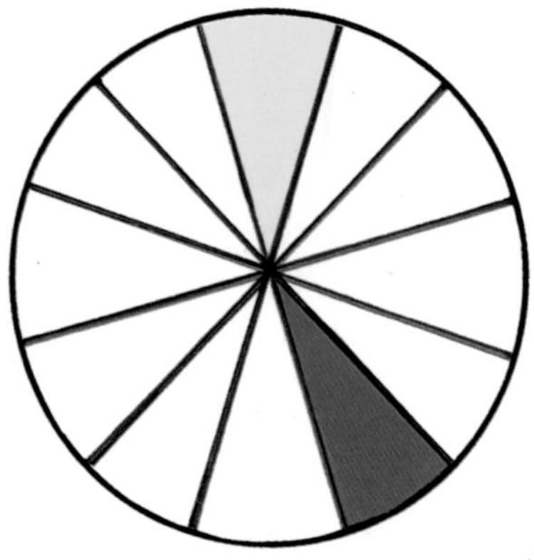

Contrast

This harmony is obtained from the colour wheel by using a colour with one that is four segments away.

Yellow and red
Green and orange
Orange and violet

A contrasting harmony can be very harsh so a tint or tone of one hue can be used with the other at full spectrum strength.

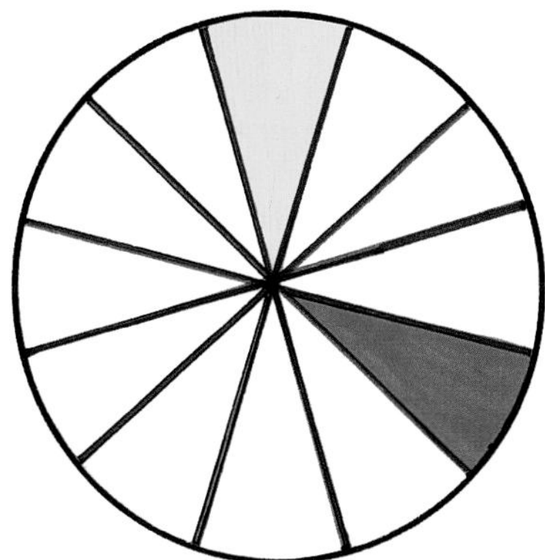

Triadic

This is made up of three colours separated by four segments on the colour wheel.

Green, violet, orange
Red, yellow, blue
Blue-violet, yellow-green, red-orange

This can be quite harsh and one colour should be dominant, with less of the second and a touch of the third colour, or there can be mix of hues, tints and tones.

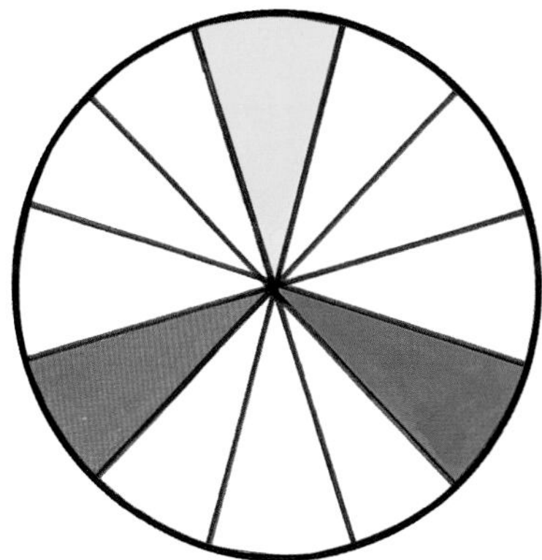

Analogous

This harmony is made up of three or four colours adjacent to each other on the colour wheel and not including more than one primary.

Yellow, yellow-orange, orange
Red, red-violet, violet, blue-violet
Green, blue-green, blue, blue-violet

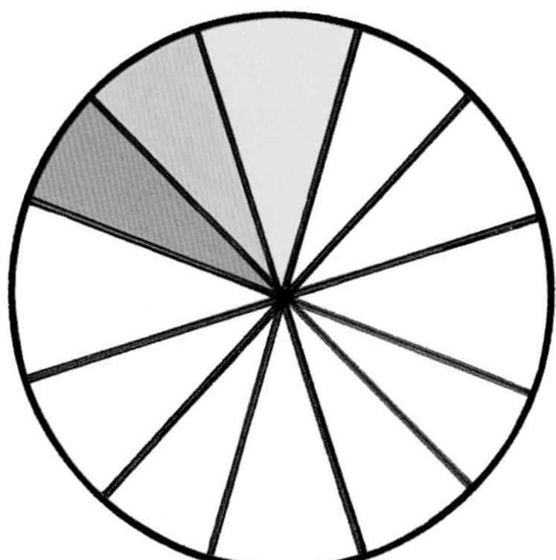

Tetradic

This four-colour harmony is separated by three segments on the colour wheel.

Green, yellow-orange, red, blue-violet
Yellow, red-orange, violet, blue-green

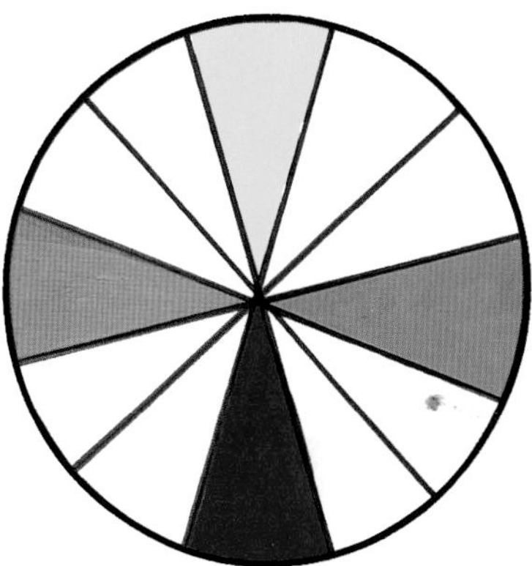

Polychromatic

This harmony is based on tints, tones and shades chosen from the complete colour wheel. It is a very popular choice in modern floristry.

ACHROMATIC OR NEUTRAL COLOURS

This is the name for colours which have weak chroma and are therefore neutral. As they do not impinge on a colour scheme, they are ideal for containers, bases and drapes which are not intended as focal areas of a design or display. The colours are black, white, grey, beige and stone.

Neutral colours often take on the surrounding colour. White is a classic example. If a selection of white flowers is made, it will be seen that there are many shades of white, as most white flowers have a very pale tint of colour in them. It may be thought that the white of an arum lily is a pure white, but when put against a white fabric it appears slightly green. A white rose set against a bright white satin will appear to be cream but against a red background it will look slightly pink.

This takes us on to juxtaposition, which comes from the word 'juxtapose', to put things side by side: colours as seen by the human eye alter depending on what colours are beside them.

Colour set against mid grey is always seen at its truest because it does not absorb any other colour and this is why flowers look so well in a grey container or against a grey drape or backcloth. When red is set against grey the grey appears to take on a greenish hue, the red appearing purer and less orange. When orange and grey are placed side by side, the grey appears to become more blue and the orange less yellow. If a rose-pink flower is used with purple, it looks lavender-pink, but when placed next to cream the pink stands out and is more intense.

WEIGHTING OF COLOUR

The amount of white, black or grey in a colour will change the degree of lightness or heaviness of the colour, hence the terms hues, tints, tones and shades.

Pure yellow is light and uplifting, whereas dark green or violet is sombre and heavy.

Colours of equal intensity and weight visually do not complement each other, although in some modern design they can be used successfully. An arrangement of deep purple chrysanthemums and dark green foliage will appear very heavy, dull and sombre, whereas a lighter version of the purple mixed in with perhaps some variegated leaves will be much more interesting and appealing.

In any floristry design the darker flowers should be recessed and lighter flowers should be used in the outline. If there are darker flowers on the outline and lighter flowers recessed, the design will appear to be visually unbalanced, because darker colour looks heavier to the eye.

Colour distribution of small areas of pure colour (grouping material) is much easier on the eye and generates more interest than strong overall colour, which is visually too harsh and tiring. It is a good idea in any colour scheme to use fewer stronger colours and more of the paler ones. However, it should be noted that the florist with a lot of experience can experiment with unusual colour weighting, particularly in continental design, and create very dramatic effects.

If a design is to be made using all one colour, then shapes and textures should be considered to generate interest: for example, an all-foliage design should have glossy, shiny, dull and velvety-textured leaves, as well as different shapes. If all the same shape, colour and texture were used, it would appear very dull and boring to the eye.

Grouping and Linking Colour

In a design a colour should be taken through from one side to the other or grouped in blocks, ensuring that an equal amount of a different colour is used to counterbalance. If colour is not grouped it will appear blobby and disorganised to the eye.

Ribbons on a design should always complement or tone. A ribbon which is a completely different colour and not related in any way to the design will look totally wrong. In a based funeral design, ribbons on the sprays should be the same colour as on the ribbon edge.

Luminosity

This is the term used for the degree of light emitted from a colour. The lightest colour is pure yellow. In planning the decoration of large areas such as churches, or hotel entrances, thought should be given to the amount of light available, as these venues are often very dark, and lighter-coloured flowers should be used if they are to be easily seen.

The lighter colours are referred to as advancing colours. These include yellow, white, bright orange, lime green, pale pinks and peach colours. Tints have a higher luminosity than shades and tones, which contain grey or black.

Blues, violets, dark greens, rust colours and deep reds have a low luminosity and are referred to as receding colours. They should be avoided in big displays in churches and large areas viewed from a distance. These colours can be used within a display which includes lighter-coloured flowers but avoid using them as outline flowers, as they will be lost.

When viewing a church for a wedding, it is important to keep in mind the time of day and the season. If the church is lit artificially, this will change the colour of the flowers, especially if candlelight is used, and the interior will look totally different from the way it would appear on a bright sunny morning. If there is no sunlight coming in the windows, the colour and shape of the display placed in front of them will be altered.

When deciding on colours for flowers in a marquee, remember that pink will become peach and blues become mauves. It is also important to take into account the colour of the marquee lining when deciding on a colour scheme.

All these situations alter colour drastically.

Flowers and Colour

Colour can be very exciting and it is always worth experimenting. It is a very personal thing and everyone has different ideas about which colour goes with another. It is a good idea to stick to recognised colour schemes in commercial work unless you have discussed any unusual harmonies with customers. Design and competitive work, on the other hand, gives a lot of scope for experimentation with colour.

A pink rose in bud will appear to be pale; when it reaches its peak it will be slightly darker, and when it starts to mature it will become even darker. At each stage of maturity the colour will change slightly. This is the case with many flowers.

A monochromatic hand-tied design might include 'Nicole' roses, nerines, 'Montreux' lilies, hypericum and 'Dark Flamenco' chrysanthemums.

Lovely rich colour appeals to some people, a combination of paler varieties to others: waxflowers, 'Starlight' gerbera, pale pink eustoma, 'Le Reve' lilies and 'Evelien' roses.

Consider putting the first group with pale peach. Exchange the 'Nicole' rose for a 'Gerdo' rose and substitute chrysanthemum 'Dark Flamenco' for 'Salmon Reagan'. This is unusual colour harmony but the rich burgundy colour with peach looks very good. It's all a question of trying out different colour schemes and making them work.

A very effective harmony is to put pale peach, pale lavender, pale pink and pale yellow together. This has been done and looks wonderful, but as previously said it's all a matter of choice.

Foliage and Colour

Most foliage available in the markets is green in colour. There is also a vast range of foliage that may be sourced locally, and if you can find some 'tame' gardens which need a prune every so often, this will give a wider scope to your foliage and twigs. Cornus in winter has lovely red, yellow or deep burgundy stems, depending on the variety, and can add colour in a different way. Pot plants are a good source for individual leaves. *Begonia rex* looks very good in a bridal bouquet based on predominantly pink flowers, and croton leaves add interest to a limited flower bouquet using yellow or orange gerbera.

A large glass vase filled with 'Professor Blaauw' irises and gerbera 'Tamara', using large fatsia leaves at the base and some yellow cornus twigs, could look stunning in the correct setting.

COLOUR AND OUTSIDE DECORATING

It is important to visit a venue before deciding on a colour scheme. The customer may want a particular colour harmony, but if on seeing the venue you find that the decor of the room is totally unsuitable for the desired colour scheme, then it is advisable to discuss this with the customer, who may be totally unaware that the colours do not look well together.

Sometimes a hotel or restaurant will have a set colour for table linen. If it is a wedding reception or private party, the customer can ask for specific colours as long as they are not way out! If in doubt, though, it is best to stick to white table linen to which any colour can be added effectively.

Often a bride will want to carry a colour scheme through to match the bridal party. If there is a conflict, it is better to decorate the reception area with flowers which are in harmony with the decor rather than the bridal flowers. A venue will always look ten times more attractive if the displays are in keeping with the surrounding colour scheme than at odds with it.

Colour can be used to great effect when doing promotional work for a special season. Blocks of colour have far more impact in a window display than lots of colours used in a muddled fashion.

Flowers in the shop look very effective if displayed in containers which are all the same colour, preferably green or neutral stone or grey, as this allows the flowers themselves to attract the eye.

Cut flowers are more attractive to the eye if displayed in blocks of one colour. They need not be kept in one area of the shop but can be displayed with sundries in the same colour scheme.

Red flowers can be displayed in an area where there are red containers, candles, balloons, etc. and blue flowers can be displayed with blue glass. The colour in the shop will have far more impact on the customer if arranged in this way.

If there is a promotion on basketware the displays could be silk and dried in a monochromatic harmony. Lots of different colours are worrying to the eye and distract from the product. Imagine a window or an area of the shop displaying terracotta ware filled with artificial sunflowers and dried fruits.

A GUIDE TO COLOUR FOR INTERPRETIVE WORK

Every country and culture has its own particular associations with colour and flowers, so when constructing a piece of interpretive work, check that it does not send an incorrect message. In France, for instance, both yellow and white chrysanthemums signify death.

The following colour associations are helpful in general work in the United Kingdom:

Red	Passion, love, fire, warmth
Blue	Water, peace, serenity, sky, space
Yellow	Spring, joy, youthfulness, sunshine
Orange	Fire, warmth, earthiness, autumn
Purple	Luxury, richness, opulence, age, humility, faith
Peach	Fresh, fruity, Mediterranean
Pink	Feminine, birth
Green	Cool, nature, calmness, woodland
Black	Night, fear, magic, sophistication
Grey	Dull, melancholy, neutral, sea
White	Pure, cool, light and airy, innocence

CHAPTER 3

Principles of Design

Most people know what they like when it comes to choosing a picture, a piece of furniture, fabrics for the home, or an arrangement or bouquet of flowers. There is something about the piece, its colours, shape or more significantly its design which triggers a reaction, an emotion in us, perhaps of recognition and appreciation. Seldom are the elements which create good design analysed; quite often their combination appears so effortless and natural that it is difficult to pinpoint any one exactly within the complete piece of work. This is surely the mark of good design! Basic design principles can be applied to all forms of art.

In floristry a good design not only combines design elements contained within the construction of the work but also takes into consideration external factors such as the setting and the purpose for which the display is intended. For example, a large vase of delphiniums or dahlias in a small room could appear overpowering, whereas a few thoughtfully placed stems arranged in a more limited or simple style would be far more suited to such a setting. Taking this idea a stage further, the clean lines and economical use of flowers in an abstract or modern-style arrangement would suit a modern room or reception area but would perhaps be at odds with a traditional or country-style room. Here an informal arrangement of garden flowers in a basket or pottery container would be more sympathetic to the overall style of the setting. Effective floral design therefore involves ensuring that the materials, style and location complement one another and work together to form an overall harmonious picture.

BALANCE

There are two kinds of balance which can be applied to a piece of floristry work: actual and visual. Actual or physical balance simply means that the object is physically stable and will not fall over or tilt to one side. Visual balance is slightly more complex and open to different or personal interpretation. Generally speaking, an arrangement will appear to be visually unbalanced if it is top-heavy, bottom-heavy or lop-sided. Although perfectly stable, the design will look uncomfortable and unbalanced because it contains visual elements which are individually too dominant and draw the eye away from the rest of the design.

Actual Balance

To achieve actual balance within a design the plant material must be placed so as to spread the weight evenly over the entire area of foam for an arrangement or throughout the design for a bouquet. If a large arrangement has too many heavy flowers grouped towards the front and all the stems are placed within the same small area of foam, it will be in danger of falling over. If the same number of flowers is grouped for exactly the same effect but their stems are placed more evenly over the surface of the foam, the design will be balanced. As a general guide, in achieving actual balance, smaller slender materials are used to form an outline and larger heavier flowers are placed towards the centre.

Visual Balance

In general the eye is drawn to the area in a design that is perceived to contain the most interest. In a flower arrangement this could be either a concentration of colour or a grouping of distinctive shapes or forms of flowers, foliage, fruits or seed heads. The materials in a visually balanced design will be arranged around an imaginary vertical or horizontal axis so the eye is drawn equally to both sides. This is not to say that equal amounts of material must be used either side of the imaginary central axis, as such rigid symmetry can make a design monotonous. Instead both sides of the axis should have the same visual weight, irrespective of the materials used. For example, a group of three roses on one side of a design could be counterbalanced with one gerbera or a dahlia on the other side. Although the quantity and type of flowers differ, the larger size and repetitive circular shape of the gerbera visually balance the three roses. Likewise, in a large pedestal display tall gladioli or delphiniums used to form a strong central point to the arrangement can be visually balanced by a few long trailing stems of ivy or a suitably strong grouping of large hosta or bergenia leaves at the base of the design. With both examples the strong linear effect of the flowers is counterbalanced by the movement and softness of the trailing ivy or the solidity and visual weight of the large hosta and bergenia leaves. In both examples visual balance has been created even though the placement of the materials is not symmetrical.

SCALE AND PROPORTION

Several factors can influence the apparent scale and proportion of a finished piece of floristry work. For instance, the effect of a beautifully made small arrangement with the correct size of vase in relation to the flowers and a careful choice of plant material can be completely lost if placed in isolation in a large room, on a large piece of furniture or in a position where it is surrounded by a large area of open space. A design of this size needs a more intimate setting. The reverse situation also demonstrates this principle. A large display in a confined space can overwhelm a room and become too dominant. These two examples show how scale and proportion can be altered by external influences.

Within the arrangement itself scale and proportion play an important part in creating a successful display. Careful choice and use of sizes and quantities of materials should ensure that one type of flower or colour does not dominate or overshadow the display. Extreme differences in size between neighbouring flowers will also highlight this problem.

It is worth remembering that scale denotes the size of materials used in a design in relation to each other and their surroundings and proportion denotes the quantities of materials used in a design in relation to each other and their surroundings.

To show an extreme example of this, a combination of large gerbera blooms and spray roses or lupins and cornflowers will not be in scale, as the flower sizes are too different. This can be overcome by introducing some carnations or spray chrysanthemums with the gerbera and perhaps liatris or larkspur with the lupins to link the two extremes. The correct quantity of these flowers within an arrangement is generally decided by the flower size itself: the larger the flower, the fewer to be used; the smaller the flower, the more to be used. For example, five gerbera flowers, nine carnation blooms and nine or even eleven stems of spray roses would provide the correct quantities to achieve the right proportions within the arrangement.

These ideas are just as important to remember when designing wedding bouquets and accessories. The height of the bride and style of the wedding dress will affect the finished size of the bouquets. Likewise the way in which the bride's or bridesmaids' hair is styled will affect the size and design of any headdress decorations.

With a little forethought and forward planning, scale and proportion are among the easier elements to achieve within a design. An awareness of the materials being used and the eventual purpose or use of the piece of work being made is all that should be required to practise this effectively. It would be difficult, not to say foolhardy, to try to prescribe exact quantities of materials needed for specific styles of arrangements. So much depends on the quality of the flowers, the size of the container and also the current fashion trend for interior design. Floral displays are closely linked with changing interior styles and can swing from a minimalistic look to extravagant designs resembling a summer garden in full bloom.

Generally the style of the arrangement will determine the quantities of flowers needed. An all-round arrangement for a table centre will require roughly the same amount of materials as a symmetrical display. A modern linear style should always consist of odd numbers of flowers: three, five, seven or nine blooms of the same type.

When decorating a room or building the success of the displays relies on the right choice of flower types. Large rooms filled with heavy mahogany furniture need equally bold flowers to avoid the arrangements becoming overpowered by their surroundings. Lilies, peonies, full-blown roses, gladioli and chrysanthemums are ideal for this situation. An old country cottage with low beams and ceilings requires a different approach using far more informal, smaller flowers such as alstroemeria, solidago, asters, achillea and sweet peas.

RHYTHM

Rhythm within a flower arrangement gives movement and continuity, which enable the finished design to be viewed easily and stimulate interest. This perceived movement can come from the progression of one flower or colour through the design or from the line or shape of a particular piece of foliage providing a strong visual line along which the eye is drawn. A good example of this is the flowing, gently curved shape of bear grass, which adds greatly to any design, or the sharp straight lines of broom, which will lift an arrangement with such a strong vertical line that it appears to soar upwards. Rhythm thus gives movement and excitement, without which an arrangement is solid, ordinary and fragmented.

Other elements also contribute to effective rhythm: repetition, transition and radiation. They might not be particularly important individually, but as a whole they can greatly change and improve an arrangement.

Repetition can be achieved by forming pattern lines or groupings of materials within a design. Usually the same type and colour of flower is grouped together; similar shapes positioned together will have the same effect. A pattern line of spray carnations can extend from the topmost bud in an arrangement down through the design and diagonally off to one side at the base. Likewise a line of distinctive flowers like irises can be placed through an arrangement from the point of a symmetrical triangle down to the focal area, which is formed by grouped iris. This focal area can then be strengthened by the addition of one or two large leaves such as hosta or bergenia. A finer or divided leaf like fern or ruscus would not add the necessary strength to the central group that the larger leaves do. This grouping of materials and of colour forms continuous threads through the arrangement that give the impression of movement. Repetition or the placement of separate groups of the same flower can also achieve this. Some flowers by their very size, shape or colour can be too dominant in a design if grouped strictly in a pattern line, as they would stand out from the surrounding smaller, lighter flowers.

Transitional flowers are those whose size bridges the gap from small to larger blooms. An example of this would be spray carnations at the top of an arrangement, dahlias at the base and carnation blooms in between the two. A gradual change in size is achieved, and the repetition of the same circular flower shape ensures a smooth transition. Transitional flowers and shapes are important to a study of rhythm as they complement the pattern lines of a design, therefore allowing the eye to travel easily from one pattern grouping to the next. Generally speaking, this transition should be as gentle and unobtrusive as possible.

Colour also plays an important part in achieving transition. By using tints, tones and shades, stronger, brighter colours can be blended together effectively to form a pleasing mix of flowers that would otherwise overshadow the rest of the design. Gerbera are a good example of this. The perfect circles of the flowers command attention even if pastel colours are used. For flowers such as these, small individual groupings within the display are more effective than a complete pattern line. Three blooms together on one side above the focal area and five or seven flowers diagonally opposite below the focal area form a far more pleasing design than a complete line. The uneven numbers of three and five or seven blooms achieve visual balance because of their positions within the arrangement, the lesser number being higher in the display than the larger number.

Repetition of colour or form within a design not only helps to achieve visual balance; it strengthens the overall unity of the arrangement and provides areas of interest and accent within the display. The gradual transition in size from small to large of any plant material within a display will always help to give a smooth overall unity to the arrangement. As a general rule for most arrangements, particularly the more traditional styles, it is always better to use a colour-themed arrangement rather than present a display of isolated patches of colour.

The direction in which flowers and foliage appear to flow within an arrangement is of the same importance as the previous elements described and is called radiation. All floral designs have a focal area, usually centrally positioned toward the base of the display, from which all materials should appear to radiate. This ensures that the arrangement has elegance and grace, and even a large pedestal arrangement should give this impression. Although the central 'working' area of foam can be very large, the finished effect should still be the same. This is achieved by placing the stems into the foam at the correct angle in relation to their position within the display. Those at the top are inserted vertically, those at the sides horizontally and those at the base almost upside down.

HARMONY

It is difficult to define the principle of harmony and describe the way to achieve it within an arrangement, as it relies not on the application of one or two elements but rather on the sum total of all the parts successfully coming together to create a harmonious and pleasing whole. To try to simplify this, harmony can best be described as the accord or unity between the various elements of a design that make it an artistically pleasing arrangement. Balance, rhythm and repetition, scale and proportion, dominance and contrast all effectively working together will create harmony within a display. None of the design principles should be in conflict with the others or with the overall design unless used as a deliberate exercise in contrast.

This harmonising of the entire display can be achieved in a number of ways, by the repetition or similarity of texture, style, shape and colour between the flowers, foliage, container and surroundings. The harmonious relationship of an arrangement with its surroundings should not be confused with scale and proportion, which rely on compatibility of size and quantity. Harmony requires not only this but also sympathetic combinations of flower types, colours and styles of designs and containers to form an integral part of the surroundings in which they are displayed. To use a familiar example again, a rustic basket of garden flowers in a country cottage illustrates this very well.

To achieve harmony it is useful to look at the combinations of materials to be found in nature. A woodland and country-style arrangement of branches, primroses, bluebells and moss displayed on a piece of wood or bark looks 'right'. The addition of flowers such as carnations or roses, even if of a suitable colour, would ruin the overall effect, as they would not be in harmony with the simple wild flowers.

Often the simplest and apparently uncontrived arrangements are the most successful in achieving overall harmony. Too much variety in materials and colours, of either flowers or accessories, can confuse and destroy the final effect. Two extremes as examples of harmonious displays would be a large stone jar filled with sheep's parsley flowers and wild oats in the sympathetic surroundings of a country-style kitchen or a cottage room. Anthuriums, on the other hand, demand a much more sophisticated treatment. Arranged in a black lustre glass vase with some equally bold leaves such as strelitzia or monstera, they make a bold statement which needs to be matched by equally bold surroundings such as a modern hotel foyer or apartment containing strong visual impact.

CHAPTER 4

Construction and Wiring Techniques

Wires are used for control, support, anchorage, lengthening of stems and binding materials together. Wiring is thus a very necessary technique for the florist, but it is important to remember to use as little wire as possible, as nowadays less wire is used than previously and more natural stems are seen. The glue gun has also replaced wire in many areas of the florist's work.

Wires Available to the Florist

Type of wire	*Gauge*	*Available as*
Fine wire	0.20 mm	reel
Fine wire	0.24 mm	reel
Fine wire	0.28 mm	reel/silver stub
Fine wire	0.32 mm	reel/silver stub
Medium wire	0.38 mm	reel/silver stub
Medium wire	0.46 mm	reel/silver stub
Medium wire	0.56 mm	reel/blue annealed stub
Medium wire	0.71 mm	blue annealed stub
Thick wire	0.90 mm	blue annealed stub
Thick wire	1.00 mm	blue annealed stub
Thick wire	1.25 mm	blue annealed stub

Most of these are available with a green plastic coating. Decorative real wires are now available in a range of colours including metallic copper and gold. These are wired as a decorative feature to wrap around a flower head such as a tulip or a rose, to twist around stems or branches, to bind stems into bundles or to create a caged effect. These techniques are more suited to contemporary design.

There is no single correct way for wiring material, especially support wire, as long as it does the job effectively, but it should be stressed that the lightest gauge or thickness for the purpose intended should be used. Some flowers, if conditioned well, need little if any wiring, whereas others are less sturdy and need more support. Wired material should not make the design stiff and heavy.

All visible wires should be covered with tape. Green-coated wire does not need to be taped except where it is used as a mount and then only over the stem end. It is important when wiring to cover the stems with tape as quickly as possible in order to slow up the dehydration process.

SUPPORT WIRING

Support wiring strengthens a stem and is used mostly for wired bouquets, corsages and any other work where material requires extra support.

In tied wedding work it is sometimes necessary to support wire a few of the longer trails. The wire should be unobtrusive and covered with tape where visible. When the work is completed the wires going through the tying point should be cut out and the ends pushed back into the tying point.

Although most funeral flowers in foam are not wired, the lateral and focal flowers may need support. Roses and carnations are very brittle and are thus vulnerable when handled, so it is a good idea to support wire some of the taller flowers, which can easily be knocked and damaged.

To test whether a flower is adequately supported for the purpose intended, hold the stem at the base. If it swings around, then the gauge is too fine. If it is rigid with no movement, then the gauge is too heavy. There should be a degree of light, controlled movement.

Tip

When mounting material for use in foam, particularly for funeral work, bend the ends into a hairpin before pushing into the foam. This will give extra anchorage.

Flowers

There are three methods of support wiring for flowers.

1. Internal

This is used on hollow-stemmed flowers and some fleshy stems, for example, anemones, daffodils, gerbera. The wire is pushed up the stem on the inside until it bites onto the inside of the calyx.

2. External

The wire is inserted into the calyx, carefully twisted round the base of the calyx and then brought down the stem. Do not twist too many times as this will make the flower rigid and heavy.

3. Semi-internal

If the stem is fleshy, it is possible to support wire the top part internally and the lower half externally. This is done on such flowers as tulips, irises and gerbera when longer length is required.

The wire should be inserted into the stem 10–12 cm below the calyx and pushed up to the calyx internally. The wire below the insertion point should be twisted down the outside of the stem.

Some flowers can be internally wired for a short length and then, when a longer length is required, both internal and external methods can be used.

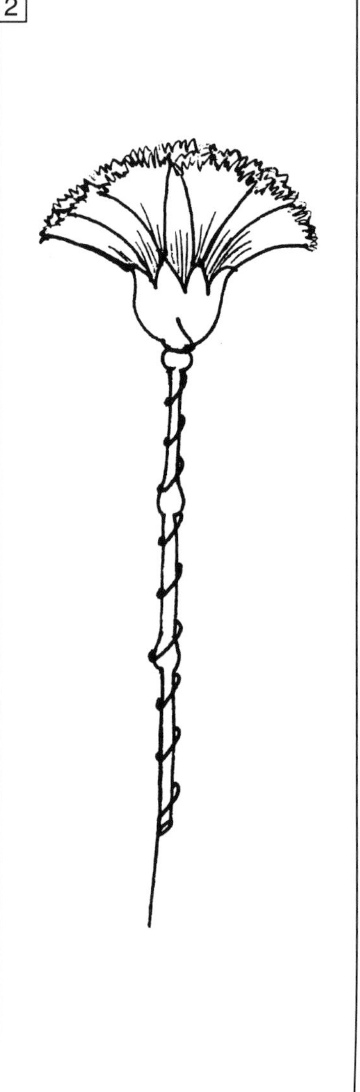

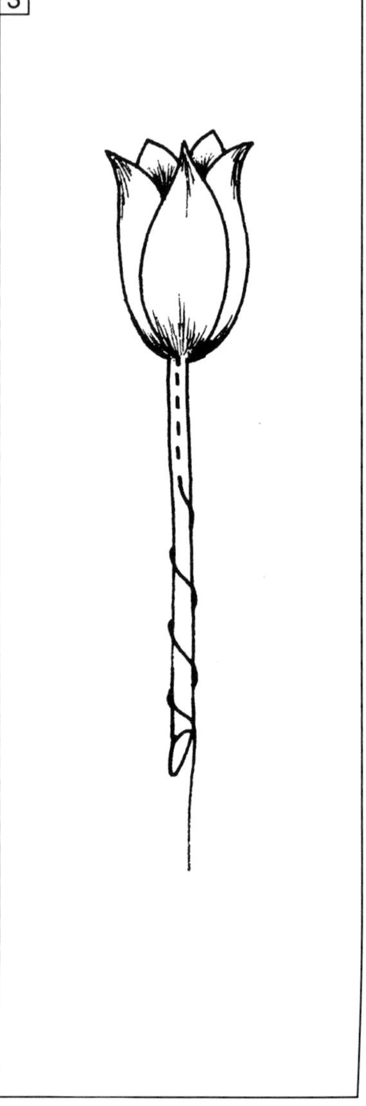

Foliage Leaves

Individual leaves can be support wired by a method called stitching, which is shown below.

Hold the leaf with the underside uppermost. Using a good length of fine wire (size depends on the leaf thickness), take a small stitch through the front of the leaf over the main vein about a third down from the tip. Form a loop with the wire ends and twist them together at the base of the leaf to form a stem.

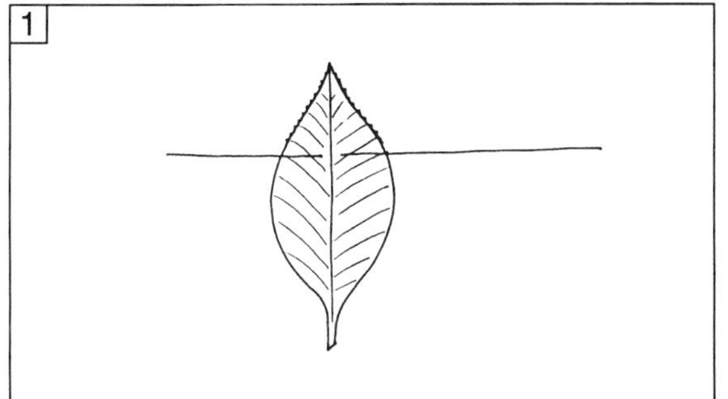

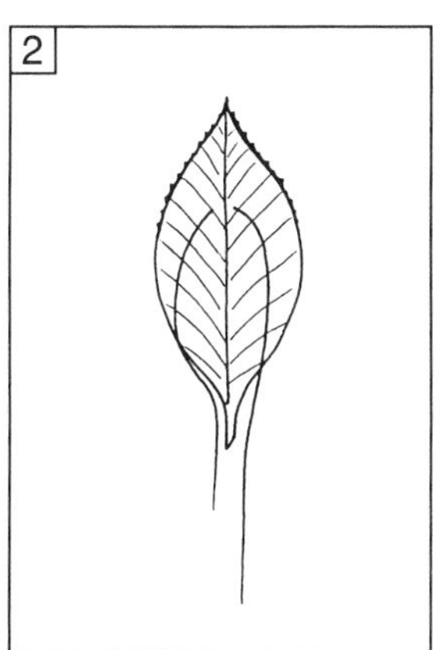

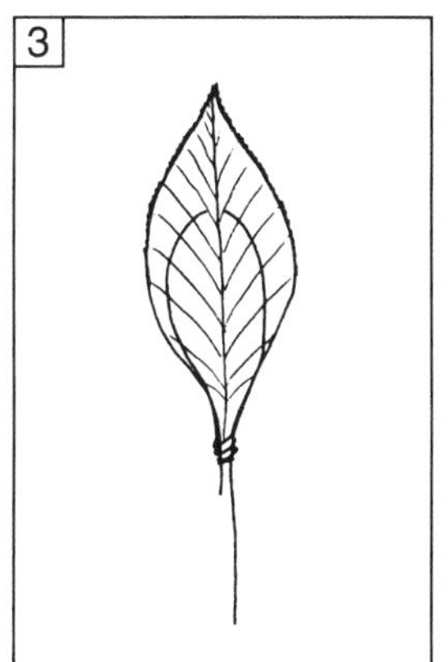

If green wire is available, it should be used; otherwise this is the one occasion when bare wire is seen, as taped wire will not go into the flesh of a stem or leaf.

Some leaves are too fleshy to support wire in the normal way, and very quickly bruising appears. It is possible to tape wire onto the back of the leaf with sellotape or pot tape (right). This should be done as unobtrusively as possible.

MOUNTING WIRE

This is the method used for anchoring the plant material into foam or moss or for creating a false stem for wired wedding work. The weight of the material being mounted will determine whether a single or double leg mount is necessary. The single leg mount will anchor a lighter stem, the double leg mount a heavier one. The mount is always a higher gauge than the support wire used, i.e. a rose with 0.71 mm support wire will require a 0.90 mm mount.

Single leg mount

Double leg mount

If the mount is for funeral work or a flower arrangement, then the base of the stem does not need to be covered in tape as the stem will be able to take moisture out of the foam, but if it is to be used for wedding work then the stem must be sealed with tape to retain the moisture. In wired wedding work the taped wires are put together at the binding point and the rest of the wire forms the handle, which is part of the design.

BINDING WIRE

This is used for attaching moss to a frame or for binding together the wire stems of a bouquet or corsage. For wedding work 0.28, 0.32 or 0.46 mm binding wire should be used, usually from a reel. Natural stems should never be bound with wire. All the stems should end and become false stems at the binding point. Sometimes when a bouquet has been made from only a small amount of material it is necessary to add wire to the handle to give more weight to balance the bouquet, but care should be taken that it does not feel too heavy.

INDIVIDUAL WIRING TECHNIQUES

The size, shape, structure and use of the flower determine wiring technique. As long as the method works and the gauge is correct for the purpose and all the visible wires are concealed, it does not matter how it has been achieved. Freesias are wired in various ways, the following being one example.

Stems

Using 0.28 mm green reel wire, wind carefully down the stem from the top bud to the largest bud. To form a false leg, push a 0.56 mm or 0.71 mm wire into the base and tape firmly.

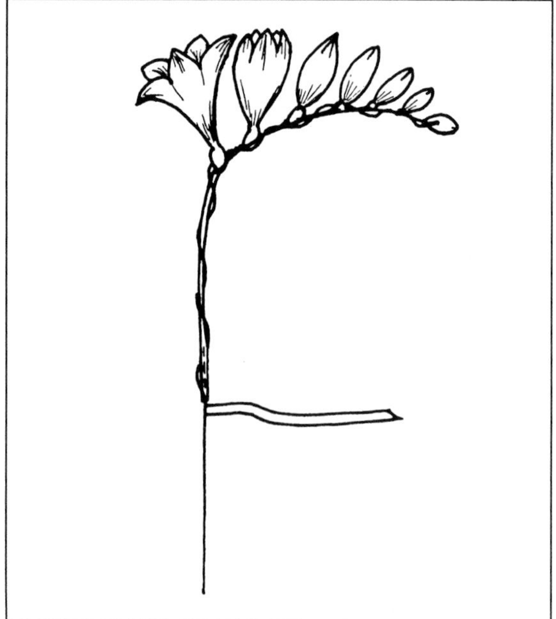

Individual Florets

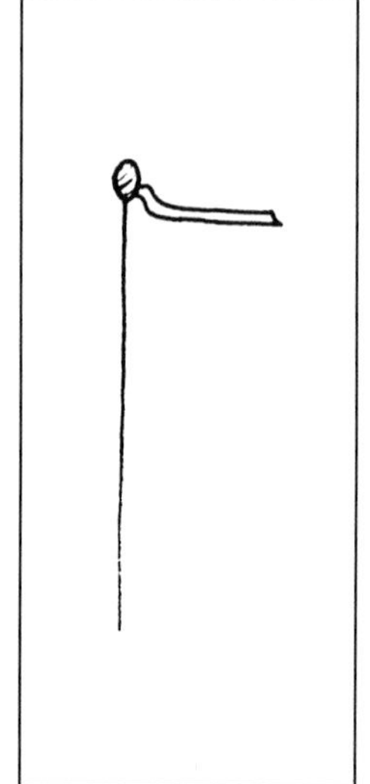

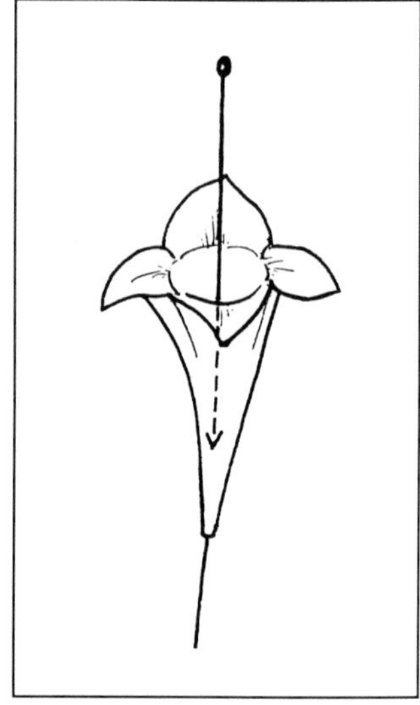

Tape the tip of a 0.28 mm wire to form a little ball. Push the untaped end through the top of the flower and pull gently down to form a false stem. Then carefully tape from the base of the flower to the end of the wire.

Tip

Remember that the last thing to do with a buttonhole or corsage is to add a steel pin at the binding point for the customer's use.

Roses

Pin sepals using small 'hairpins' of green 0.28 mm wire. Insert two 0.32 mm silver wires to form a cross through the seedbox. Carefully bring down the wires as shown in the figure and tape from the top of the seedbox to conceal all wires.

Use 0.46 or 0.56 mm for cross wires, on larger roses, and 0.71 or 0.90 mm for the stem wire.

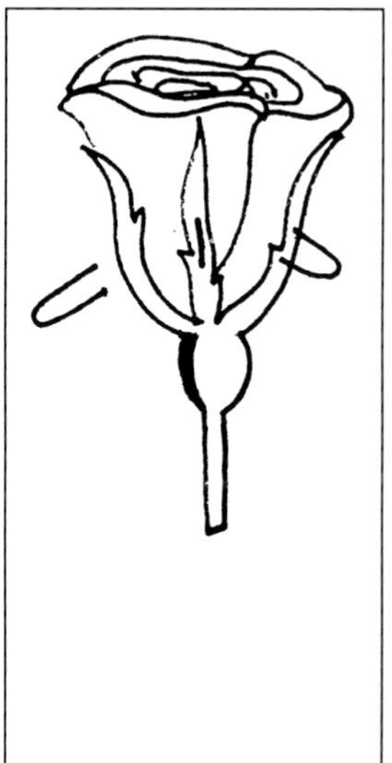

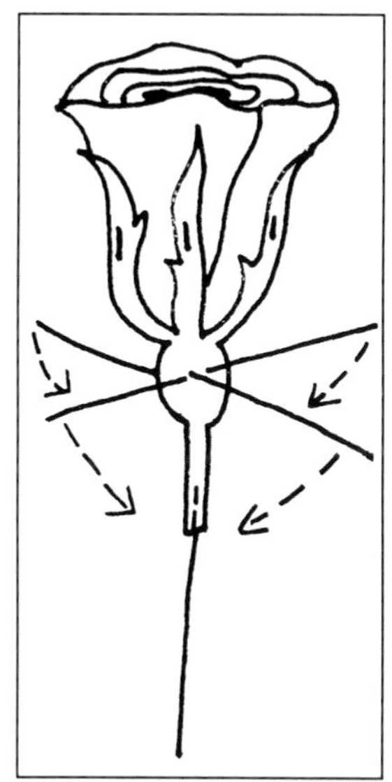

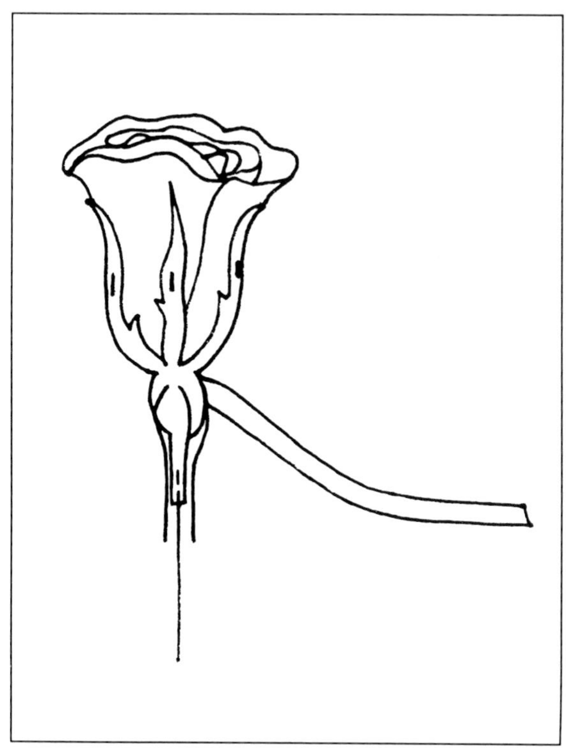

Spray Carnations

Push 0.71 mm wire up through the calyx and out of top of flower. Make a hook at the top and pull wire down until the hook reaches the base of the calyx. Tape the stem and the wire.

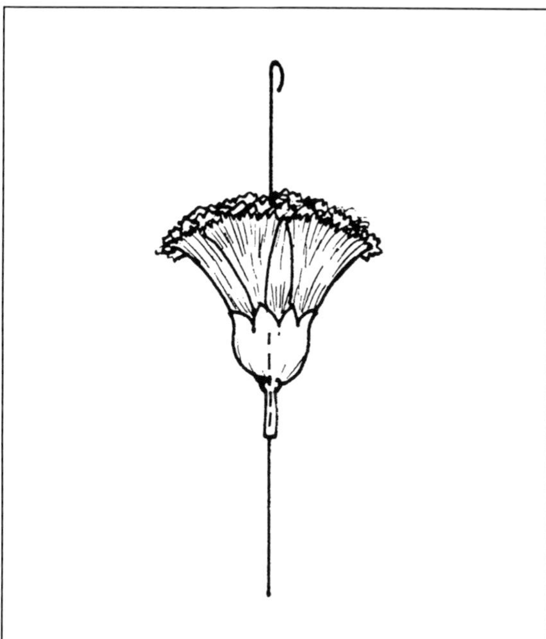

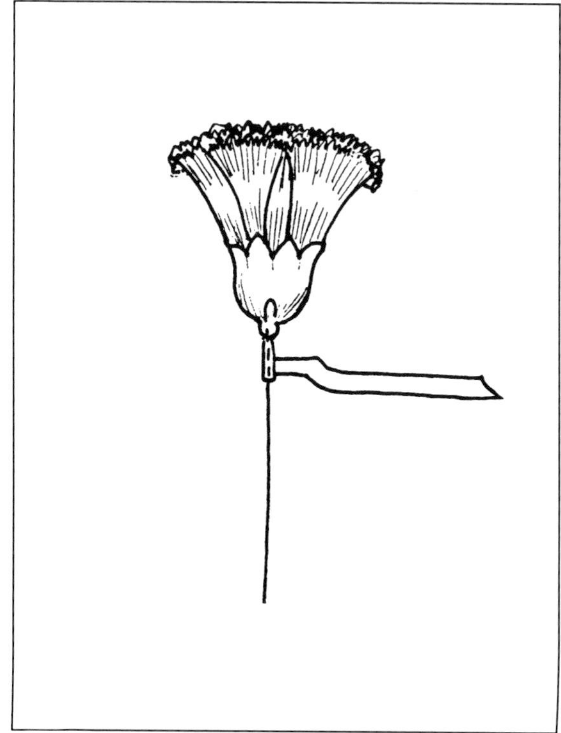

Lily of the Valley

Use 0.20 mm green reel wire. Start at the base of the stem and wind the wire round in between the florets, finishing at the top around the base of the last floret. Cut the wire as close to the floret as possible.

Small materials like violets which have weak stems should be mounted on a fine wire with a double leg mount.

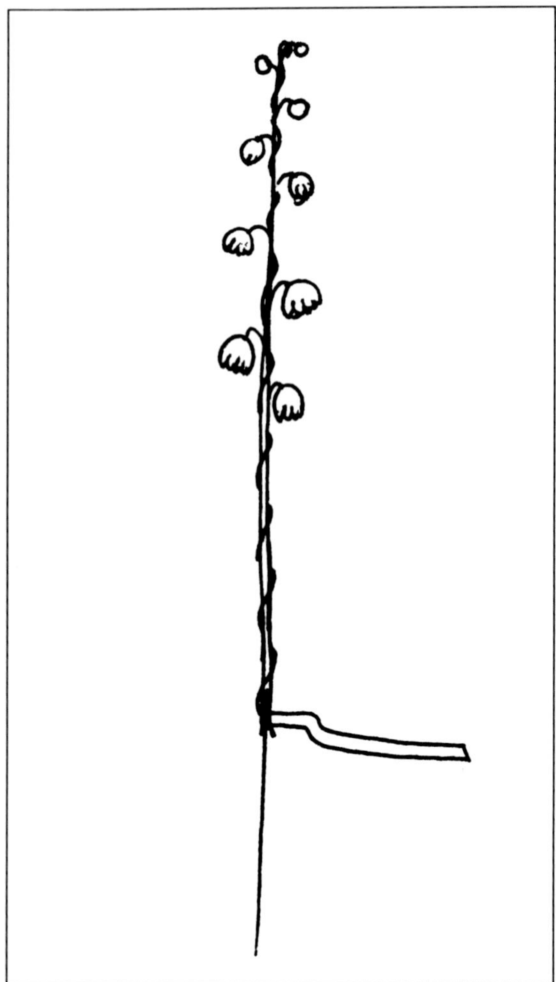

Fruits and Nuts

The use of fruits and nuts in floristry adds a great deal of interest and individuality to a piece of work. For instance, a wired Victorian posy, corsage, wedding bouquet, flower arrangement and festive garland can all be made to look unusual or special by the thoughtful use of a few nuts, berries or fruits within the design.

These materials must be support wired to provide a sufficiently long stem to insert in the design and to ensure that the material remains secure during its use.

Fruit and berries should rarely be left on their natural stems, especially for fine delicate work. Not only are the stems too thick or woody to include in the construction but also most fruits and berries have a tendency to fall off their branches when they dry out in a warm atmosphere.

For most small berries a fine stub wire used as a single leg mount is all that is required. The wire is passed through the base of the berry. Fruits that do not bleed when pierced, such as cotoneaster or small crab apples, can be wired this way.

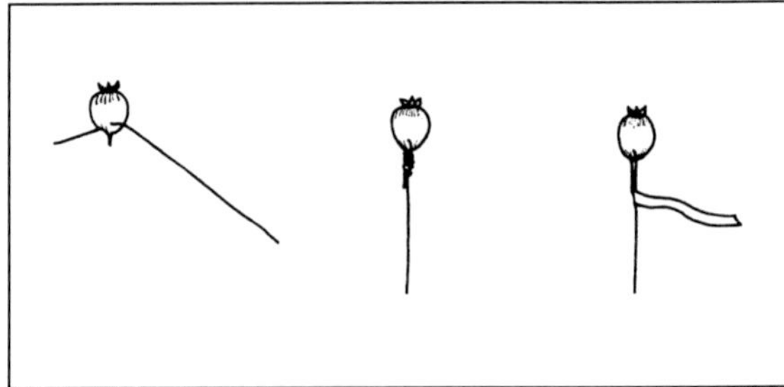

Most nuts do not have stems and are far too hard to pierce with a wire. A solution to this is to bend one end of a suitable gauge of stub wire into a small ring or loop. Carefully place a generous amount of hot glue onto this and then press the nut into the molten glue until it sets. This provides a secure fixing and also adds a stem.

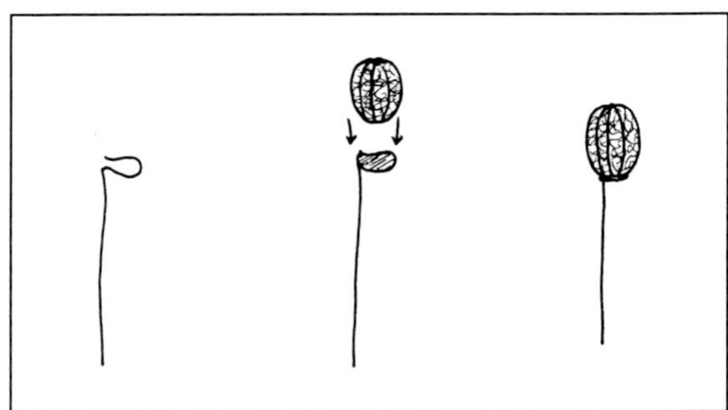

Larger, heavier fruits such as apples, oranges and lemons need to be supported on a much heavier wire such as 0.71 mm or more often 0.90 mm. The wire is pushed through the lower half of the fruit so that an equal amount protrudes from each side of the fruit. Both wires are then bent down over the fruit and twisted together underneath, leaving two wire 'stems' which can be inserted into foam for arrangements or into garlands.

If several fruits are being used in a display, a more natural effect can be achieved if some are wired from the base and some from the top so that, when clustered together, the stalks and tops as well as the undersides of some fruits are visible.

Fruit wired in this way for use in a table centre arrangement is for visual effect only and not intended for eating!

TYPES OF UNITS USED FOR MAKE-UP WORK

These are materials of one type which have been individually wired and are then put together to form a wired unit. The size is graded from small at the top to larger at the bottom to give the impression that the unit is natural and is growing. This is often referred to as pipping and is a method commonly used for headdress work where individual florets are required.

Branching Unit

Support wire leaves on 0.28 mm wire. Then tape together individual leaves to form a branching unit.

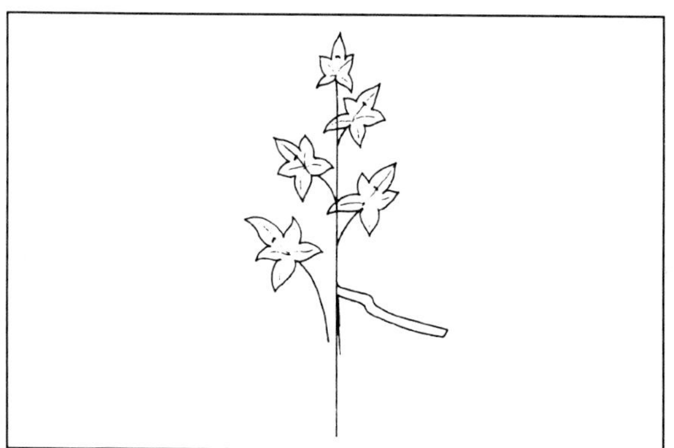

Natural Unit

Put a group of stems together on a single or double leg mount, depending on the weight of the material used. Waxflowers, little bunches of gypsophila and foliage which has been left on natural stems can all be wired in this way. A lot of foliage such as leatherleaf and asparagus can be broken down into smaller pieces for wiring like this.

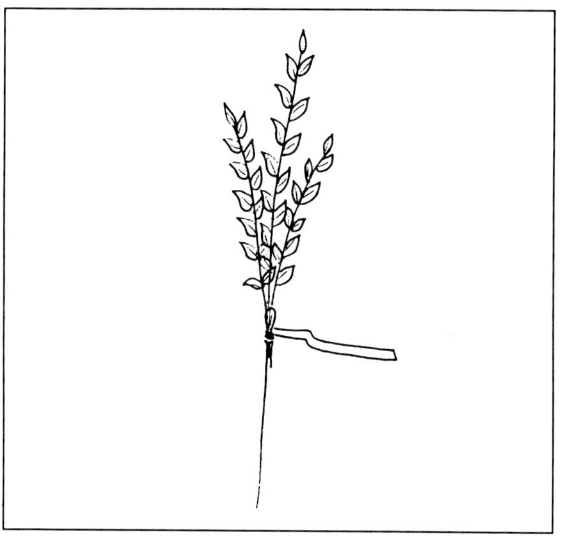

Ribbed Unit

This method is particularly effective when using hyacinth florets. Thread individual florets onto stay wire which has a hook on the end. Taping below the bottom floret stops the florets moving.

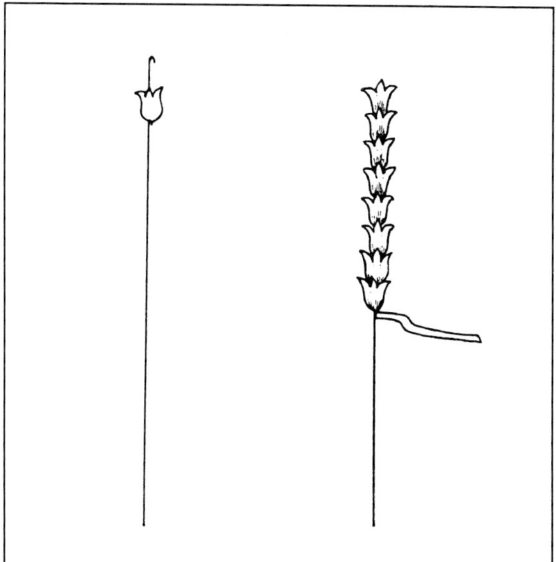

PINNING

This is another method of securing material and is used particularly in funeral work for single-leaf foliage bases (e.g. laurel and ivy). Different kinds of mosses are pinned, and some flower bases such as violets or hydrangea heads are grouped into a small bunch and then pinned.

There are three sizes of German pins, which are sold by the box:

10 mm × 25 mm short
10 mm × 40 mm medium
10 mm × 75 mm long

Pins can also be made in the form of a hairpin in whatever gauge or length is required.

Small sepal pins are sold for pinning the sepals on a rose; these can also be made of fine green wire to the length required, because the manufactured ones are usually too long for small roses.

Steel dressmaker's pins are used to secure ribbon edging in funeral work and also for corsages and buttonholes. For a corsage or buttonhole, pins with pearl heads look very attractive.

GLUE

The use of glue is now widely accepted as a quick and efficient alternative to many wiring and construction techniques. Fresh flowers and leaves can be glued directly onto headdress bands, combs and hats, as well as into foam bouquet holders for extra security. This reduces the amount of time needed for preparation and wiring before the item of work is put together. Glue is also used in the make up of dried flower displays, pictures and wall hangings, as well as silk and fabric flower arrangements and novelties.

Some points should be made about the safe and effective use of these appliances. The glue itself is bought as a solid cartridge which is inserted into the gun. A heating element melts the glue and a trigger forces the cartridge through the gun and pushes the molten glue out of the nozzle. Only the smallest amount is necessary to secure a flower, and a little practice may be required to judge the right amount of pressure needed so as not to expel too much glue in one go. The glue takes a few seconds to dry and some heavier flowers may have to be held in position until it sets. Great care must be taken to ensure that the glue does not come into contact with fingers and skin, as this is very painful. If this does happen, immerse the affected area in cold water immediately until the glue has set and can then be carefully removed.

A certain amount of discoloration or scorching of fresh flowers or leaves is unavoidable but, providing the amount of glue used is kept to a minimum, this should not be visible.

An advantage of the glue pot is that it leaves both hands free to hold and secure materials at the same time. It can also be used by more than one person at a time, and it melts the glue at a lower temperature than the gun. Small pellets of glue are melted in a shallow heated pan and the flowers can then be easily dipped into this and applied to whatever is being made. With this method it is also easier to control the amount of glue used.

There are also other forms of cold adhesives available for use with fresh and dried material. These are usually available in a pot or in spray form and can be used for the same purposes as hot glue.

Tip

Take extreme care when using hot glue and always follow the manufacturer's instructions.

CHAPTER 5

Flower Arrangement

To achieve success in constructing any arrangement, the following points should be observed.

- All material used should be absolutely fresh and well conditioned.
- The container should be watertight.
- The materials should always be in proportion to the size of the chosen container and the purpose for which the arrangement is intended. Small flowers are not suitable for a large pedestal; similarly, large gerbera are not correct in an arrangement using an O-bowl.
- The foam should be soaked correctly and all the stems should be pushed well into it so that materials will not fall out. The stems of all material should be cut at an angle with a sharp knife and the leaves removed at the point of insertion into the foam. This will ensure that the hole in the foam is not too big and will keep the stem secure.
- Always ensure that the foam is not visible and that there is space to add water at the back of an arrangement.
- There should be a recognisable colour harmony.
- If the design is for a special purpose, the colour choice should be appropriate, for example, golds and yellows for a golden wedding gift.
- The design should be stable for ease of transport.
- Spray the finished arrangement lightly. A care card should be attached to enable the customer to care for the arrangement properly.

There should be a selection of flower shapes in a design: spikes, rounds and intermediate shapes (see pages 28–29). This will create interest and transition.

The choice of foliage is unlimited, and two or three types should be used. The foliage should be an integral part of the design, not just something to cover the mechanics.

Commercial foliage is so expensive that it must be as carefully placed and used within a design as the flowers themselves. Distinctive leaves can play an important part in the overall effect of a design either because of their shape, colour or texture. Some beautiful displays can be made entirely from foliage, providing they are carefully chosen to either complement or contrast with each other. An all-foliage or all-green arrangement has a restful and calming effect and should not be overlooked when planning an event.

Other materials such as ribbon, artificial fruit, baubles, moss, bark, cones, dried fruit, fresh fruit or suitable accessories such as a teddy bear for a birth arrangement may be used, providing they are in keeping with the design, relate to the purpose for which the arrangement is intended and do not dominate it.

For most flower arrangements you will need the following basic sundries:

Knife	Pot tape
Scissors	Frog
Glue gun or sticky plasticine	Water mister spray
Containers	Ribbon
Wet or dry foam	

PREPARING CONTAINERS

The choice of container depends on what the customer requires, but do make sure it is clean and suitable for the purpose. There are so many to choose from, including crystal, wood, fine china or plastic. If the container is intended merely as a means of holding an arrangement and is not seen, such as a plastic O-bowl for an all-round design or a spray tray for a table design, then there is no need to match the colours or choose flowers which complement the container.

Some arrangements can be made without foam (see page 39). Most, however, are based on it.

There are various brands of foam on the market. Whichever is used must be soaked correctly according to the manufacturer's instructions.

Wet foam should never be pushed down into the water, as this destroys the structure, resulting in uneven soaking and dry areas within the foam. The foam should be placed in a bucket of water and allowed to soak on its own. A large block of foam will take about ten minutes to soak thoroughly, and smaller pieces will take less time.

Any soaked foam not required should be wrapped in polythene and put aside for future use. It should not be allowed to dry out, as it will not take up water a second time.

FLOWER SHAPES

Spikes

Gladioli
Liatris
Delphiniums
Ornithogalum thyrsoides
Solidago
Scilla
Aconitum
Crocosmia
Eremurus
Forsythia
Campanula
Celosia
Antirrhinums
Amaranthus
Prunus
Tuberose
Lilac
Strelitzia
Muscari
Freesias
Euphorbia
Irises
Molucella
Heliconia

Rounds

Gerbera
Carnations
Roses
Scabious
Chrysanthemum blooms
Spray chrysanthemums
Anemones
Dahlias
Hydrangeas
Zinnias
Protea
Hellebores
Agapanthus
Nerines
Ranunculus
Peonies
Ornithogalum arabicum
Narcissi
Hyacinths
Sweet williams
Craspedia
Alliums
Centaurea
Bouvardia
Calendula
Guelder rose
Achillea
Tulips

Intermediate Shapes

Solidaster
Lilies
Alstroemeria
Open irises
Trachelium
Saponaria
Spray roses
Spray carnations
Phalaenopsis and dendrobium orchids
Astilbes
Alchemilla
Limonium
Gypsophila
Statice
Lavatera
Hypericum
Sweet peas
Genista
Eustoma
Eryngium
Waxflowers
Asters

MEDIUM AND SMALL ARRANGEMENTS

Flowers

Roses
Spray roses
Carnations
Spray carnations
Asters
Gypsophila
Narcissi
Anemones
Dahlias
Muscari
Convallaria
Waxflowers
Centaurea
Freesias
Trachelium
Tulips
Spray chrysanthemums
Scabious
Ranunculus
Nerines
Limonium
Amaranthus
Alstroemeria
Agapanthus
Alchemilla
Liatris
Lilies
Bridal gladioli
Mini gerbera
Genista
Eustoma
Dendrobium and cattleya orchids

Foliage

Hebe
Euonymus
Leatherleaf
Ivy
Eucalyptus
Ming fern
Bear grass
Ruscus
Senecio
Cupressus
Evergreen oak
Escallonia
Tree heather
Cyclamen
Croton
Box
Choisya

LARGE ARRANGEMENTS

Flowers

Gerbera
Roses
Carnations
Lilies
Strelitzia
Hydrangeas
Lilac
Delphiniums
Aconitum
Euphorbia
Eucharis
Eustoma
Gladioli
Irises
Hippeastrum
Chrysanthemum blooms
Spray chrysanthemums
Dahlias
Anthurium
Heliconia
Larkspur
Asters
Liatris
Peonies
Lavatera
Limonium
Stocks
Phlox
Prunus
Solidago
Asters
Sedum
Zantedeschia

Foliage

Laurel
Portuguese laurel
Arbutus
Senecio
Bergenia
Viburnum tinus
Tree ivy
Ivy trails
Bear grass
Fatsia
Blue pine
Beech (copper and green)
Eucalyptus
Dracaena
Phormium tenax
Hosta
Jasmine
Honeysuckle
Holly
Large fern
Privet
Gaultheria
Tsuga pine
Escallonia
Cornus

The foam will need to be cut to the correct size for the container required. It is easier to cut the foam after it has been soaked, as a cleaner cut will be obtained and there is less wastage.

There must be enough foam above the rim of the container to enable stems to be inserted at an angle.

A frog should be glued or stuck with sticky plasticine to the base of the container. This will help to secure the foam, which is pushed down on to the frog. The foam is then taped to the container with pot tape, which is available in green or white.

Pot tape does not stick easily to a basket, so if using one, bring the tape round the handle and across the top of the foam to secure it. When taping over the foam, do not cover the centre part where the larger and focal flowers will be placed.

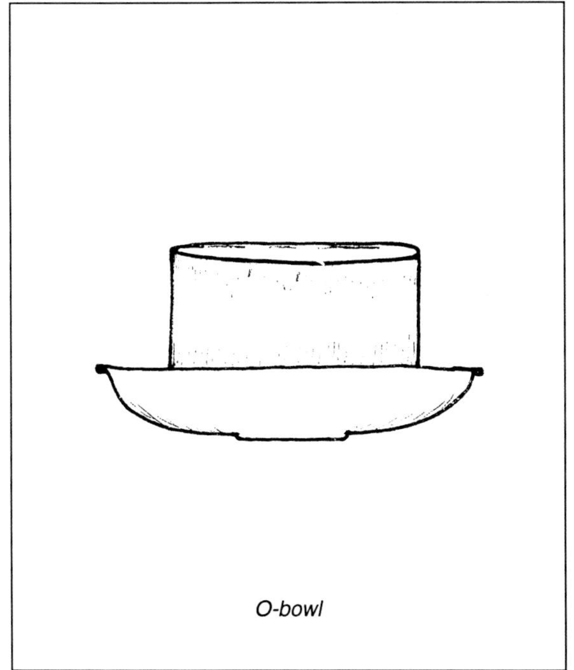

O-bowl

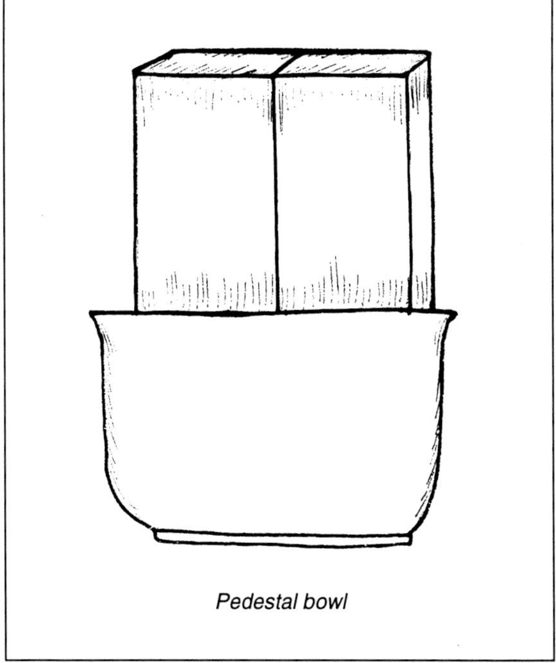

Pedestal bowl

Symmetrical arrangement

SHAPES OF ARRANGEMENTS

Symmetrical Arrangement

A symmetrical arrangement, also called front-facing, is balanced on both sides. It can be made in a container of virtually any shape or size.

Flowers	Foliage
Freesias Roses Waxflowers Alstroemeria	Leatherleaf Pittosporum *Hedera canariensis*

Method

1. The proportions should be as follows:

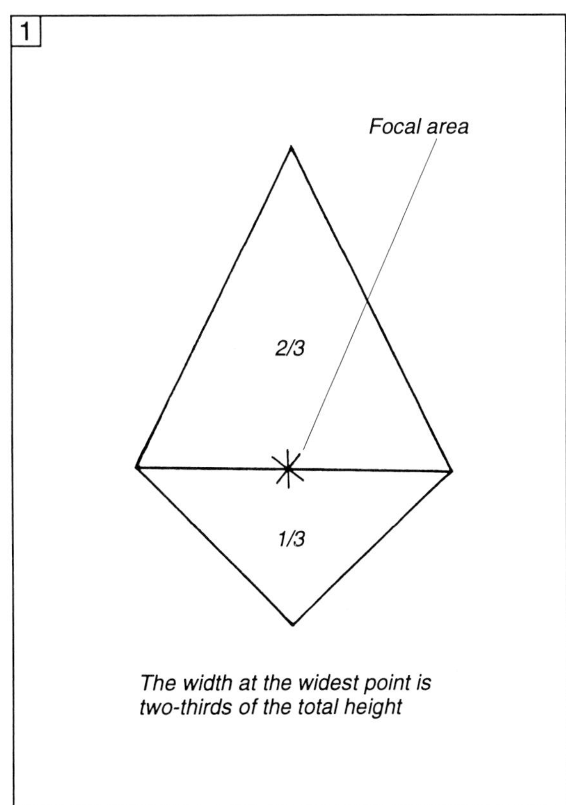

The width at the widest point is two-thirds of the total height

2. Start by placing the foliage in the foam to create the required outline. The foliage should be grouped at this stage, and the first placements will determine the height and width of the overall design.

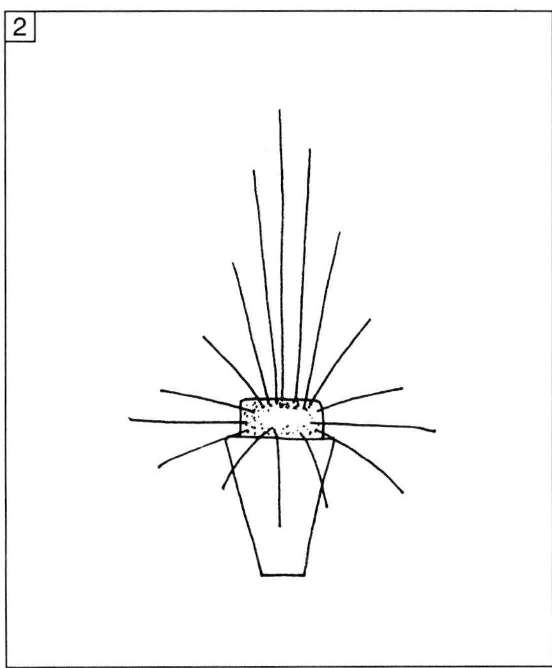

Some shorter pieces of foliage can be added behind the tallest stem. This gives a 3-D effect. The design should also be pleasing to the eye from the side and not appear to have a flat back. All stems, foliage and flowers should look as if they radiate from the focal area.

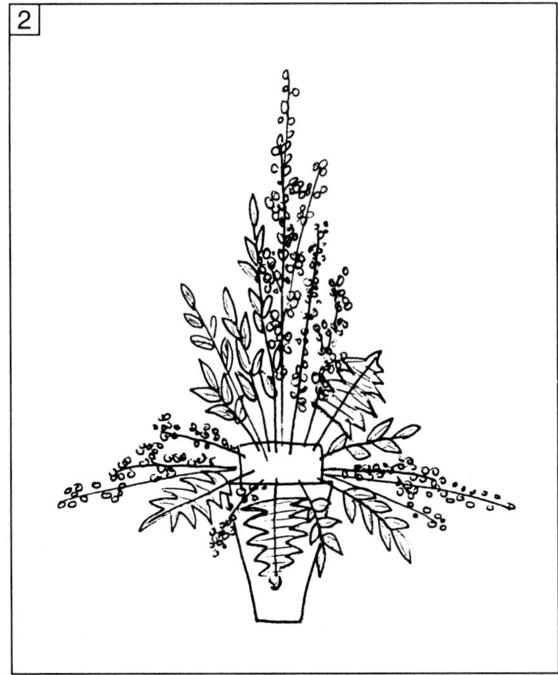

3. The flowers can be grouped through the design, forming pattern lines. Once the outline has been established, all material should be placed within it. Smaller flowers and buds should be used at the edge, larger flowers and stronger colour in and around the focal area. Start with the freesias, using the tighter buds at the top, and group through to the front and right side.

   Take the roses from the top right side through to the left side. The largest rose should be the focal flower. To strengthen the focal area, add the hedera leaves well recessed below the focal flowers. Add the alstroemeria broken down into single flowers through from one side to the other. Fill in with the waxflowers.

3

Asymmetrical Arrangement

Although the two sides of this design's axis or focal area are different, the arrangement looks visually balanced. It may be referred to as an L-shaped design, and all the usual design principles apply to it. The shape is very versatile. It can be used for small or large arrangements, in pedestal containers or on a flat base, and it is ideal as an arrangement incorporating a gift or accessory. It is also suitable for a pair of mirror designs on an altar, fireplace or a buffet table. Fruit may be added to a design for a buffet table.

Flowers	***Foliage***
Spray carnations	Eucalyptus stems
Bridal gladioli	Rubus leaves
Sweet peas	Leatherleaf stems
Roses	

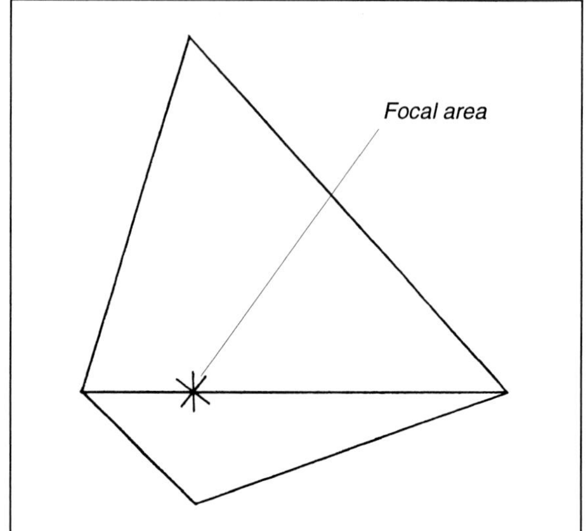

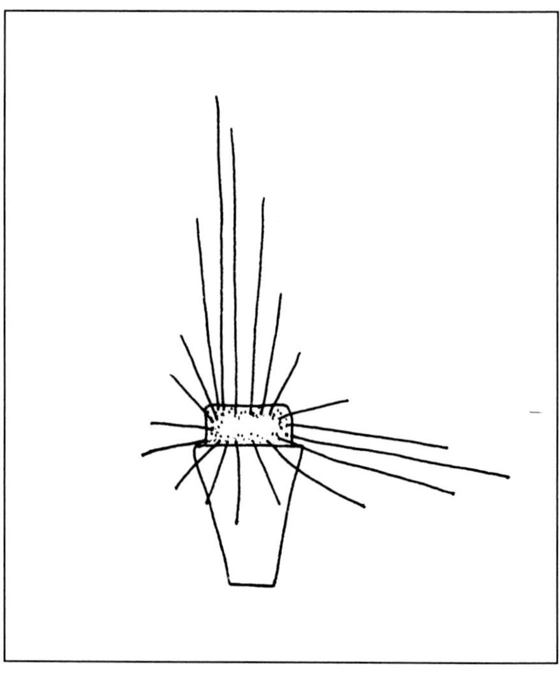

Asymmetrical arrangement

Method

1. Place a long piece of eucalyptus into the centre of the foam. Place another piece of eucalyptus to the right-hand side, flowing down at an angle. Add more pieces of eucalyptus following a line through.

   Break down the leatherleaf and take it through from the right-hand side to the left, using shorter stems to keep the L-shape. This will create an outline.

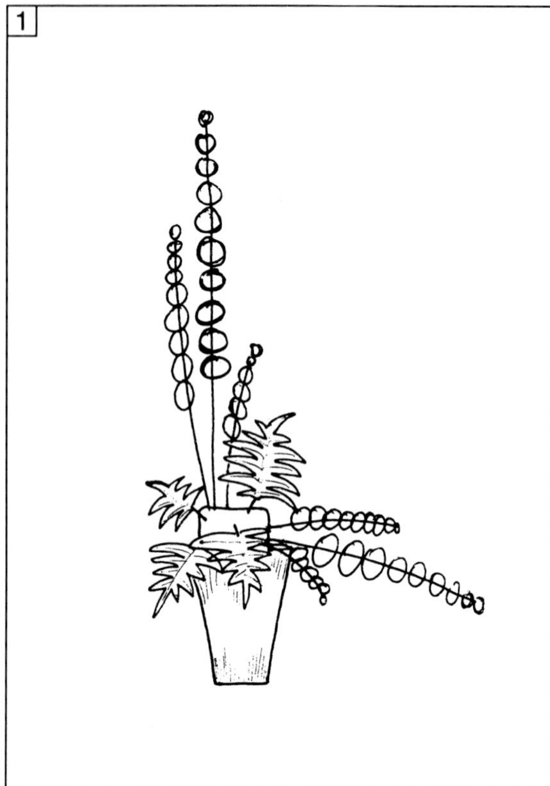

2. Take the gladioli and follow the line of eucalyptus. The spray carnations can also be brought through with the gladioli, using the larger heads towards the focal area, which will be at the widest point of the design.

   Place the roses around the centre with the largest flower as the focal point. They should be at different levels, using recession. Place the rubus leaves around the focal roses to reinforce the focal area. Take the sweet peas through, following the line of leatherleaf.
3. The material placed on the inside of the L should be kept fairly short so that the shape remains recognisable.

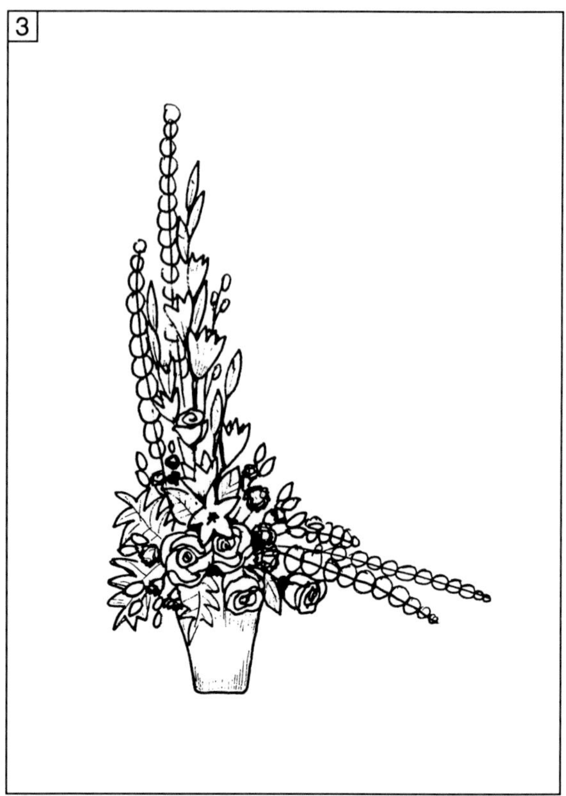

All-round Arrangement

This is a very versatile design which can be made for many purposes. As it is a circular design, it should be perfect from every angle.

Posy arrangements are very popular, either as a small gift or as a table centre, perhaps with a candle in the middle. An arrangement for a large circular table in a hotel foyer will need to be all-round to follow the shape of the table.

The same method is used to achieve the all-round design whether it is small or large and whatever its use, but the proportions will differ depending on the size required. (See pages 114 and 138.) The following method is for a small posy design.

Flowers	Foliage
Spray roses Nerines Spray chrysanthemums Alchemilla	Hebe Euonymus Leatherleaf

All-round arrangement

Method

1. Make the posy outline with five small pieces of foliage of the same length, pushed in at an angle.

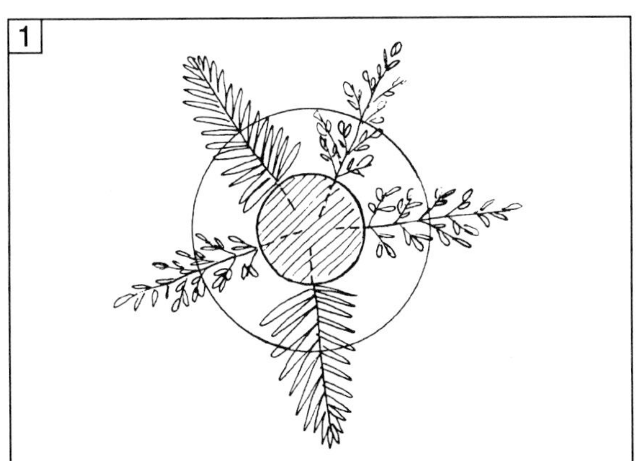

2. Group the hebe from one side to the other; then take the euonymus through, staying within the outline created. Fill in with more foliage. When taking the material through the centre, the stems should be positioned to create a domed effect. Add some small pieces of leatherleaf through from one side to the other.

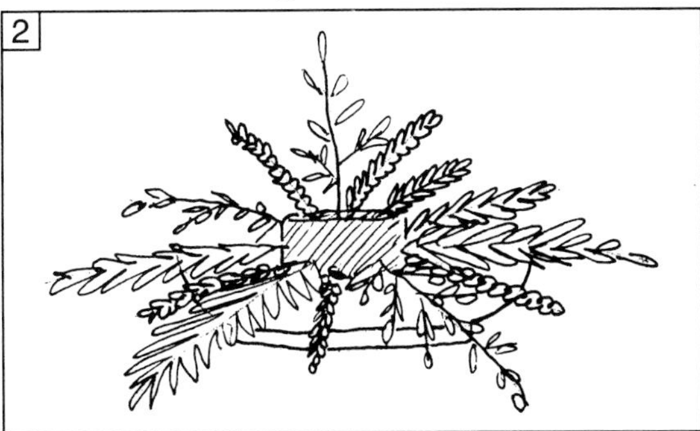

3. Use a nerine as the tallest flower and recess one on either side of the focal flower. With the remaining nerines follow through with a pattern line within the imaginary outline to either side.

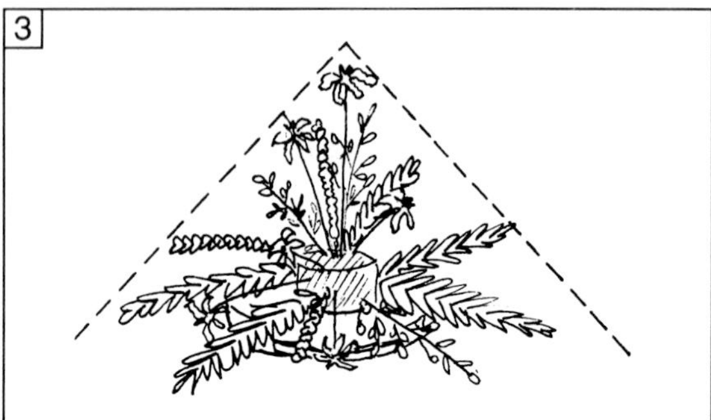

4. Cut the spray roses and the spray chrysanthemums into individual flowers. Arrange the roses around the focal area. Take the spray chrysanthemums through on the opposite side to the nerines. Place the alchemilla throughout the whole design.

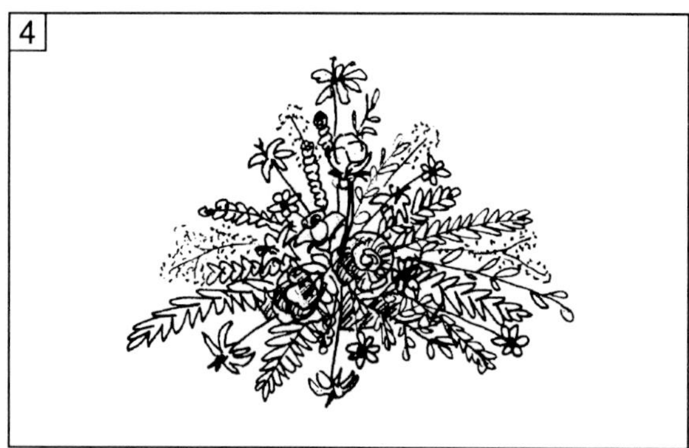

5. If a candle is used, it will take the place of the tallest flower and foliage. The materials around it should be kept low enough not to be damaged by the candle's burning.

Line Arrangement

As the name suggests, this design is made in the form of a staggered line of flowers, usually of one type. It can be for a hospital locker, a ledge or a shelf where space is limited. It is also suitable as a gift arrangement.

Materials
5 irises ranging from bud to full flower 3 croton leaves Handful of clear marbles

Line arrangement

Method

1. Study the diagrammatical drawing to show placement of the irises.

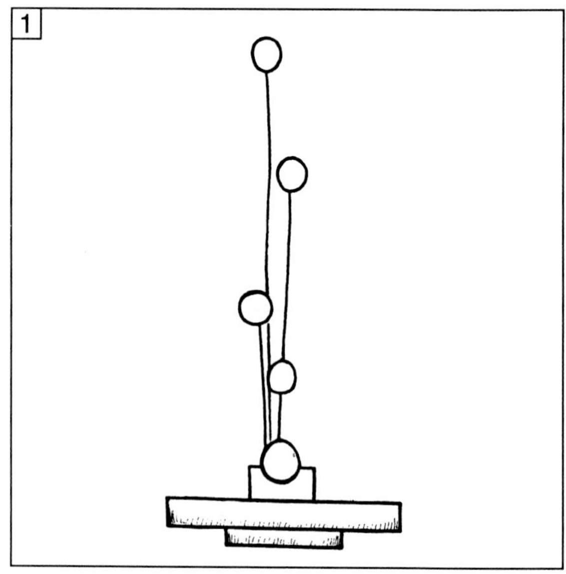

2. Place an iris, which should be in bud, into the centre of the foam. Insert the next iris, which should be a little shorter, slightly to the side of the first stem.

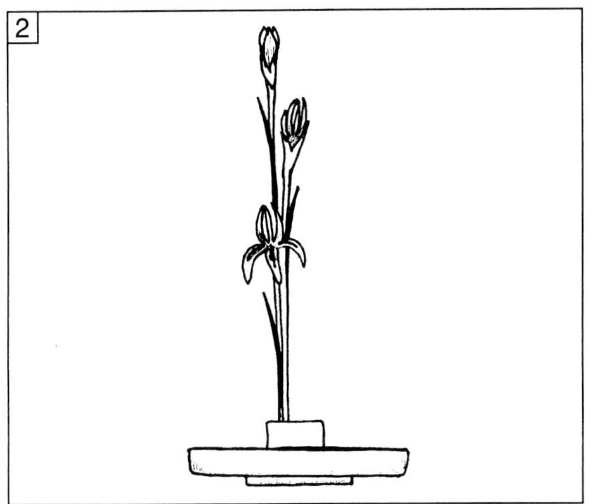

Place the third iris lower and slightly to the left of the second and the fourth iris lower still and slightly to the right of the third iris. Last will be the focal flower, placed low, almost level with the container.

The irises should range from a bud at the top of the arrangement to fully open at the bottom.

3. Arrange the leaves around the base, placing one behind the focal flower and the other two to either side of it. Scatter the marbles in the container.

As a variation on this simple design, some catkins or contorted willow can be added, but it is important not to make the design of a line arrangement too visually confusing. Avoid using fussy flowers or foliage, as this spoils the strong clean lines. Accessories such as cones, berries, fruit or bark can be an integral part of the design.

BASKET ARRANGEMENTS

Baskets come in many varied shapes and sizes, and they are very popular as a gift arrangement. Any of the styles previously mentioned is suitable: even a line arrangement can be made in a flat basket without a handle. The basket encourages the very popular country or rustic look.

Many polythene-lined baskets are watertight, but it is a good idea to check by putting some water directly into the basket and leaving on a dry surface for a few minutes. If the basket is not lined, a plastic container can be fixed in it to hold the wet foam. Alternatively the basket can be lined with thick plastic and the foam placed onto the plastic.

Most flowers and foliage are suitable for use in a basket design, although arum lilies, heliconia, eucharist lilies and anthuriums would be a little sophisticated. Garden-type flowers and foliage or a mixture of small spring flowers look very attractive in a basket design.

Any handle on a basket should be visible as an integral part of the design and should be usable. The design will need to be well balanced in order to do this.

Small Basket of Spring Flowers

Flowers	
Narcissi	Ming fern
Muscari	Hebe
Anemones	

Method

1. It is usually difficult to stick pot tape to basketware, so take it from one side of the handle to the other side twice, to hold the foam in place.

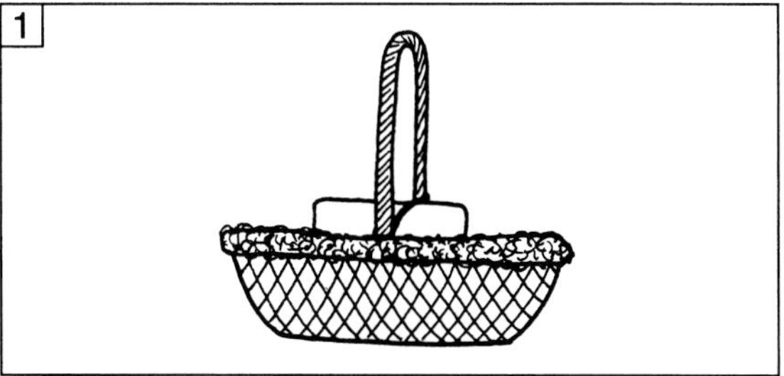

2. For an all-round design, make five points with foliage and then add more foliage within the outline, grouping the material through the centre from one side to the other.

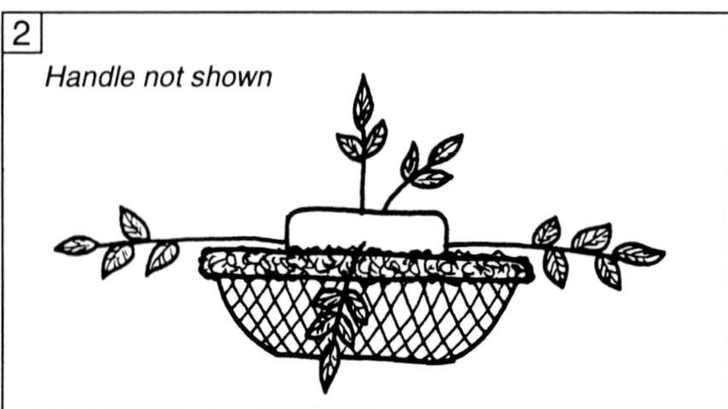

3. Take the narcissi from one side to the other, placing the tallest flower in the centre far enough below the handle to enable the basket to be picked up by the handle. Take the muscari in an opposite diagonal across the centre. Remember to keep within the circular outline while maintaining a domed profile.

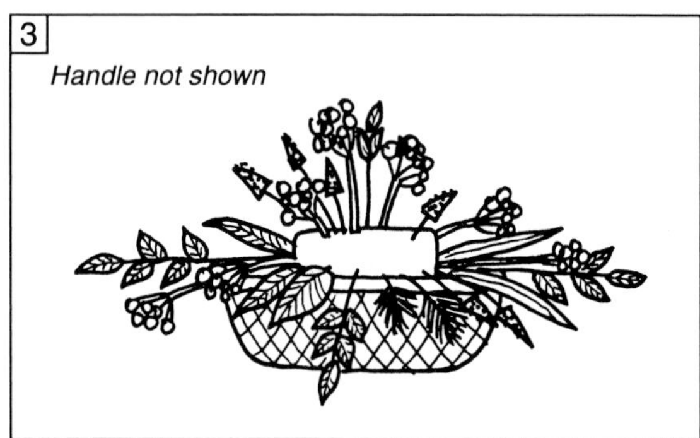

4. Make a ribbon bow, mount on a double leg mount and insert into the foam near one side of the handle.
5. Add the anemones. Place all over the design, the darker, larger flowers towards the centre. Cover any areas of visible foam with foliage.

Square Flat Basket without Handle

A continental parallel style (see page 145) is very suitable for this kind of basket, which can be placed on a low coffee table.

Flowers	Materials
2 lilies 5 liatris 5 roses 7 carnations	Bun moss 2 bundles of cinnamon sticks Fir cones, small and medium Box foliage Ivy leaves Nephrolepis leaves

Method

1. Insert a piece of foam to cover the entire inner area of a waterproof flat basket and glue it in place. The foam should extend about 3 cm above the basket rim. Glue half a large block of foam off-centre.

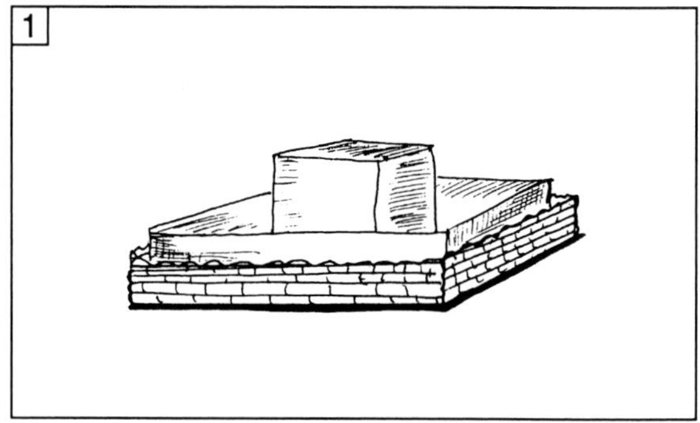

2. Place the main group, the tallest placement, using five liatris, into the larger piece of foam. This larger piece of foam gives more support and extra height. There is no focal point in this design. Material should be grouped together and placed either vertically or horizontally.
3. Arrange the two stems of lily to one side in another group, slightly shorter than the tallest liatris. Arrange the roses in another group slightly to the left of the lilies. Then place the carnations around the base of the roses, blocked together at one level to give a carpet effect.
4. Arrange the bun moss around the base of the liatris and across the other side. Secure with German pins.

5. Mount the fir cones on a single leg mount using 0.71 mm wire and arrange them around the base of the lilies. Arrange the cinnamon sticks in small bundles lying horizontally on the edge of the design and attach to the foam with wire. Support wire the ivy leaves and arrange in a stepped design on visible areas of foam. Arrange the nephrolepis leaves by placing two to the right-hand side and two coming over the front.

ARRANGEMENTS IN VASES WITHOUT MECHANICS

A design without foam or any sort of mechanics can be arranged in any vase, from a small circular posy vase to a very large one. To achieve an all-round design, the vase should have a wide neck to allow for a lot of stems. Most flowers and foliage are suitable.

This is a design which needs to be done in situ as it does not travel well. It can be placed in a hotel reception area or in a private home.

For larger designs choose foliage which is fairly bushy, such as *Viburnum tinus*, tree ivy or arbutus. Linear foliage like bear grass or soft ruscus and bare twigs such as tortured hazel, willow or cornus also look very attractive.

A single type of flower material such as lilies, gerbera or roses looks as good as a mixed arrangement. When using mixed flowers, remember to select different shapes: alstroemeria, carnations, lilies and asters would look very effective together.

Method

1. Fill the vase with water and flower food. Wire netting secured with pot tape at the top of the vase will provide extra support for large branches.
2. Arrange the foliage in a circular effect with the stems crossing below the water level so as to form a support for the flowers.

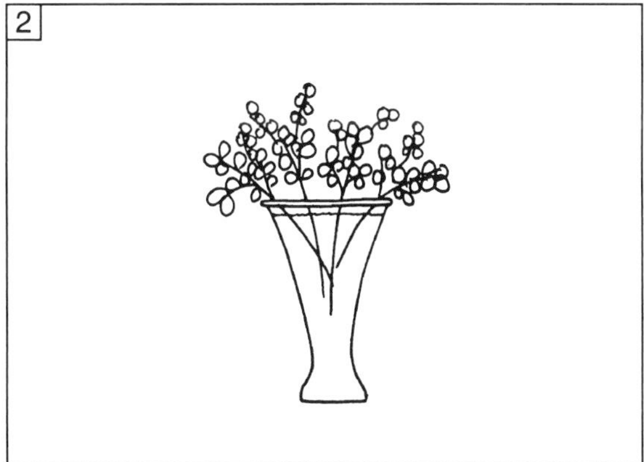

3. Place the flowers, one type at a time if mixed, in circles and then add any bare twigs.

Arrangement in vase without mechanics

CHAPTER 6

Hand-tied Assembly

The application and use of tied bunches crosses over into all areas of floristry. All designs are extremely adaptable and make ideal wedding bouquets, funeral tributes, flower arrangements and presentation gifts. By the clever use of different and exciting materials the effects achieved can range from a starkly minimal look for an arrangement to a soft full romantic bouquet for a wedding or a delightfully casual 'just picked' look for a gift bunch.

Whilst the construction techniques are basically the same for all tied bunches, the key factors involved are the correct choice of flower and plant materials and the correct size of the finished design. For instance, whilst spray chrysanthemums, spray carnations, standard carnations, roses and statice are ideal for use in a round hand-tied bunch to be given as a gift, smaller flowers would be more suitable in a bridal bouquet.

Likewise, all gift bouquets are best wrapped either in paper or cellophane. This improves the presentational effect and with the addition of ribbon and a bow adds the finishing touch. The wrapping can either be as an aqua-pack or just as a decorative collar around the flowers (see page 166).

Tied work for weddings or funerals is usually left unwrapped. The flowers are intended to fulfil an important role on such occasions and should be displayed to their best advantage without any additional sundries or unnecessary extras. The natural stems are usually cut slightly shorter than for a presentation bunch, but they still form an important part of the design. A suitably coloured ribbon bow is always added to disguise the tying point and to make an attractive finish at the back of the bouquet.

Hand-tied bouquets are exactly that: flowers and foliage held and arranged in the hand and finally tied with a piece of string. They can range in size from a small posy suitable for a token gift or for a small bridesmaid to carry, up to very large presentation bouquets for birthdays or anniversaries and large funeral sheafs.

Tied bunches are just as suited to wedding work as to the more obvious gift market and can be made in a variety of styles to suit all types of weddings from the natural informal country bunch or posy to the limited modern style of continental design or the larger formal shower or trailing bouquet. Whatever the shape or occasion, tied bunches have a natural appeal, giving the flowers a greater sense of movement and freedom than wired work and allowing them to be fully appreciated.

Tip

The stems of tied bouquets to be used for weddings are usually left unwrapped. Always make sure the flower stalks are clean and dry, and remove all leaves, leaf stalks and especially thorns. Any wires used for support wiring which have come through into the stem of the bunch should be carefully cut off as short as possible and the sharp ends pushed back into the tying point so as not to snag on dress materials.

Hand-ties are quick and simple to make and can be placed in a vase without the need for any further arranging – an important selling point.

The versatility of the hand-tied makes it an established design within most of the areas of commercial floristry work.

Furthermore, the finished bouquet gives a value-for-money appearance as the same quantity of flowers used in this style can look fuller than in a flat bouquet. Yet another advantage is that it can be placed in a vase without any further arrangement. This should surely be an important selling point!

The type of flowers and foliage depends on the finished size and style of the bouquet. Generally anything which has a reasonably firm stem can be used, although some flowers are more suited to this type of work than others. The method of construction for all types of tied bunch is basically the same. The key to success is to arrange the stems of the flowers in a spiral. This naturally forms a spreading open top to the bunch. The clever combination of unusual or unexpected materials or colours can create some eye-catching results.

A bridesmaid's posy bouquet for a spring wedding would be very easy to make using small sprays of mimosa and eucalyptus as the main part of the bunch with muscari, scilla and anemones. An outer collar of larger ivy leaves would complete the effect.

A much more elaborate cascading bridal bouquet could be made from natural trails of asparagus fern and soft ruscus with the main body of the bunch formed from two or three stems of well-chosen bush ivy. Into this foliage framework would be added natural sprays of cream *Euphorbia fulgens*, white spray roses, white tulips and a couple of greenish-white hippeastrum blooms to add body and depth to the design.

In contrast a simple but impressive bouquet can be made from only one or two types of choice flowers such as perfect long-stemmed roses or white lilies, used with only one type of complementary foliage like eucalyptus or ruscus.

Whatever the purpose of the bouquet, care should be given to the finishing details. It is a good idea to cover the string on the tying point with pot tape for neatness and added strength. The stems

Tip

Flowers and plant material which may mark clothing or cause skin irritations should be avoided in bouquets if possible. Stain from lily pollen is a common problem and so always remove the stamens from open flowers. Another point to remember is to remove all rose thorns from the *complete* length of stem, not just from the part of the stalk which will be held. If left on they can snag or catch on clothing.

Circular hand-tied bouquet

should be cut to the correct length (about one-third of the overall arrangement length) and be perfectly clean. If intended for use as a gift, the bunch can then be wrapped in cellophane and finished with a bow. Wedding bouquets and tied funeral tributes should always have the tying point covered with a ribbon bow of a suitable colour and size. As with all gift-wrapping and presentation, the accessories should not dominate or overpower the effect of the flowers.

The position of the tying point determines the finished size of the bunch. A high tying point will produce a small posy; a lower tying point, a much larger bouquet. Whatever the size of the bunch, all the stems must spiral in the same direction.

Circular Hand-tied Bouquet

All flowers with a reasonable stem length can be used. Those listed below are useful because of their structure, which forms a framework of support for smaller individual flowers

Flowers	
All types of lilies	September flowers and aster types
Single spray chrysanthemums	Solidaster
Alstroemeria	Statice
Spray roses	Eustoma
Waxflowers	

Foliage	
Filler	
Pittosporum	*Asparagus umbeillatus*
Eucalyptus	*Euphorbia marginata*
Bunch ivy	Senecio
Soft ruscus	Bear grass
Hard ruscus	
Outer ring	
Leatherleaf	*Asparagus plumosus*
Begonia leaves	Nephrolepis fronds
Hosta leaves	Douglas fir

Fruits and seed heads	
Cotoneaster	Mountain ash (sorbus)
Blackberries	Poppy heads
Ivy	Small fir cones
Symphoricarpos	Lotus heads
Small crab apples (malus)	Nigella
Rose hips	Linseed
Hawthorn	Eucalyptus
	Cereals

The following construction techniques for a hostess or circular hand-tied bouquet apply basically to all hand-tieds.

Method

1. Choose a selection of flower and foliage shapes: rounds such as carnations or roses; iris or liatris spikes; fillers such as spray chrysanthemums, statice or solidaster, gypsophila, eucalyptus and leatherleaf.
2. All flowers and foliage should be well conditioned before use. Remove all foliage, side shoots and buds which will be below the tying point. Clean stems will lock together more easily and form a better spiral.
3. Lay out all prepared materials ready for use. It can be difficult to stop to prepare more material once the bunch has been started. Keep flowers and foliage separated into colours and types. Cut a length of string for tying and make a ribbon bow with long tails for tying around the stems.

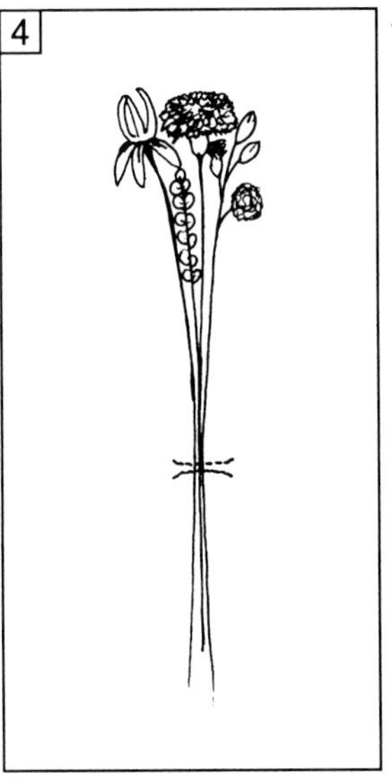

4. To start the spiral a central 'core' must be made first. Bunch together three or four pieces of mixed flowers and foliage. Hold these lightly in one hand so that they are supported between the thumb and forefinger. It is then quite easy to add further materials by simply opening the finger and thumb and laying the new stems at an angle on to the existing core of stalks. Two or three pieces of

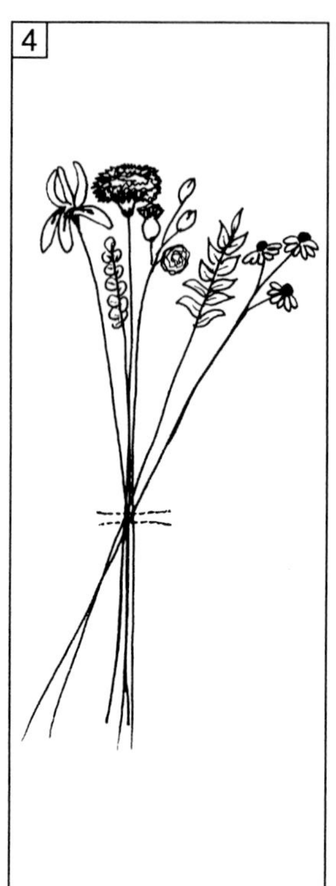

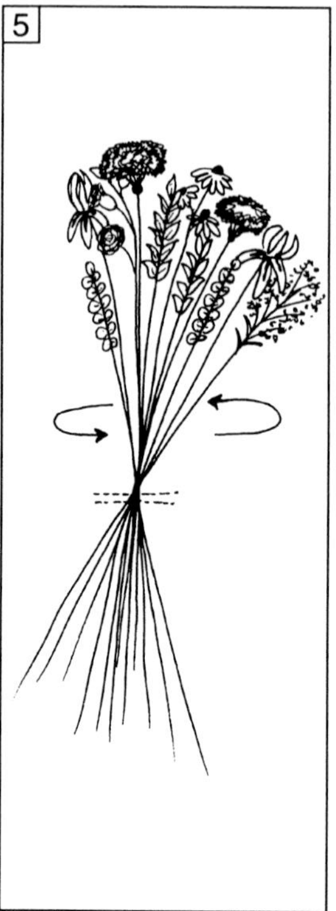

material can be added together, care being taken to ensure that the bunch forms a slightly domed top and is roughly circular.

5. Turn the bunch to receive more material by holding the stems lower down with the free hand, releasing the grip with the other and simply turning the whole bunch by about a quarter turn. Hold the bunch again with the other hand in exactly the same place as before. Add two or three more flowers in the same way and in the same position by opening the finger and thumb and turn the bunch again. This process is continued until the bunch is the desired size.

   The stems will easily spiral and the flowers will be well spaced within the bouquet if you construct it this way.
6. Finish the bouquet before tying it by adding an outer ring or 'collar' of foliage. Leatherleaf fern is ideal for this purpose; other leaves such as begonia, hosta or pittosporum can be used. This collar not only frames the flowers attractively but also protects the outer flowers from damage.
7. Tie the bunch firmly with string. Nylon string or garden twine can be used. Holding the bunch firmly in one hand, bind the stems several times with string, leaving a length at the beginning for the final knot. Binding the stems several times makes it possible to lay the bunch down without it falling to pieces so that both hands can be used to tie the knot. Cover the tying point with pot tape for neatness and added security.

8. The stems should then be cut to the correct length, approximately a third of the overall length of the bouquet. Hold the bouquet upside down and close all the stems together in one hand. Cut through the bundle of stalks as evenly as possible. Release the stems and tap the base of the stalks lightly on a work surface to level them. The bunch should now stand upright on its own stems.
9. If the bouquet is to be used for presentation it can be wrapped in cellophane. If for a wedding, simply cover the binding point with a ribbon bow and trim the ribbon tails to just below the base of the stems. The stems can be cut slightly shorter than for a presentation bunch to allow the bouquet to be carried more easily.

Natural Posy

This small tied bouquet can be used as a bridesmaid's bouquet or an informal gift for any occasion.

Flowers	
Anemones	Hellebores
Muscari	Alstroemeria
Small narcissi	Lily of the valley
Freesias	Solidaster
Nerines	Gypsophila
Snowdrops	Waxflowers
Scilla	Erica
Matricaria	*Viburnum tinus*
Smaller rose varieties	Dianthus
Spray chrysanthemums	Calendula
Spray carnations	Mimosa
Spray roses	

Foliage	
Pittosporum	*Asparagus umbellatus*
Small eucalyptus	Box
Hebe	Euonymus
Bush ivy	

Bridesmaid's natural posy

The construction is exactly the same as for the circular bouquet, all materials forming a spiral. Because of the smaller size, fewer flowers will be used and this reduced quantity of materials can make it difficult to achieve the same spiral as in a larger bunch. With careful choice of materials, though, it should not be a problem. The flowers and foliage used must be in proportion to the finished size of the bouquet. This can limit the choice of materials at certain times of the year.

Because of the reduced size of this design there is a tendency for the flowers to be more tightly packed than normal. To avoid this, use short filling material such as pittosporum, erica, viburnum or box lower down in the bunch to keep the flowers apart. A narrow ribbon should be used to form a small bow.

Tied Sheaf

A sheaf of flowers is by no means a new idea, although today it is mainly confined to funeral work. However, by varying the size and type of flowers used, sheaves have a wide range of applications from wedding bouquets to gift bouquets. From about the end of the First World War until well into the late 1920s, a sheaf of white lilies was the most fashionable bouquet a bride could carry on her wedding day. This idea has become acceptable again, and simple tied bunches of lilies or just blossom are being used as bridal bouquets.

Whatever the purpose of a sheaf, the construction methods are exactly the same. By changing the overall size and flower types it is possible to make a wide range of bouquets. A tied sheaf should be roughly triangular with a narrow tapering top and a wider fuller base. It is a front-facing design and should have a flat foliage back. The stems must form a spiral in order to allow the flowers to spread out to create the width and profile and they are an important feature of the finished design.

If mixed flowers are being used, care should be taken to form groupings and pattern lines of one flower type or colour within the design. A variety of flower shapes will make an interesting design combining spikes, round flowers, larger open blooms and small, fussy material such as gypsophila or September flower. This design can be equally effective when only one type of flower

Tied funeral sheaf

is used, in which case the flower must be sufficiently bold or distinctive to create an eye-catching effect. Longiflorum lilies, large long-stemmed roses, arum lilies or branches of lilac blossom provide the necessary impact to make this idea work.

Because of its large size, which can be anything up to a metre in length, it is much easier to construct a funeral sheaf on a work bench or table rather than trying to hold all the material in one hand. To do this make sure the tying point and the stems extend over the edge of the table to allow a spiral to form whilst the flat back of the design is supported on the table top.

The tied funeral sheaf is an impressive tribute and something different from the more usual wreaths, crosses and hearts.

For a funeral sheaf a strong backing foliage must be used to support all the flowers and to provide a strong shape to the design. Laurel, tsuga pine, spruce and thuja are ideal.

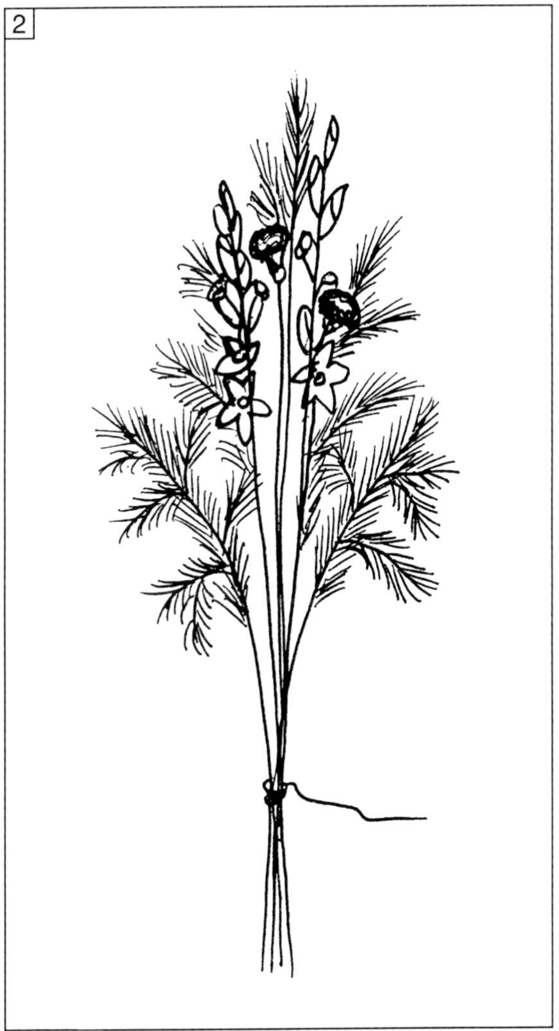

Method

1. Start the sheaf by selecting a strong, well-shaped branch of backing foliage. Ideally this should be narrow at the top and wider at the base. If all available material is a bit thin, tie several pieces together.
2. Lay two or three of the longest flowers onto the foliage to form the top of the design. All the stems are parallel at this stage. If making the design on a work surface the stems can be lightly held together at the tying point, which should be just over the edge of the table.
3. Continue to add flowers to form the shape of the sheaf. Pattern lines should already be established within the design.
4. Graduate flowers down through the design and begin to create a spiral of stems. Holding the

stems just below the tying point, angle the stems nearest you to the left and those underneath to the right. This will automatically begin to form a spiral as well as allowing the flower heads to fan out and fill in the wider parts of the base of the design.

5. The profile of the sheaf should also be built up during the construction so that it contains some materials which are raised towards the base. This is achieved by adding small 'packing' pieces of foliage such as conifer during construction. Not only does this help to raise any flowers which are placed on top of it but also strengthens the overall construction of the bunch. These small pieces of foliage must have enough stem to pass through the tying point.
6. To help fill in and raise the centre of the design, flowers such as spray chrysanthemums and lilies are very useful. Their branching flower heads enable them to fill in quickly without making the design too heavy. Finer, thinner flowers can then be threaded through them and are supported by them as well.
7. Larger flowers are grouped towards the centre and base of the design to provide visual weight. The base of the sheaf can then be finished off with a 'collar' of foliage such as leatherleaf or bergenia leaves tied securely and finally with a ribbon bow.
8. These tied bunches will not be required to stand up on their stems so the base of the flower stalks can be trimmed into a slight curve if desired instead of a straight cut.

Faced hostess bouquet

Faced Hostess Bouquet

This form of tied bunch is like a small tied sheaf. It is constructed in exactly the same way and should have the same triangular shape. The only difference is the size.

It should have a flat back of foliage like a sheaf, groupings of flowers and colour within the design, and a raised profile with a fullness and depth around the widest point at the base. It is finished off with a ribbon bow and the stems are wrapped in cellophane. This design will not stand up, so the wrapping cannot be filled with water.

As this design is generally intended as a gift, choice and expensive flowers like roses, lilies, orchids and freesias are generally used. Like the circular hand-tied bouquet, this is a ready-made flower arrangement and can be placed in a vase without any further attention.

Informal Presentation Bouquet

The informal presentation bouquet is ideally suited for carrying at a civic function or presenting after a ballet or theatre performance.

It is constructed in the same way as previously discussed, but made to be carried on one arm, like cradling a baby. This allows one arm free for receiving guests and shaking hands.

The bouquet is one-sided with a flat plain backing of foliage. Instead of being arranged in a circular formation, the flowers are graduated from a point to a wider base and are all front-facing. The stems of the bouquet should nevertheless spiral and the profile of the bunch should be raised and fuller nearer the binding point. Within the

Informal presentation bouquet

design, some materials should be recessed to provide depth to the arrangement and stronger colours or larger flowers should be grouped towards the centre and base of the design.

Flexible stems and naturally curved materials such as spray carnations, *Euphorbia fulgens*, dendrobium orchids and September flowers are particularly useful to help form the trailing side of the bouquet which will be farthest away from the body when held. The bouquet is finished off with a ribbon bow and a greater length of tails can be left on it. The stems are trimmed neatly. As this design is not expected to stand on its own stems, the ends of the flower stalks can be trimmed to form a curved base, which looks more attractive than a straight edge.

Cascade Wedding Bouquet

A variation of the standard circular tied bunch is a trailing form. It closely resembles the traditional wired shower bouquet, although it tends to be larger and fuller and provides a more informal or natural look. It works particularly well with semi-wild or shrubbery-type materials such as philadelphus, lilac, cytisus, ivy and viburnum.

The construction techniques are the same as for the ordinary hand-tied, all the stems spiralling to allow the flower heads to spread outwards. The main difference is in the materials, which obviously need to include some which trail down naturally or have very pliable stems. Ivy trails, asparagus fern, smilax, soft ruscus, wild clematis and old man's beard are ideal.

Start with three or four stems of bushy foliage such as ivy to form a central core around which the spiral is formed. Once the basic structure has been established, the flowers can be threaded through the foliage framework. The stems must all follow the same direction. It is advisable to support wire some of the flowers used in the trail of the design, so that the stems can be gently bent into the required angle without breaking. The larger flower heads should be recessed towards the centre of the bouquet.

This style of bouquet responds particularly well to a greater mixture of materials than a traditional wired bunch, and fruits, berries, seed heads and grasses can be used to create some interesting designs. The flowers should be chosen with care and generally the choicer types are best. All types of lilies, standard and spray roses, tulips, gerbera and freesias as well as blossoms like prunus, cytisus, mimosa, waxflowers and viburnum are especially effective.

Upright style bouquet

Limited Upright Bouquet

Also called a continental upright bouquet, this type is very different in its finished appearance from the tied bunches already described, as it resembles a modern-style flower arrangement. It is very easy to carry and ideal for a modern bride or perhaps for a second wedding.

Unlike other tied bouquets in which most of the material is arranged on one level, this style relies on dramatic contrasts of level and form for its impact. The flowers and foliage are more strongly grouped than in other styles and a limited choice of flower types is preferable to a great mixture. Unusual materials such as fungi, wood, dried seed heads or stalks are often included, as well as more dramatic flowers like orchids, anthuriums, nerines or lilies. Each piece of material must be of sufficiently strong appearance in shape, texture or colour to provide visual contrast with the others.

A limited hand-tied bouquet consists of an upright central grouping, lower filling materials around the tying point for stability, one or two strong focal items and some naturally trailing or curved material to provide a balance to the height.

Flowers

Linear shapes

Liatris	Antirrhinums
Delphiniums	Bridal gladioli
Irises	Veronica
Larkspur	Molucella
Stocks	

Focal flowers

Roses	Tulips
Lilies, smaller star-flowered types	Camellias
	Hyacinths
Anenomes	Orchids
Ranunculus	Small gerbera
Scabious	Carnations

With pliable or naturally curving stems

Euphorbia fulgens	Gypsophila
Alchemilla mollis	Eustoma
September flowers	Cytisus
Crocosmia	Honeysuckle
Spiraea	Jasmine
Spray carnations	Sweet peas

Foliage

Trailing

Soft ruscus	Jasmine
Asparagus sprengeri	Ivy
Asparagus plumosus	Nephrolepis
Smilax	Bear grass
Cytisus	Willow
	Vine

Larger leaves

Syngonium	*Aucuba japonica*
Hosta	Rhododendron
Bergenia	Mahonia
Hedera canariensis	Camellia

Tip

During the construction of the arrangement, some flowers may move from their original positions. After you have finished the bunch, but before tying it off, lightly shake it and carefully reposition any flowers as necessary. Because of the spiral of stems this is quite easy to do. Some materials can even be taken out and replaced without seriously affecting the design of the bouquet.

Method

1. Start the bunch with the tallest central grouping of flowers. Wherever possible these should be of a linear shape such as liatris, larkspur, delphiniums, irises or stocks. Depending on the size of the flowers, three or five stems should be sufficient.

These flowers should be held together to form an upright group. Graduate the levels of the flowers so that they are stepped down from each other rather than all

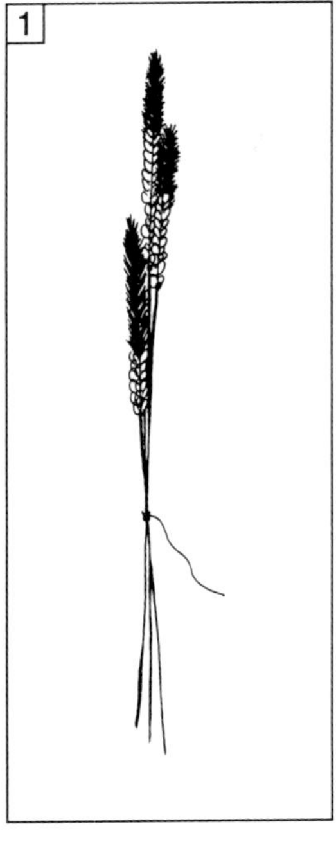

on one level.

The tying point must be established at this stage, usually at a distance of approximately 20–30 cm below the tip of the tallest flower. If it proves difficult to keep these first flowers in position because of their height, it is a good idea to tie them together before adding any further material.

2. Group some lower material around the base of the tall flowers to provide stability and to form the central area of the bouquet. The stems should be placed in a spiral and the bouquet designed as an all-round piece.
3. Add a second lower grouping of flowers and the focal or largest flowers towards the centre of the design.
4. Include the trailing materials to provide a contrast and visual balance to the height of the central group.

   Colours and types of flowers and leaves should be linked through the design, rather than being used singly or in isolation. The groupings need not be equal in size or quantity to achieve balance. Three syngonium leaves on one side of the bouquet and two on the other, for example, or three rose buds grouped together can be balanced with one fully open rose lower down in the design.
5. When the bouquet is finished, tie it with string in the usual way and cover the tying point with pot tape.
6. Trim the stems to one-third of the overall length and add a ribbon bow in a complementary colour to cover the tying point. The tails of the bow can be left slightly longer than usual to echo the trailing foliage or flowers.

3

4

CHAPTER 7

Wedding Design

USEFUL TIPS WHEN TAKING WEDDING ORDERS

- Keep a large desk diary solely for wedding orders.
- Have handy a portfolio of your own work as well as books of wedding designs.
- Make an appointment with the bride well in advance of the wedding date. Take down as many details as possible:
  - Name, address and telephone number of the bride
  - Date of wedding
  - Time of wedding
  - Delivery time and any other delivery addresses (e.g. buttonholes)
  - Approximate cost of each piece
- If a church is to be decorated, a site visit should be made with the bride to discuss the designs and to advise what is possible. It is a good idea to draw a plan of the venue and give a price for each design in the form of a floor plan. The customer can then decide whether she wishes to have all the designs or some of them. The same applies to the venue for the reception.
- For a large wedding which includes bridal, church and reception flowers, a quotation should be sent and signed by the customer. It then becomes a contract.
- Ask for a deposit, usually 50%, two weeks before the wedding. Brides have been known to cancel or to go to another florist without informing the first florist. A deposit should ensure that the flower cost is covered.
- Specific details for each piece of work to be made should be noted. (It may not be you making up the work on the day.)
- Ask for a piece of the fabric of the bride's/bridesmaids' dresses to help with matching flowers to fabric.
- Never promise a particular flower unless you are absolutely certain it will be available. If in doubt, always tell the bride you will get the nearest thing.

CONTENTS OF WORKBOX FOR WEDDING WORK

Scissors
Knife
String
Secateurs
Pot tape in white and green, wide and narrow
Reel wires of different gauges
Selection of stub wires from fine 0.28 mm to 0.90 mm
Box of steel dress pins
Box of pearl-headed dress pins for corsages
Sellotape
Double-sided adhesive tape
Plastic binding tape in green, white and brown
Stapler and staples
Glue gun and glue sticks
Cloth/duster
Water mister spray
Kitchen roll
Tissue paper
Box of ready-made sepal pins
Several 0.32 mm silver wires with taped balls attached for wiring individual blooms such as freesias
A quantity of split plastic binding tape
Tape measure or ruler

It is usually a good idea to lightly spray all finished pieces of wedding work. By reducing the amount of moisture the flowers and foliage lose, this will help to keep them looking fresh. Only a light covering of water is needed, as the flowers should not look wet. The easiest way to do this is by using a hand mister or spray which can be obtained from any good wholesaler.

Whilst the majority of flowers benefit from this treatment, there are a few where care must be taken to avoid damaging the blooms. Some orchids such as phalaenopsis and other delicate flowers like gardenias, sweet peas and stephanotis will develop brown spots and stains on their petals from too much water. It is a better idea to cover these with damp tissue instead of spraying directly with water.

Buttonhole/Boutonnière

It might perhaps be thought that a buttonhole hardly warrants any explanation, consisting as it does of just a single flower. However, this is not strictly true, because as any good florist knows, just as much care and attention to detail should go into making something simple as into the construction of a full bouquet.

The wearing of a buttonhole or lapel flower is mainly restricted these days to special occasions such as weddings or other formal functions. This was not always so, as in earlier times a flower was just as an important a part of a gentleman's general attire as his hat or tie. The Victorian and Edwardian eras saw the greatest use of buttonholes as a fashion accessory consisting of anything from a simple cornflower or sprig of heather to such sophisticated exotics as gardenias or camellias.

The flower was usually backed by a small spray of foliage or a leaf, and the fashion-conscious Edwardian gentleman even went so far as to wear a specially made silver or glass tube containing water at the back of the lapel to keep the flowers fresh all day.

Most people today would choose either a carnation or a rose, both of which are ideal because of their lasting qualities. The rose was long the favourite but at the beginning of the 1950s it was overtaken in popularity by the carnation, backed with a piece of *Asparagus plumosus* fern. During the last few years, however, the rose has again become popular. Often a single rose or bloom matching the colour and focal flowers of the bride's bouquet is chosen by the groom to set him apart from the rest of the bridal party.

Whenever possible, a buttonhole flower should be worn through the buttonhole and not pinned onto the front of the lapel. For this reason the

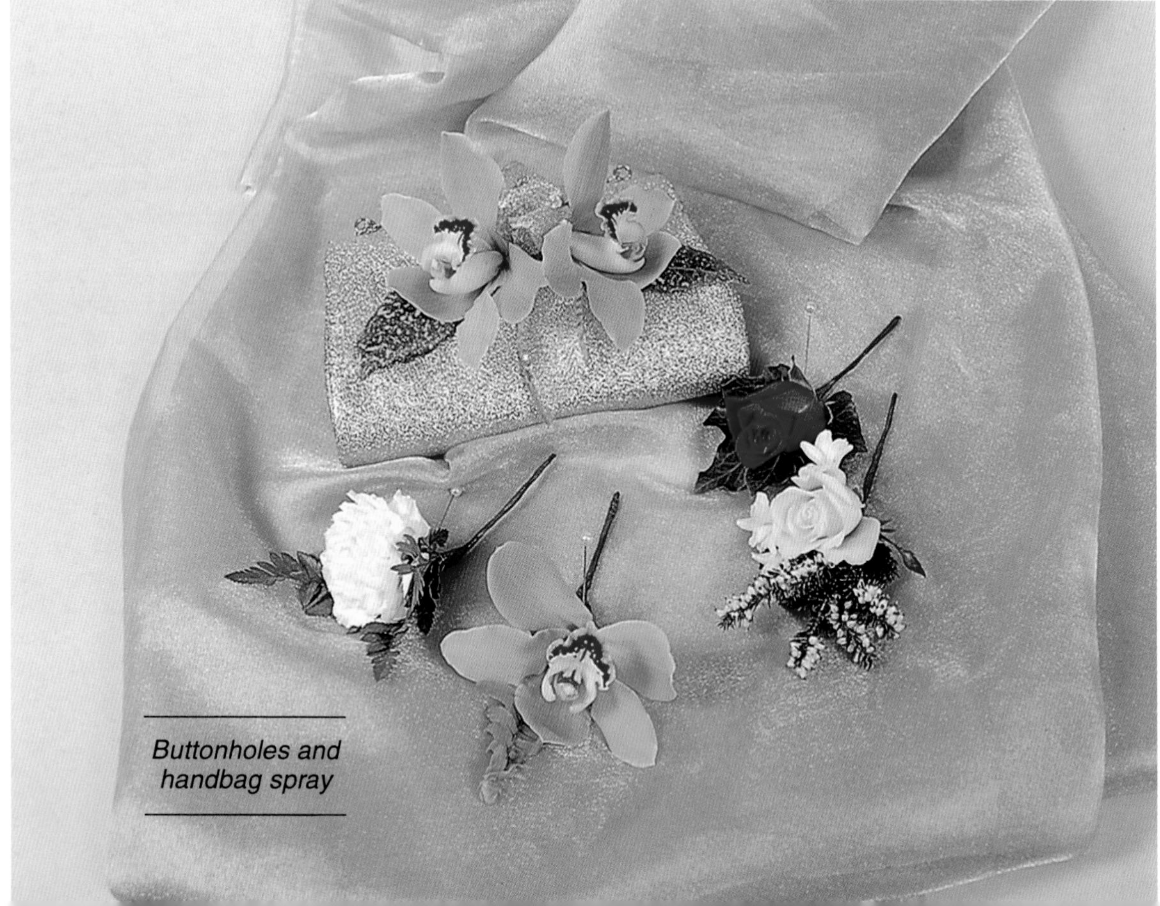

Buttonholes and handbag spray

flower stem needs to be very fine and thus it is important to mount the flower heads of thicker-stemmed blooms such as carnations or larger roses on a taped wire, so providing a thinner stem.

Large, flat leaves such as those of the ivy or rose should also be wired by stitching with a silver wire and then binding with plastic tape. Traditionally a rose bloom is always accompanied by its own foliage.

Boutonnières are made up of a number of stems of small headed flowers and foliages such as spray rose, heather, stephanotis, lily of the valley or cornflowers.

Making a buttonhole or boutonnière consists of taping together the chosen materials after any necessary support wiring or mounting has been carried out.

Flowers
(chosen mainly for their lasting qualities)
Carnations
Roses
Heather
Gardenias
Camellias
Cornflowers
Stephanotis
Dianthus
Anemones
Violets
Helleborus niger

Foliage and leaves
Camellia leaves
Myrtus communis
Buxus sempervirens
Mature rose leaves
Ivy leaves
Asparagus plumosus and *A. sprengeri*
Adiantum cuneatum (maidenhair fern)
Euonymus leaves

Tip

The rose will form the focal flower in a buttonhole so it is important to select carefully a perfect bloom of an appropriate size.

Method

1. Select a well-formed rose bud and remove stem just below the seedbox. Insert a short 0.71 mm stub wire into the stem and up into the seedbox. Bind with plastic tape. It is may be necessary to remove one or two of the outer petals if they are marked.
2. Choose three mature rose leaves, a large one and two smaller ones, and support wire by the stitch method. Bind with plastic tape.

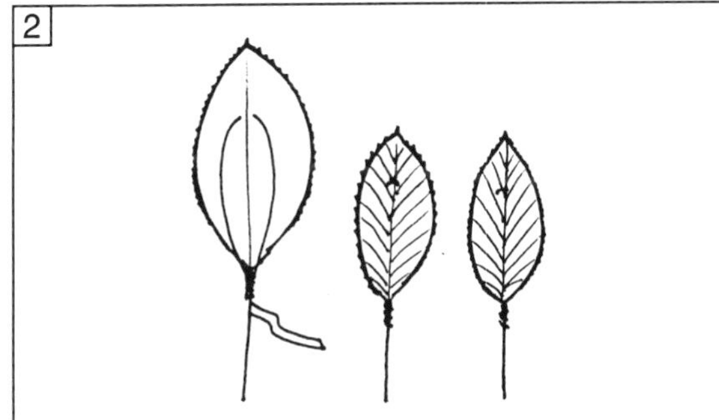

3. Tape the largest leaf onto the rose stem so that the leaf forms a backing to the bloom. Add the two smaller leaves to the front of the buttonhole so that their fronts face the bloom and the support wire is visible at the front. Trim off the wire stem to the required length (usually about 3–4 cm) and bind with plastic tape, taking care to cover the ends of the cut wire.

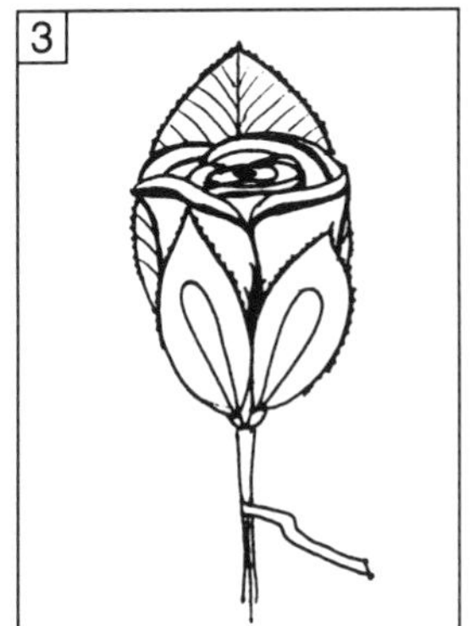

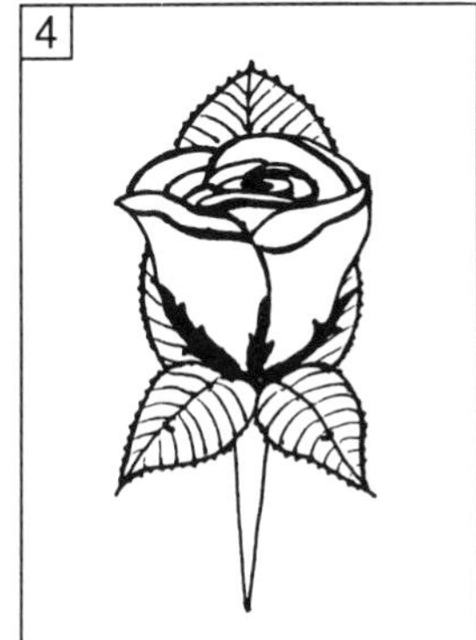

4. Gently bend the two front leaves down in front of the rose, thus providing an attractive collar for it when worn. Attach a pearl-headed dress pin to the stem.

Corsage

The corsage is traditionally worn for formal occasions. With a little thought and imagination it can be made into a beautiful accessory for even the most glamorous ballgown or wedding wear and be every bit as eye-catching as a piece of jewellery.

It is also quite versatile, as one can be attached to hats or handbags, coat lapels or belts, wrists or shoulders.

A corsage should always be as light as possible, its weight depending on the type of materials used. A typical wedding corsage would be made of freesias, hyacinth pips and ivy or euonymus leaves, all mounted onto the finest of silver wires. Larger flowers such as orchids or even lilies can be used to great effect with a few well-chosen leaves to create a simpler look.

Corsages

Modern corsage

For parties, small pearls or beads can be incorporated into the design, as well as bows, silver or gold thread and ribbons.

Flowers

- Hyacinth pips
- Small statice sprays
- Sedum florets
- Freesias
- Alstroemeria
- Spray roses
- Dendrobium and small cymbidium orchids
- Spray chrysanthemums such as 'Penny Lane' or 'Cassa'
- Helleborus bells
- Heather sprays
- Small pieces of safari pack berries
- Smaller lilies such as 'Enchantment' or 'Sterling Star'
- Feathered carnation petals

Foliage

- Ivy leaves
- Peperomia leaves
- Senecio leaves
- *Ficus benjamina*, green and variegated
- Euonymus leaves
- Hebe sprays
- Camellia leaves
- *Rubus tricolor* leaves
- Portuguese laurel leaves

Method

1. Wire and tape all materials using fine silver stub wires such as 0.28 mm and 0.32 mm.
2. Tape together some of the leaves and also a few of the smaller flowers or buds to make small units of material. This reduces the number of individual stems to be bound into the binding point and adds strength to the design.

3. Tape together three or four pieces of foliage to form the outline as far as the binding point will be. Add some flower material, which should be graduated in size towards larger flowers in the centre of the design.

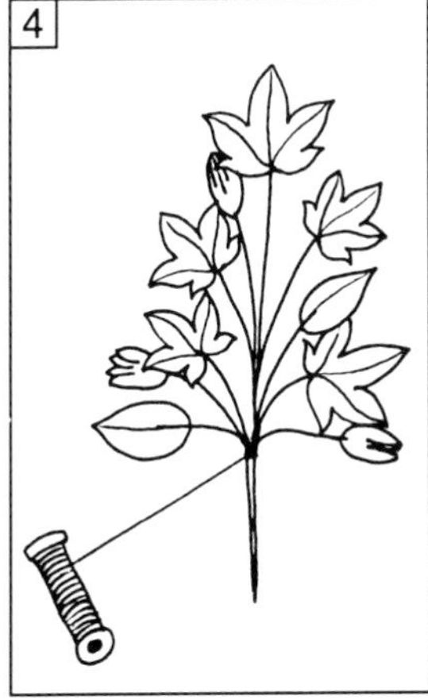

4. Attach silver reel wire to the stem of the corsage. This has now determined the binding area or centre of the design. It is from this point that all materials should appear to radiate.
5. Position the focal flower directly above the binding point and bind in.
6. Continue to add more outline materials, taking care to carry any pattern lines or colour groupings of material through the design. Materials placed behind the focal flower are bent backwards to cover the stem of the corsage, which is called the return end.

7. Trim the stem wires to the correct length, which should be just shorter than the return end flowers. The stem can be thinned if necessary by cutting off some of the wires. The stem and binding point can then be taped to cover the binding point and cut wires.
8. Re-position any materials that may have been moved during completion. The finished corsage should be roughly triangular shaped. Its profile should rise slightly up to the focal flower and recede down again into the return end. Attach a pin into the stem before despatch to the customer.

HEADDRESSES

Floral headdresses, whether of fresh, dried or artificial flowers, form an important part of any wedding order and should be treated with as much care and attention as the bridal bouquet itself.

Styles and designs of headdresses are many and varied and like any good bridal bouquet are made to the specific requirements of the customer. As the headdress often provides the finishing touch to the bride's or bridesmaids' appearance, it is important to choose a suitable style. This will be determined by the style, colour and length of hair in which it is to be worn, as well as the type of dress and age of the wearer.

Only the lightest materials should be used. Quite often the headdress is one of the last items to be made for a wedding order to ensure that it remains as fresh as possible for the few hours it will be worn.

Fresh flowers and foliage are widely used but must be well conditioned, as a great deal of body heat is lost through the head. To prevent wilting, use only mature foliage and leaves. For obvious reasons dried materials and artificial fabric flowers are very popular for this type of work.

The basic styles are as follows:

- ***Circlet*** – A complete ring of flowers, sometimes finished off at the back with a ribbon bow.
- ***Half circlet or alice band*** – This can be worn in three different positions: at the front of the head, at the back or over the top.
- ***Comb spray*** – This can be worn at the back of the head, on one side above the ear or on top of the head. It is sometimes used to fix the bridal veil.
- ***Flower heads and leaves*** – To be fixed randomly into a hairstyle giving a romantic informal look or pinned together to give detail to a French plait.

There is very little difference between the head circumference of a child and a young adult, and most circlet headdresses will be within the range of 46–50 cm. When measuring for a circlet or half circlet, always remember to make allowances for the hair style to be worn on the day.

The choice of materials is endless, and some stunning effects can be achieved by using the unusual or unexpected. The following lists are based mainly on lasting qualities when wired.

Flowers	
Spray roses	Delphinium florets
Smaller standard roses	Ivy flowers and berries
Freesias	Feverfew
Hyacinth pips	*Alchemilla mollis*
Stephanotis pips	Gypsophila
Helleborus bells	Waxflowers
Viburnum tinus	Muscari
Fresh statice	Pussy willow
Mimosa	Single spray chrysanthemums

Foliage	
Ivy leaves and berries	*Pittosporum tenuifolium*
Soft ruscus	Variegated euonymus leaves
Asparagus sprengeri	
Senecio leaves	

Circlet Headdress

Circlet headdress

Method 1

1. Mount all materials on as fine a wire as possible and then tape.

2. Make a bow using narrow satin ribbon leaving the tails long. These can then be cut to the desired length when being worn. Attach a taped silver wire as stem.

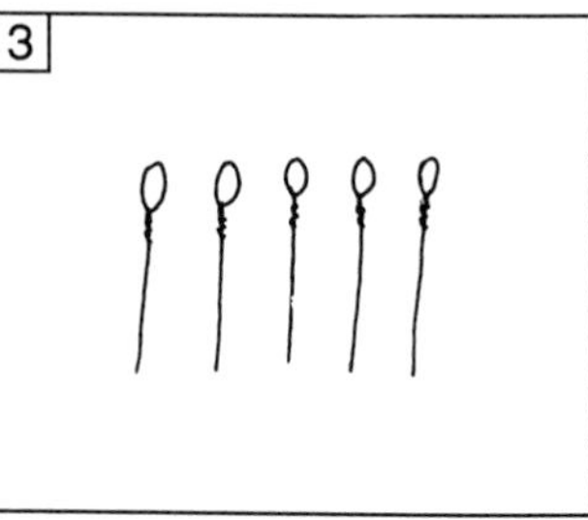

3. Make five or six small 'eyelets' from taped silver wire for attaching the circlet with hair grips.

4. Begin taping the materials together to form a continuous band of flowers and leaves to the required width. Start with an eyelet and cover this with a leaf. Place each piece of material so that it slightly overlaps the base of the previous piece.

5. Continue taping material until the required length is achieved, adding the remaining eyelets at regular intervals. Make sure the width of the design remains the same along its entire length.

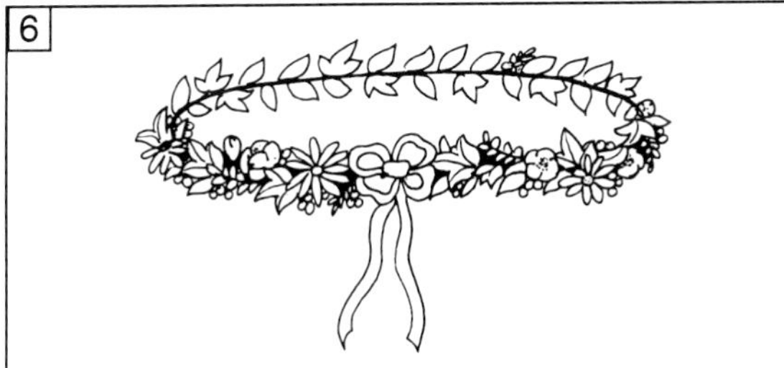

6. Trim off the last few wires leaving a short stem of approximately 2–3 cm. Bend into a circle and pass the stem through the first eyelet to form the circlet. Add the bow to cover up the join by twisting the stem wire around the wire of the circlet.

Method 2

Exactly the same method of preparation and construction is used as in Method 1 but instead of taping the materials onto each other to form a flexible circlet, they are taped directly onto a stay wire of the correct length. This can be made from taped 0.71 mm wires which are joined together to form the required length.

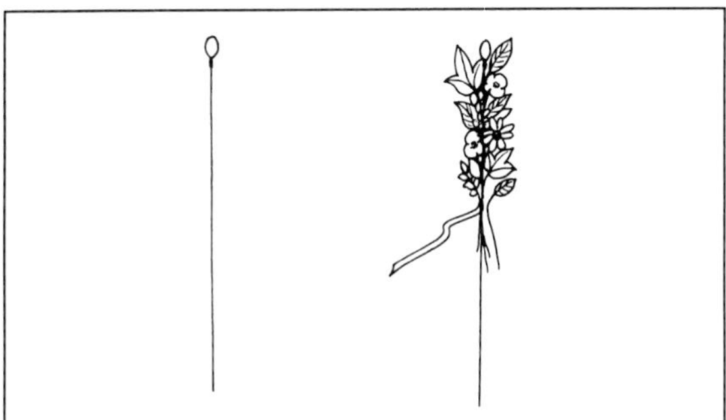

Wired circlet headdress and a glued Alice band headdress

Half Circlet or Alice Band Headdress

A half circlet of flowers is made in exactly the same way as a full circlet except that the direction of the flowers is reversed at the middle point of the design. As half circlets are usually worn over the top of the head from side to side, the middle area of the design can be made slightly fuller, and the finished effect when worn resembles a tiara.

The headband can be made of two separate pieces which are bound together at the centre with flowers and leaves arranged in such a way as to conceal the join, or the materials can be taped directly onto a 0.71 mm stay wire.

Start binding the materials from each end, working towards the centre and incorporating some larger open flowers in the middle to give the required fullness and height to the design.

Alternatively a ready-made alice band can be used, the materials being taped directly onto it in the same way as described above.

Tip

Ask the customer to provide their own Alice band or hair comb for you to work with. Give the customer the option of supplying their own choice of Alice band or hair comb for decoration as these can vary considerably in quality and comfort.

Comb Spray Headdress

A comb spray consisting of perhaps just one perfect lily bloom, one or two lily buds and two or three choice leaves can look absolutely stunning when worn with an upswept hairstyle. This form of hair decoration is particularly suited to the older bridesmaid but also has its uses for the bride's going-away outfit or even for parties.

A comb spray is best described as a corsage attached to a comb. Choose a comb with a thick, strong spine which will provide a good base for the flowers.

Comb sprays

Method

1. Using the finest wires possible, mount and tape the chosen materials.
2. With a fine silver binding wire begin to assemble the spray, binding in three or four pieces of material together.

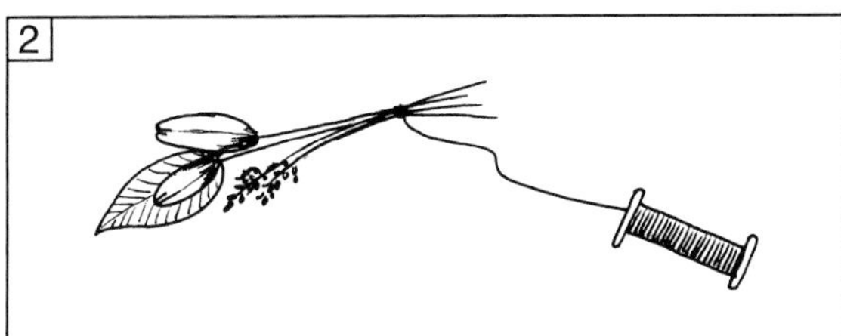

3. Form a return end to the design in the same way as a corsage.

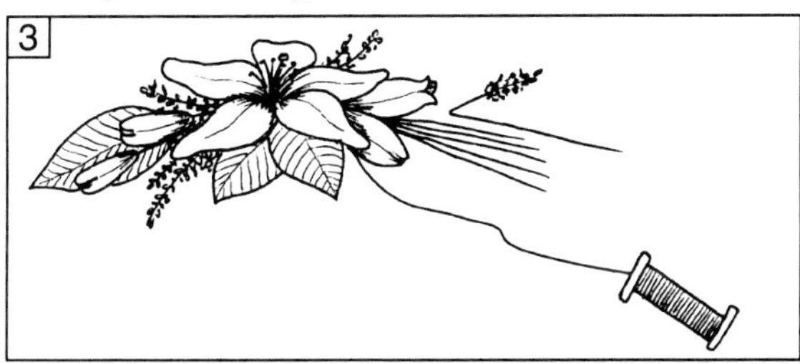

4. Cut and reduce the width and length of wire stem with scissors and then carefully bind with tape to conceal the binding point and any cut wires.
5. Attach the binding wire to one end of the comb.
6. Lay the flower spray against the spine of the comb and very carefully bind together with the reel of wire. Great care must be taken to move the materials to allow the wire to pass right through the design so as to bind it securely to the comb.

7. Bind along the length of the comb and finish off by twisting the wire tight and cutting off as close to the comb as possible.

This form of decoration can also be worn without the comb. Make the flower spray in exactly the same way but incorporate three or four eyelet hooks as previously described for hair grips.

The Glued Headdress

The methods of construction previously described tend to be rather time-consuming. One way of really reducing the time is to use a glue gun.

For this you will need a strong base to glue the flowers onto such as a plastic circlet band, alice band or comb.

There are two methods of construction, either by gluing the flowers and leaves directly onto the framework or by wiring and taping the materials as usual and then gluing them onto the frame instead of binding them together. An advantage of this second method is that it allows you to move or rearrange the flowers after the gluing is finished.

Tip

When making a hot glue headdress, use a length of thin flower stem to hold materials in position whilst the glue sets.

Flower Heads and Leaves

Choose flat flowers such as spray roses or daisy-type spray chrysanthemums for this type of hair decoration. Longer or trumpet-shaped flowers such as freesias protrude too far from the hairstyle and look awkward.

Method

1. Select flowers and leaves of varying size, leaving approximately 1 cm of stem attached.

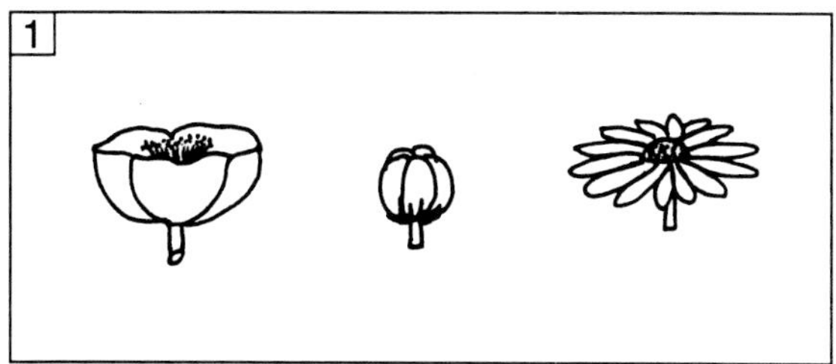

2. Using a 0.32 mm silver wire support, wire the flower in the appropriate way and bind with plastic tape. Brown tape is a good idea, as it is almost invisible when the flowers are worn.

3. Twist the taped wire stem back onto itself to form a small eyelet and carefully cut off any remaining wire. Each flower can then be fixed into the hair by a single hair grip passed through the eyelet.

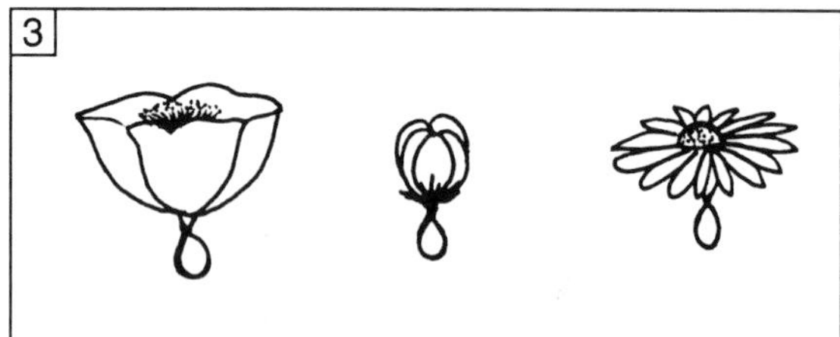

Bible or Prayerbook Spray

This design is suitable for either the bride or bridesmaids to carry and provides a simple but very attractive alternative to a more traditional bouquet or posy of flowers. It consists of a small spray of flowers and leaves stitched onto a ribbon, which in turn acts as a bookmark in the Bible or prayerbook for either the marriage ceremony or the Lord's Prayer. The book is carried so that it can be opened and read in the normal way with the long ribbons at the top of the book away from the body.

Tip

Because of the limited amount of materials that are used for a Bible or prayerbook spray, choose only small and choice flowers and leaves.

Flowers	Foliage
Small roses	Ivy leaves
Stephanotis	Asparagus fern
Muscari	Nephrolepis fern
Hyacinth pips	Small eucalyptus leaves
Dendrobium and small cymbidium orchids	Peperomia leaves
Freesias	Euonymus leaves
Spray roses	
Jasmine	
'Paper White' narcissi	
Gypsophila	

Method

1. Choose a small or medium-sized Bible or prayerbook. A white cover looks effective. Pass a length of wide silk ribbon through the book at the appropriate page so that the ribbon comes out at the bottom of the book. Take the ribbon up and over the front cover, and then stitch the two pieces neatly together along the top edge of the cover. This forms the bookmark and makes a secure base onto which the spray can be attached. The ribbon should trail down to approximately 30–45 cm.

Prayerbook spray

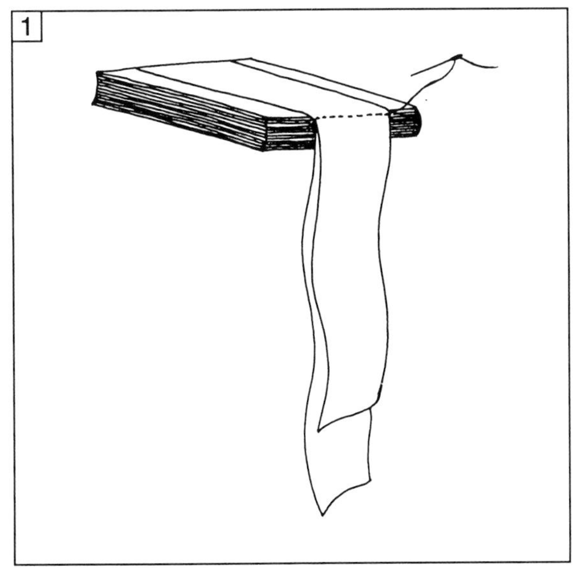

2. Construct a suitably sized spray of flowers and foliage in the same way as for a corsage. Its width should not exceed that of the cover.
3. Place the finished spray onto the ribbon so that it sits in the centre of the book. The tip of the spray should extend just over the top of the book and the return end should not extend below the bottom of the book. In fact it is a good idea if the flower stops short of the bottom of the book to avoid being damaged. Carefully move some of the wired flowers along the main spine of the spray and securely stitch them to the ribbon. It is a good idea to stitch both the top and bottom ends of the spray for added security. An alternative to sewing the spray onto the ribbon is to use a hot glue gun, taking care not to mark the cover of the book with molten glue.

   Re-arrange the flowers back into position and bend one or two leaves or flowers over the top edge of the book to curve down over the ribbon tails.

4. Cut off the ribbon tails neatly, the front ribbon slightly shorter than the back one. A very small cluster of leaves and flowers or just a single rosebud with one or two ivy leaves can be sewn onto the end of the ribbons. Sew through both ribbons to stop them twisting around when the book is carried.

Flower Basket

The range and variety of baskets available today is so great that it would be impossible to define a particular style as being suitable for a bridesmaid to carry. Much depends on the ideas of the bride herself and the dresses to be worn, although it has to be said that generally baskets are best suited to a wedding with an overall country or natural look to it. Many materials are used to make baskets, from the traditional stripped willow or cane to large chunky branches with bark and twigs, or even roots, still attached. Lavender, heather, strips of bark, fir cones, even nuts, are all used to provide a bewildering choice of styles and finishes.

For a wedding it is perhaps more appropriate to choose a style which is not too rough or heavy and which will not detract from the flowers. The basket itself should obviously be in proportion to the size of the person carrying it, and shallow, flatter designs are generally more suitable to take flowers.

Whatever style is used, some sort of container or waterproof lining must be attached to hold the flower foam. A deep basket can be discreetly lined with black plastic and the foam positioned directly in it, or a shallow plastic dish can be glued into place before the foam is added. The foam can then be taped onto the dish for added security.

Baskets can be 'dressed' with ribbons before adding the flowers. This needs careful thought, as it is very easy to use too many ribbons and bows and spoil the finished effect. One popular idea is to bind the basket handle with a narrow ribbon of a suitable colour and attach two small bows with trails at the points where the handle joins the basket base.

Remember that these designs are intended for carrying, so allow enough room for hands between the top of the flowers and the handle itself.

Nearly all flowers are suitable, depending on the size of the design. Remember that the flowers should be in direct proportion to the basket itself. However, some flowers and foliage look particularly effective when used this way.

Flowers	
Roses	Waxflowers
Anemones	Gypsophila
Bouvardia	Primroses and polyanthus
Small narcissi	Lily of the valley
Muscari	*Helleborus niger* and *H. orientalis*
Nerines	Cornflowers
Alstroemeria	Sweet peas
Freesias	

Foliage	
Nephrolepis fronds	Hebe sprays
Ivy leaves and trails	Box foliage
Pittosporum	Ruscus
Rosemary	

Bridesmaid's basket

Method

1. Line the basket with plastic or attach a plastic dish. Cut and trim wet foam to the correct size and place in position. Usually only a very small piece of foam is required as the finished design is quite low.

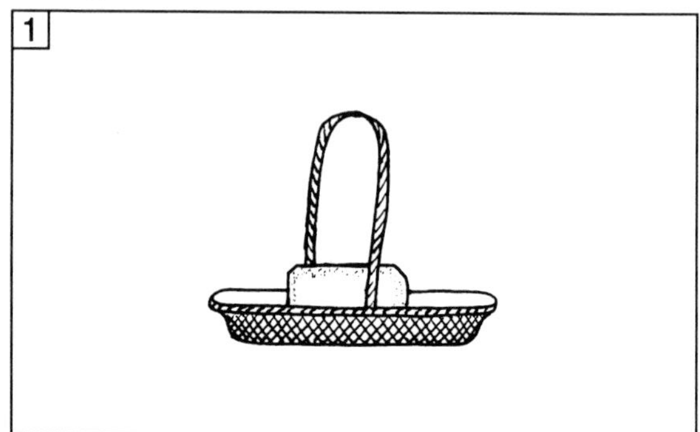

2. Add ribbons or bind handle if required.
3. Insert longest pieces of material first, making sure the length is in proportion to the basket. Continue to form the outline of the design with foliage.

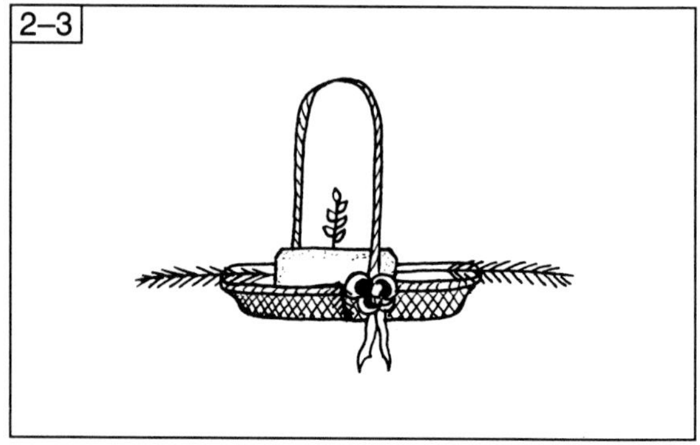

4. Cover foam with short pieces of foliage before adding flowers.
5. Add flowers, placing any choice blooms such as roses or freesias so as to form a line from one end of the design to the other. Cluster larger open flowers towards the centre of the design.

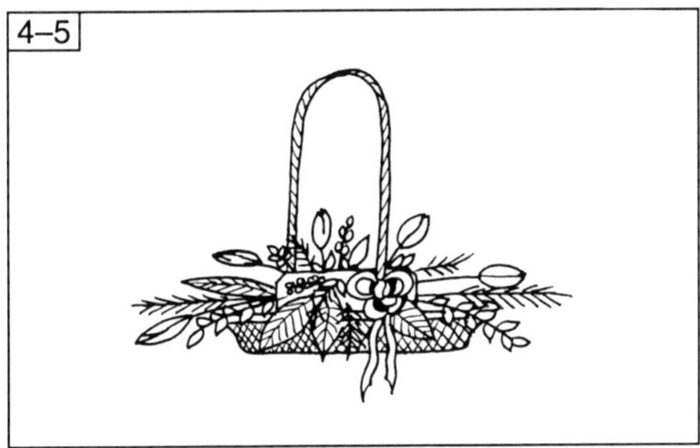

4–5

6. Finish by adding small 'detail' materials such as gypsophila, waxflowers or stephanotis.

6

POMANDER

The pomander or flower ball is particularly suited to the younger bridesmaid and can look extremely pretty when used with a pinafore or smock-style dress. It can vary from a ball covered in one type of flower, with just a few rose buds and leaves added around the base of the handle at the top, to an overall mixture of small flowers and foliage.

Historically the pomander owes its name and shape to the French *pomme d'ambre* or amber apple. The term was applied to a mixture of herbs and spices which was mixed with scented resin and then made into small spheres to be carried on a ribbon or cord to ward off unpleasant smells. As it was commonly thought that the plague was spread by noxious odours, pomanders became widely used during the 16th and 17th centuries.

The use of small, flat-headed flowers and small-leaved 'dense' foliage makes it easier to retain the spherical shape. There are two methods of construction, either on a foam ball or as a fully wired ball of flowers.

Both wet and dry foam spheres can be used for a fresh flower pomander. The obvious advantage

Pomander

of pre-soaked foam is that the moisture ensures the materials remain fresh for a longer period. Disadvantages are that soaking can make the pomander quite heavy and the foam will break up if handled carelessly.

A dry foam sphere, on the other hand, is much lighter, will not disintegrate so easily and can be assembled just as easily.

For dried or silk flowers, a dry foam sphere should always be used.

Flowers	
Spray carnations	Spray roses
Statice (fresh or dried)	*Alchemilla mollis*
Sedum	Hyacinth pips
Trachelium	*Helleborus foetidus*
Lilac	Heather sprays
Viburnum tinus	Sea lavender
Small double spray chrysanthemums	Cornflowers
	Delphinium florets

Foliage	
Small-leaved hebe	Ivy flowers and berries
Box sprays	Small types of safari pack foliage
Asparagus	Decorative crab apples
Pittosporum	Cotoneaster berries
Rosemary	

Tip

As the pomander is an adaptation of an historical item, use so-called 'old-fashioned' looking flowers, foliage and even nuts and berries.

Foam Pomander

Method

1. Cut all chosen material to the same length (approximately 2–3 cm) for a finished size resembling an orange. If a larger pomander is required, the material will not need to be much longer but a greater quantity will be required to cover a larger area.
2. Wire the material with either a short 0.46 mm or 0.56 mm wire using a double leg mount. This is done for added security, as a flower stem on its own could shrink and fall out of the foam.

3. Cover the foam sphere (pre-soaked if wet is used) with fine plastic netting.

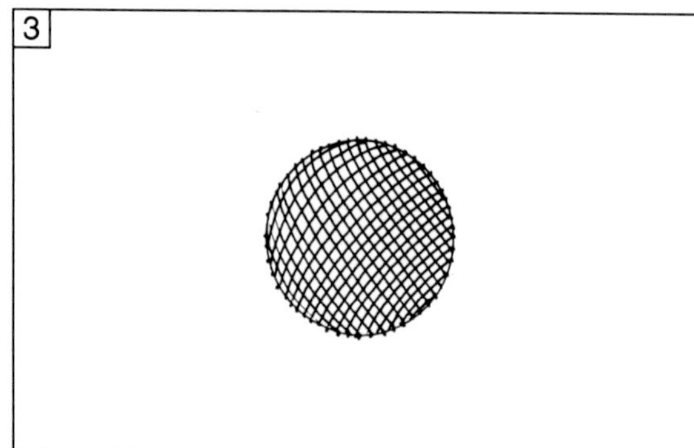

4. Make a wired ribbon handle and attach.

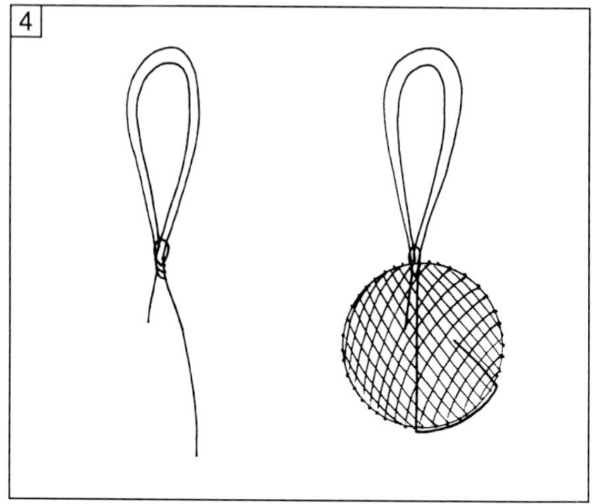

5. Starting at the top, place flowers in the foam to achieve an even coverage. Continue until the sphere is completely covered.

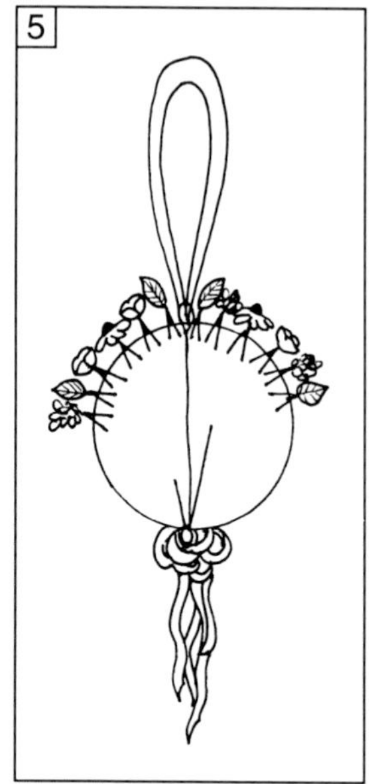

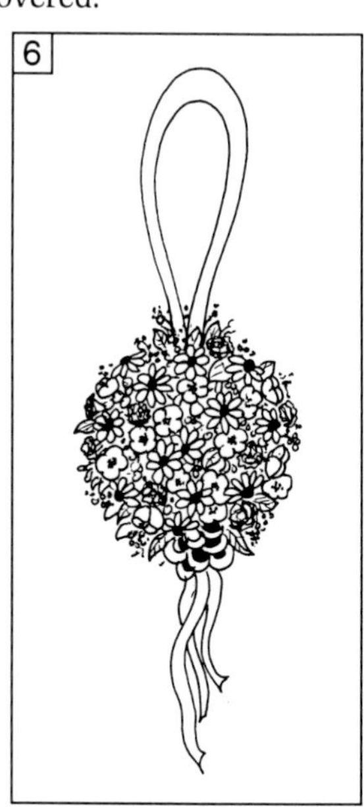

6. Add bow and tails to base of pomander.

Wired Pomander

Method

1. Cut all material the same length. Support wire and tape all materials, using as fine a wire as possible. It should not be necessary to use any wire thicker than 0.56 mm.
2. Make a loop of ribbon to form the handle. Secure the base of the ribbon on a single leg mount and cover the join with binding tape.

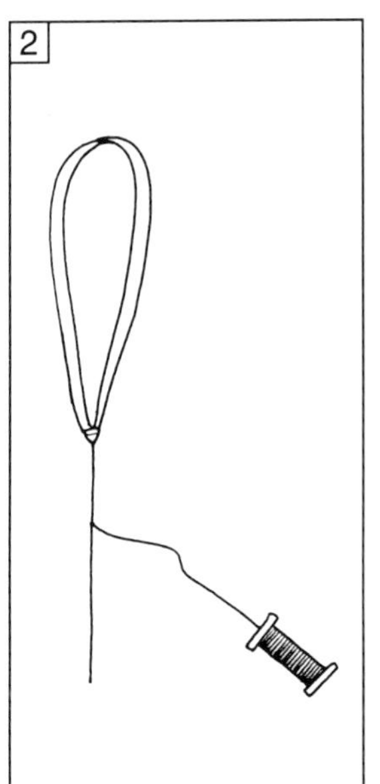

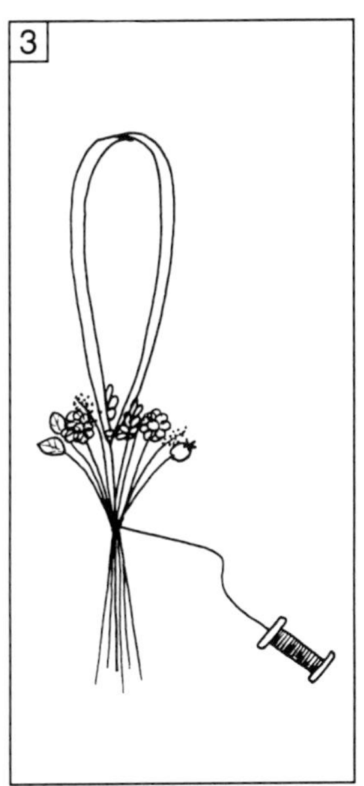

3. Begin the assembly by attaching the binding wire to the handle wire approximately 6 cm down from the base of the ribbon. Bind in the materials all of the same length, ensuring that the binding point stays in one place.

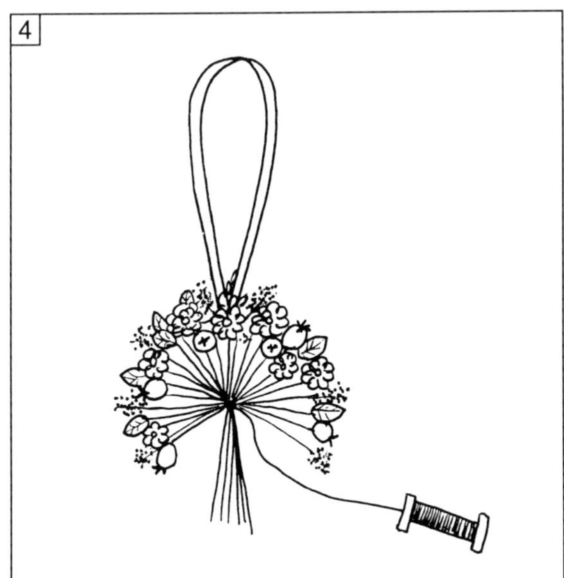

4. As more material is added, gradually pull it down to form a sphere.
5. When the pomander is nearly finished, add the final materials and the wired bows, leaving the construction handle and binding point clear.
6. Once the binding wire has been securely finished, cut off the construction handle leaving a stump approximately 3–4 cm long. Cover this with binding tape.

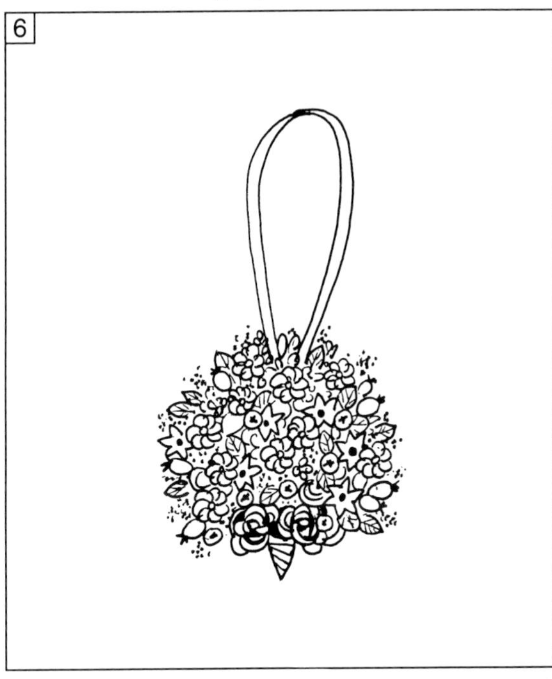

7. Pull the bows and some of the last material added over the cut stump to complete the spherical shape. The bows should be directly in line beneath the ribbon handle.

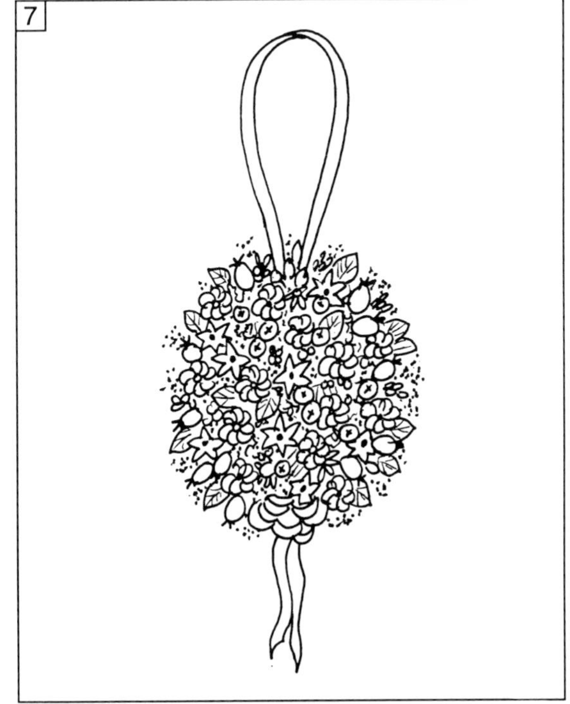

Victorian posy

Victorian Posy

Victorian posies look especially effective when carried by a young bridesmaid. They are compact and easy to hold and as they are usually backed by a starched lace or plastic frill, they are less vulnerable to damage. Today the posy is mainly used at weddings but previously it was carried as an accessory when out visiting, at evening parties or at the theatre.

An authentic posy consists of a central flower, usually a rosebud, surrounded by four concentric circles of colour, each band of colour being formed by one type of flower or foliage. The posy can also be made of a random mixture of flowers. The flowers are tightly arranged to form a domed shape, and the posy is finished by an outer ring of leaves or foliage and finally a lace frill.

A traditional look can be achieved by using a selection of so-called 'old-fashioned' flowers. Although the flowers which are commercially available today are not the original varieties, of course, many of them at least give a similar effect.

Colour also plays an important role in creating the right look and again an 'old-fashioned' colour scheme of lilacs, blues, dusky pinks and rose would be particularly suitable. This is not to say that the Victorians did not have or use brighter colours such as yellows, reds, etc., but the shades of orange, peach and apricot and the sharp lemons and fluorescent reds and corals of many of today's flowers were not available to them.

The Victorians with their great sense of sentimentality developed the language of flowers into a fine art. A carefully or indeed carelessly arranged posy could speak volumes!

Flowers

Sedum	Heliotrope
Spray chrysanthemums	Lavender
Spray carnations	Lilac
Heather	Trachelium
Gypsophila	Achillea
Cornflowers	*Alchemilla mollis*
Helichrysum	Viburnum
Small roses	

Foliage

Pittosporum, variegated varieties	*Asparagus densiflorus*
Euonymus	Santolina
Hebe	Ivy
	Senecio

Edging leaves

Hedera helix	*Rubus tricolor*
Elaeagnus ebbingei	*Prunus lusitanica*
Eucalyptus gunnii	

Method

1. Mount all materials on as fine a wire as possible (0.46 or 0.56 mm) and tape. The centre flower – usually a rose – is the only flower that requires a 0.71 mm wire.
2. Attach the binding wire to the wire stem of the central flower approximately 6–8 cm down from the flower head.

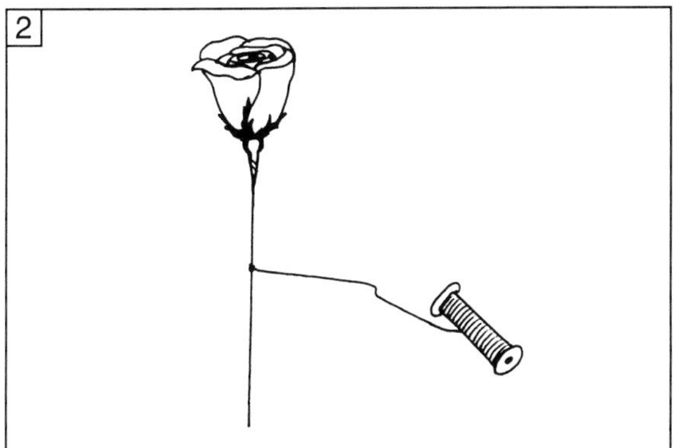

3. Bind in first ring of materials a fraction lower than the central flower head.

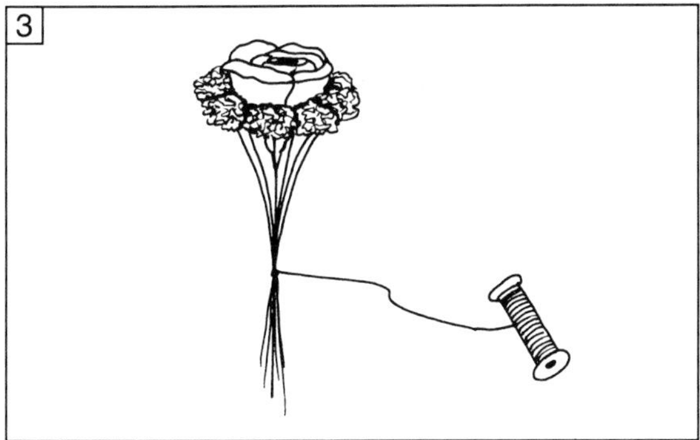

4. Continue binding rings of colour around the central flower. Ensure that each band of colour is of equal width and that a circular shape is retained. The binding point must remain constant.

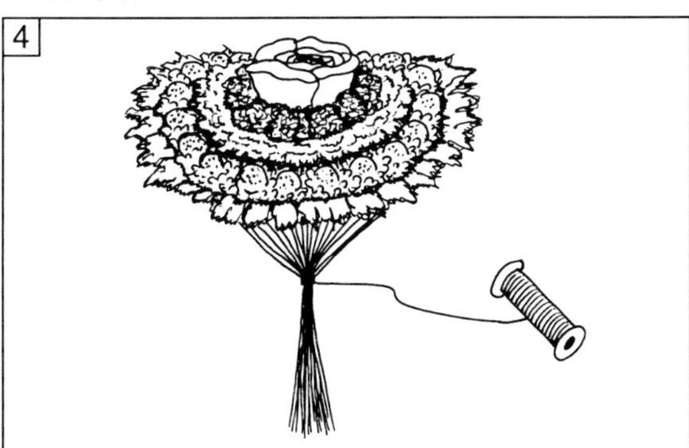

5. As each ring of materials enlarges the posy, bend the wires slightly so that the surface of the posy remains even but slightly domed. Material towards the edges of the posy will need longer wires.
6. Finish with an outer ring of leaves, which should be half visible beneath the flowers.
7. Cut stem to correct length and bind handle with white tape.
8. All wires when viewed from beneath the posy should radiate out from the centre like the spokes of a wheel. Attach the lace frill next. It is usual to slightly enlarge the small hole at the base of the frill to allow the handle to pass through. The frill should be pushed up to the top of the stem to frame the posy and conceal the wires.
9. The handle can now be neatly covered with ribbon and two or three bows attached to the top of the handle to conceal the base of the frill. This design is particularly effective if several ribbon tails are left on the bows and cut to varying lengths.

Tip

For an authentic touch, try to incorporate some scented flowers or foliage such as lily of the valley, lilac, heliotrope, mignonette or stocks in a Victorian posy.

Loose posies

Loose Posy

As its name suggests, this is a design which, although wired, should look like a natural mixed posy. Always popular for weddings, it is suitable for both the bride and bridesmaids. A loose posy for the bride would be slightly larger and contain choice or different flowers.

This design is also known as an Edwardian or colonial posy and is a development from the tightly packed Victorian posy to a more natural, informal style. A mixture of flowers and foliage is usually used, but some charming effects can be created by combining just one or two varieties of flower with a complementary foliage, such as anemones with wild ivy leaves and berries or lily of the valley with asparagus fern.

Part of the appeal of this design is its versatility. There are no rules as to its correct size or to the mix of materials used, although for the most pleasing effect avoid so-called sophisticated flowers such as lilies or orchids and do not allow large flowers to dominate the design. Differences in flower shape create interest.

Flowers	
Smaller varieties of roses and spray roses	Cornflowers
Spray carnations	Sweet peas
Freesias	Asters
Hyacinth pips	Muscari
Anemones	Small narcissi
Statice	Tulips
Waxflowers	*Viburnum tinus*
Lily of the valley	Escallonia
Gypsophila	Lavender
Solidaster	*Helleborus corsicus* and *H. foetidus*

Foliage	
Ivy leaves, trails and berries	*Escallonia* 'Edinensis'
Pittosporum tenuifolium	*Senecio greyi*
Hebe pinguifolia 'Pagei'	*Elaeagnus ebbingei*
Ferns such as asparagus and nephrolepis	Small *Eucalyptus gunnii* sprays
Snowberry	Box
	Myrtle

Tip

Try to incorporate more unusual materials such as ivy berries, sprays of rosemary and other garden foliage to add extra interest to commercially grown flowers in a loose posy.

Method

1. Prepare all materials by using the appropriate method of wiring and suitable wire gauge. The wires used must support the materials but still allow a certain amount of natural movement. It is unlikely that any wires over 0.71 mm will be needed. All materials should be neatly taped.
2. Using toning colours of ribbon, make two small bows with long tails. Either tie these onto the posy handle or mount on a taped wire and bind into position during construction.
3. Attach the binding wire to the flower which will form the centre of the design. This should be done approximately 6–8 cm below the flower head for an average-sized posy. Add five pieces of foliage/leaf units and bind into the same length as the first flower. Bend the five foliage units down so they form a rough circle around the central flower.

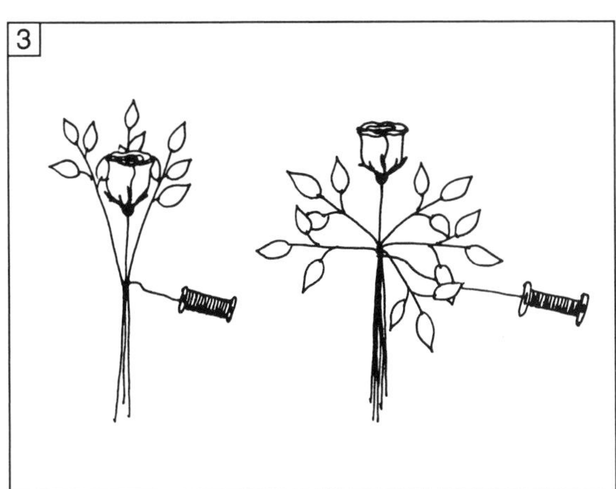

4. This has now established the overall dimensions of the posy. Add a further five pieces of foliage and bind in slightly shorter than the first five. Bend down as before to strengthen the circular outline. Continue to add further flowers and foliage to infill the posy, recessing some for added interest. If using choice flowers such as roses, freesias or tulips, it is more effective to group them through the design in an informal line rather than dotting them about all over the posy.

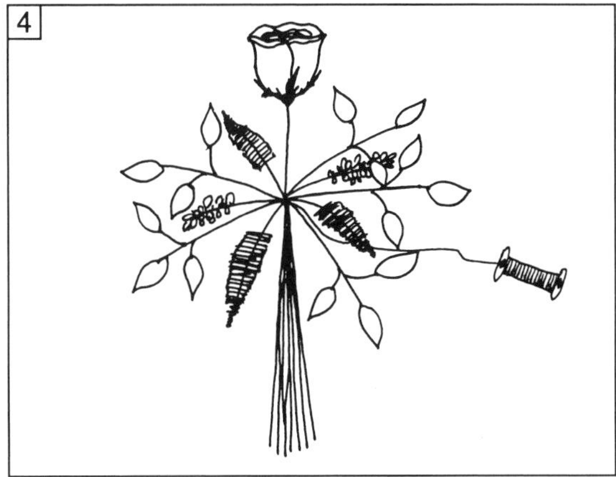

5. To make the handle, bind the wire stems with white plastic tape, ensuring that the base of the handle is well covered. Cover the handle with finishing ribbon, which should be tied off neatly at the top of the handle. Then tie the two bows to the top of the handle.

The finished posy should be circular in outline and slightly domed in profile. It should be light and feel secure to handle.

FLOWER HOOPS

This design is particularly suited to the younger bridesmaid and looks effective if small ribbon bows are added among the flowers or at the carrying point.

Flower hoops can be made either by wiring or by gluing the materials onto the frame. This piece of work is more easily prepared with a glue gun than with wire, but care must be taken to ensure that the flowers are held in position until the glue has set. There is a tendency for heavier flowers such as rose buds to slide out of position while the glue is drying. Flowers and leaves can either be attached so as to form a solid ring of material, or small sprays of flowers can be attached at intervals.

The frame can be made up from 1.20 mm stub wire joined together with plastic tape to form the required size circle. It should then be lightly padded with strips of tissue paper and bound with a narrow satin ribbon in the chosen colour scheme. This will give a surface thick enough to take the addition of the flowers. A plastic hoop can be bound with ribbon straight away as it is of sufficient width to provide a base for the flowers.

Whatever the method, a uniform finish should be created by repeating similar designs or flowers throughout the design.

Flowers	
Spray roses	Freesias
Spray chrysanthemums	Spray carnations
Gypsophila	Dendrobium orchids
Stephanotis	Alchemilla
Hyacinth pips	Mimosa
Waxflowers	Sedum
Hydrangea florets	Delphinium florets
Cornflowers	

Foliage	
Sprays or individual leaves of any small-leaved foliage	
Ivy	Euonymus
Pittosporum	Asparagus
Ruscus	

Wired Hoop

Method

1. Wire and tape all materials on fine stub wires. Construct two small ribbon bows. Carefully lay out materials in groups of the same type and size ready for use.
2. If the hoop is to be completely covered with flowers, start by taping a leaf or flower with white binding tape at the top of the hoop where it will be held.
   - Continue taping more flowers and leaves, gradually working around the ring. Each new piece of material should slightly overlap the last and all should lie in the same direction.
   - Ensure that enough material is used to cover the ring base. This can mean taping two or three pieces of material onto the ring together and gently bending them outwards so that they cover the ring base.
   - When the ring has been filled, cover any remaining wire stems with tape. Remember to leave a section of ring empty of flowers so that it can be held.
   - Finally attach a small bow beside the first piece of material placed on the ring and against the last piece. This provides a neat finish, covers any obvious stems and emphasises the carrying point.
3. If small sprays of flowers are to be attached, the following method may be used.
   - Prepare all materials by wiring, taping and laying out ready for use. Make ribbon bows if required.
   - Construct small sprays and clusters of flowers by the same method as for a corsage. The size of these sprays will vary, depending on the finished design. They should always be as light as possible.
   - Trim the stems of each spray and neatly cover with binding tape. Decide on position for fixing on the ring.
   - Attach a 0.32 mm silver binding wire to the hoop and place a spray onto the hoop frame. By carefully moving some of the leaves and flowers, the binding wire can be passed through the spray so as to bind it tightly to the hoop frame.

     The clusters and sprays need to be bound several times to ensure they are secure and will not move when the hoop is carried.
   - Once the flower spray is secure, cut off any remaining binding wire and neatly bend the end back into the flowers for safety. Re-arrange flowers and leaves back into desired shape.
   - Finish off by adding ribbon bows.

Glued Hoop

A hot glue gun makes the construction of a flower hoop much easier and less time-consuming. Clusters and sprays still have to be constructed by wiring and taping as previously described, but once they are made they can then be glued onto the hoop frame.

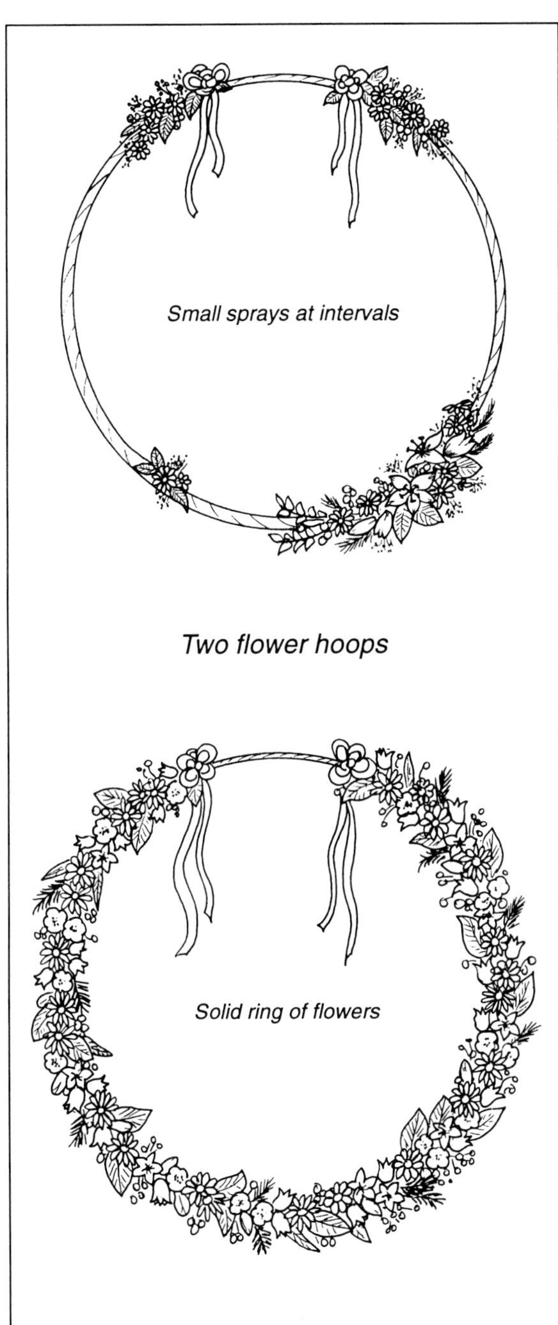

Two flower hoops

The following method will form a complete cover of flowers around the ring.

Method

1. Prepare all materials by removing all excess foliage and stems, leaving approximately 3–4 cm of natural stem on each item. Fragile or heavier flower heads such as roses may require support wiring and taping before use.
2. Start by placing the first flower or leaf into position on the ring and attach with a small amount of molten glue.
3. Add glue in lengths of 5–10 cm onto the frame and gently press flowers and leaves into it. Hold flowers in position until the glue sets, which takes only a few seconds. Make sure flowers are secure before moving on to the next ones.
4. Work around the ring in small sections. Ensure enough flowers are used to cover the width of the ring and also the glue.
5. Finish the design by leaving a space for carrying and then attach two ribbon bows either side of this to conceal the start and finish of the flower material.

Tip

When making a glued hoop, use a thick piece of flower stem or the closed blades of a pair of scissors to press the flowers into the hot glue until it sets.

Limited Wired Bouquet

With the right materials and the right style of dress this type of bouquet can look very dramatic. Its success depends on the choice of a suitably bold flower and the restrained use of foliage and accessories.

Larger, more obvious flowers such as gerberas or lilies are ideal and should be used with only two or three different types of foliage at best. These would consist of a few large dramatic leaves such as croton, some small sprays of filler foliage and possibly a few stems of bear grass.

Pieces of *Salix matsudana* 'Tortuosa' branch, small fruits or fir cones, or safari pack seed heads can add an extra point of interest but should be used with care so as to keep the lines of the design clean and uncluttered.

Tip

When using flowers of one sort in a limited wired bouquet, always try to get some variation, however small, in flower size and shape. With a flower such as a lily, use different stages of flower development from green buds to fully open blooms.

Flowers	
Standard carnations	Gerbera
Lilies such as 'Star Gazer', 'Mont Blanc', *L. longiflorum*	Anthuriums
	Hippeastrum
	Tulips
Arum lilies	Large roses

Foliage	
Croton leaves	Ivy leaves of larger varieties such as *Hedera canariensis* or 'Gloire de Marengo'
Dieffenbachia leaves	
Aspidistra leaves	
Syngonium leaves	
Prunus laurocerasus	
Aucuba japonica	Bear grass
Small bergenia leaves	Hebe sprays
Philodendron leaves	Pittosporum sprays
Dracaena leaves	Safari pack

Limited bouquet

Method

1. Use five or seven flowers of the same type and colour, three or five large leaves of varying sizes, a few sprays of filler foliage and a few cones or seed heads if required.
2. The flowers are left on their natural stems and support wired along the entire stem length. Add a 0.71 mm mount wire to the base of each stem to form the handle of the bouquet.

   The correct length of stem can be difficult to judge. On a table top lay the flowers out in the shape of the bouquet and cut the stems off where the binding point will be. The large leaves should all be stitched for support. Tape all wires.
3. Attach 0.32 mm silver binding wire at the base of the natural stem of the longest flower and bend down.

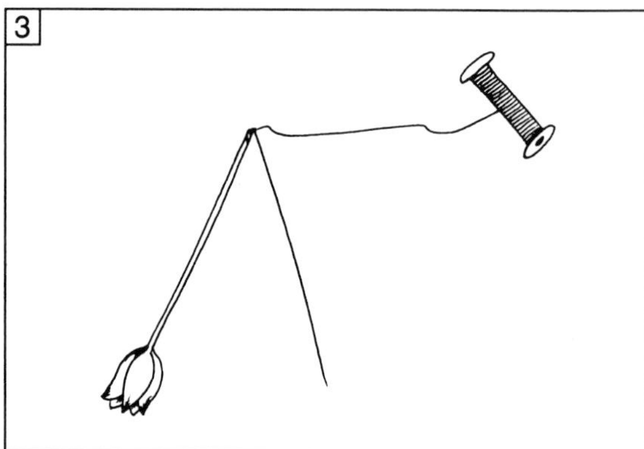

4. Continue adding the remaining flowers to form a line of flowers. Remember that the focal flower should always be in direct line with the handle and never bent. Recess one flower immediately beneath the focal flower to give visual strength to the centre of the design and also to cover the binding point.

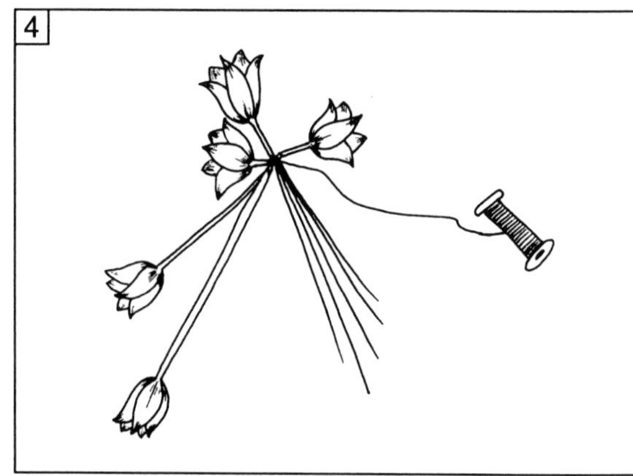

5. Add the foliage, taking care to form a well-balanced design. Part of the beauty of this bouquet is its simplicity, so try not to cover the flower stems with too much foliage as this will diminish the design's clear lines.

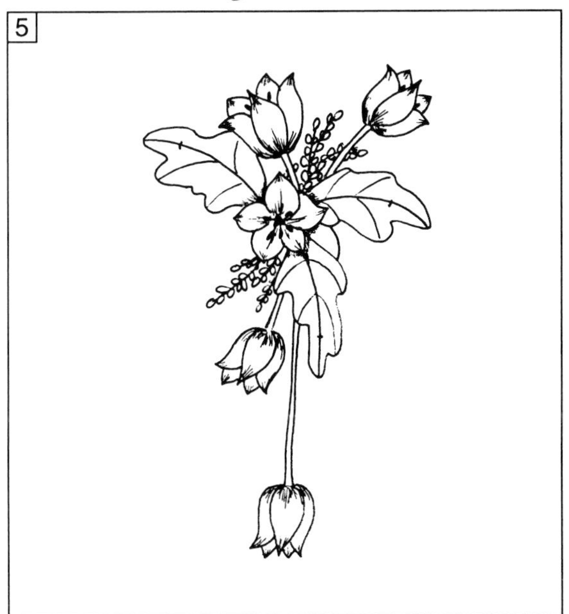

6. Cut the handle to the correct length and bind with white tape.
7. Finish by binding the handle with ribbon and a bow at the top of the handle. Choose a complementary- or neutral-coloured ribbon and make the bow fairly small so as not to detract from the flowers.

Extension Bouquet

The extension bouquet is similar in many ways to a limited wired bouquet. The main difference is that the length of the bouquet is formed by mounting individual flowers onto a decorative 'extension' stem instead of taped wire or instead of using the natural stems. This extension can be made of a range of materials such as velvet or silk tubing (with an internal wire for support), lengths of bear grass, contorted willow or ribbon-bound wires.

The finished effect of the bouquet is structured and formal, although quite minimal. It is well suited for use at perhaps a registry office or for a second wedding. As with a limited bouquet, the flowers must be distinctive and of a suitable size. Often only one type of flower is used, along with only two or three types of well-chosen complementary foliage. Accessories such as beads, cones, twigs, etc., will add extra interest.

The most common size is three extensions, although for a larger bouquet five can be used. The extensions form the length or trailing part of the design. The upper part of the bouquet is made in the same way as a limited or even a shower bouquet, using materials wired and taped in the usual way.

Flowers	
Cymbidium orchids	Tulips
Gerbera	Gladioli florets
Lilies	Camellias
Roses	Gardenias

Foliage	
Ivy leaves	Fatshedera
Nephrolepis fern	Maranta
Peperomia leaves	Eucalyptus

Method

1. Support wire and tape all materials, including lengths of materials for extensions.

   If using natural materials such as bear grass or willow stems, first wire and tape flower heads on fine silver wires. Attach a 0.71 mm mount wire to the base of the extension material and tape as usual.

   Extensions should be graduated in length so that flowers will be individually displayed and not covered by one another. For this reason start with the longest extension and shorten the length toward the top of the bouquet. Having judged the correct length of the extensions, carefully attach a flower to the end.

2. If velvet or silk tubing is used, remove the inner string or cord after cutting to the required lengths. Insert a 0.71 mm wire into the tubing so that it protrudes from each end. The wire should extend only slightly from the end to which the flower will be attached. A longer section of wire at the other end will form part of the bouquet handle. It should be taped in the usual way. Ensure that the plastic binding tape is taken up onto the end of the tubing to secure it to the wire.

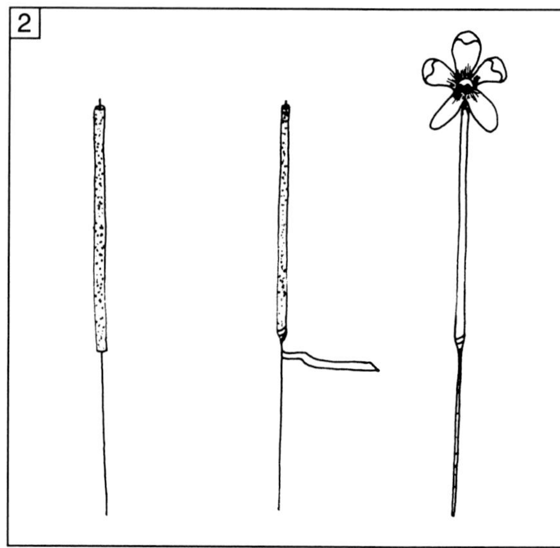

3. Start making the bouquet by bending the longest extension down to form the length and attach the binding wire at the binding point.

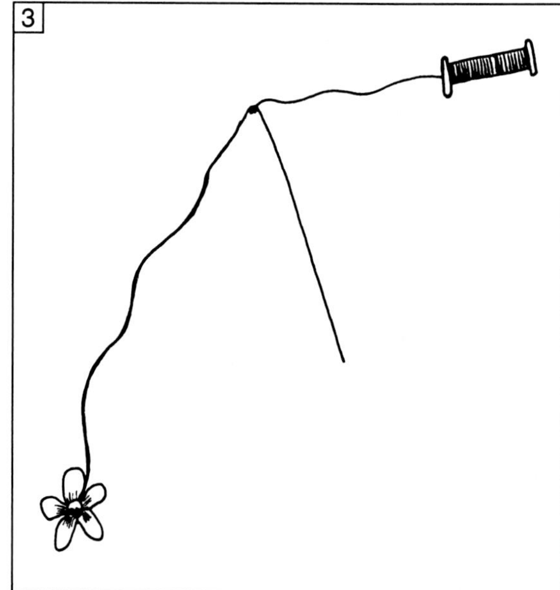

4. Bind in the remaining extensions and add leaves and sprays of foliage to form the width and return end of the design.

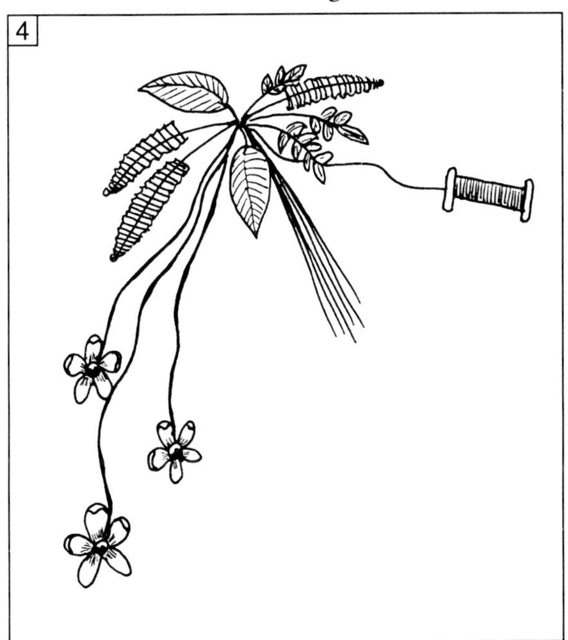

5. Place remaining flowers into the design to form a line through the bouquet.

6. Strengthen the focal area by adding one or two recessed leaves and finish by adding any accessories to be used.

7. Trim off the wire stems and bind with white plastic tape to form the handle. Bind the handle with ribbon and finish off by adding a ribbon bow to the top of the handle.

Shower Bouquet

This is perhaps the most popular of all the wedding bouquet styles. It is often described as pear or teardrop shaped, and a loose, open style should be aimed for. The size of the bouquet depends on many things – the height of the person carrying it, the style of dress and the types of flowers used. Generally a shower bouquet is thought of as being a somewhat larger and fuller traditional design than most other wedding bouquets.

The overall effect should be of a graduated cascade of material from a concentration of larger flowers or stronger colour towards the centre of the design, not only down into the length of the bouquet but also at the sides and partially at the back.

Both natural and wired units of material may be used; the more natural stems that are included, particularly of foliage, the more movement is achieved within the design. This consideration is important in any floristry work but particularly with this type of bouquet, where the amount of material used can make the design look too heavy and solid. When using natural stemmed materials make sure they are mounted on sufficiently strong wire.

For example, unless long trails of ivy are attached to perhaps two 0.71 mm or even a 0.90 mm wire, they will tend to become loose when the design is carried. This should not be confused with natural movement, as the two are very different. As previously mentioned, it is visually pleasing to see a degree of flexibility of flowers and foliages within the finished design, but at the same time all materials should be securely fixed in position at the binding point.

There are so many combinations of flower and

Shower bouquet

foliage types as well as colour schemes for this style of bouquet that they are too numerous to mention. Usually a mixture of perhaps four or five types of flower is used with two or three types of foliage. A typical mixture would be roses as the main focal flowers, along with freesias, dendrobium orchids, spray carnations and stephanotis, with ivy trails, nephrolepis fern and a few scindapsus leaves.

However, some eye-catching and distinctive effects can be achieved by using only one or two types of flower with a complementary foliage of just one colour. White is particularly effective on its own, as are some of the strong colours such as reds, blues and purples.

For this idea to work well the flowers themselves must be of a bold shape and size. 'Casablanca' or 'Star Gazer' lilies look superb on their own with only some dracaena or fatsia leaves. For a winter wedding a full shower bouquet of deep red or burgundy roses, some full blown and some in bud, with wild green ivy trails, leaves and blackberries, can look stunning.

Shower bouquet

Flowers	
Roses	Tulips
Spray roses	Small spray chrysanthemums
Spray carnations	Alstroemeria
All types of lily	*Gladiolus nanus*
Stephanotis	Hellebores
Freesias	Gypsophila
Dendrobium and cymbidium orchids	Waxflowers
Hyacinth pips	

Foliage	
Ivy	Hebe sprays
Nephrolepis fern	Box foliage
Scindapsus leaves	Soft ruscus
Asparagus sprengeri	

Method

1. Prepare materials by support wiring where necessary. With a single leg mount wire provide an extended stem length for *all* materials. Bind all wire stems neatly with tape.

   Include as wide a range of flower/foliage sizes as possible in your selection. For example, wire not only rose buds but some larger half-open blooms and one or two fully blown flowers. Vary the length of natural units of material from long pieces for the 'tail' of the bouquet to some very short pieces to infill the centre.

   Repeating the same foliage or flower through the bouquet gives continuity to the design, and having a wide choice of sizes and lengths of material makes the construction of the bouquet much easier.

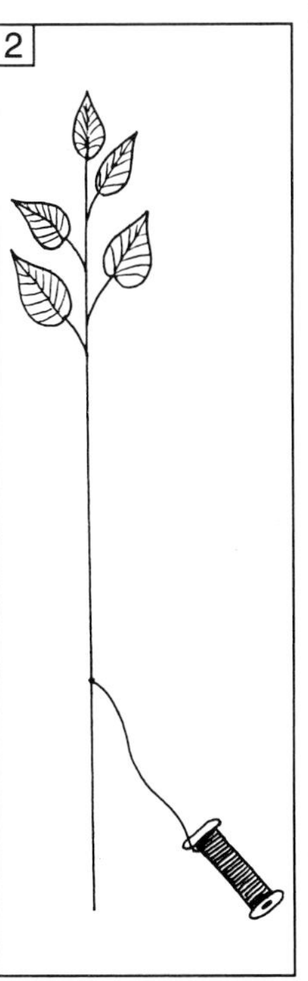

2. Start the construction of the bouquet by attaching the binding wire to the longest piece of foliage which will form the maximum length in the tail. The return end should not be too long, as this would make the bouquet difficult to hold, but it must be low enough to balance the tail of the bouquet and partially cover the hands when it is held. The golden rule of proportion can be applied here: two-thirds of the length and material bulk below the binding point and one-third above or at the back.
3. Add further foliage and flower units, graduating the length up to the binding point, so that the

tapering outline of the bouquet is formed from its longest point to its widest point either side of the binding point.

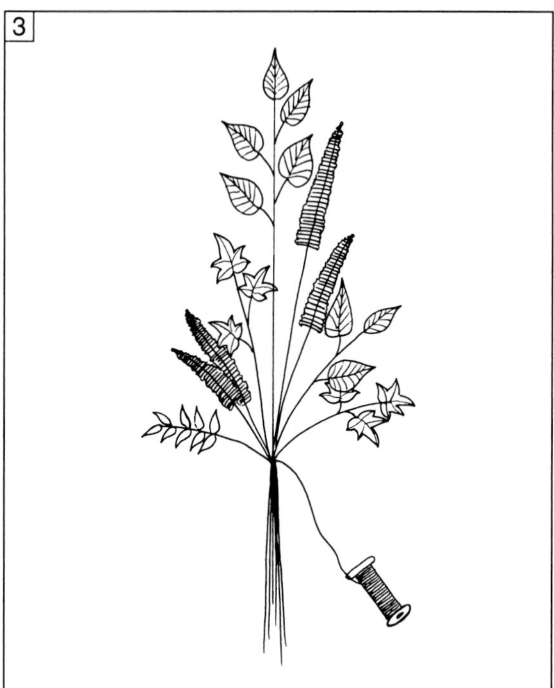

4. Add flowers into this basic outline, remembering to start some of the groupings or pattern lines of the main flowers from the bottom of the design. These will then be brought through the design up to the focal area and into the return end. It is much easier to bind in place all the flowers which are needed than to try to add some later, so each stage of the bouquet should be finished as you work up to the centre.

5. At this point of the construction all the material already bound together which is still straight must be bent over to form the trail of the design as well as the handle. Remember that the handle of the finished bouquet must be parallel to the body line.

   Hold the wires below the binding point as you would hold the finished handle of the bouquet and carefully bend over all the material so that it forms a fall or shower effect. Re-position any flowers as necessary.
6. Next add pieces of material roughly the same length either side of the binding point. These should be at angles to the bouquet handle which is being formed by the wire stems of the flowers already used. Complete the shape by adding more material bent backwards to form a return end.

7. To establish the height or profile of the bouquet, place one of the focal flowers immediately above the binding point so that its wire stem is directly in line with the handle and not bent. The height of this flower depends on the finished bouquet, 8–10 cm usually being sufficient for one of average size.

8. Once the focal/profile flower has been bound into position, strengthen this with another flower of the same type just below and perhaps even a third deeply recessed onto the binding point. This gives a sense of visual strength and solidity to the centre of the design.

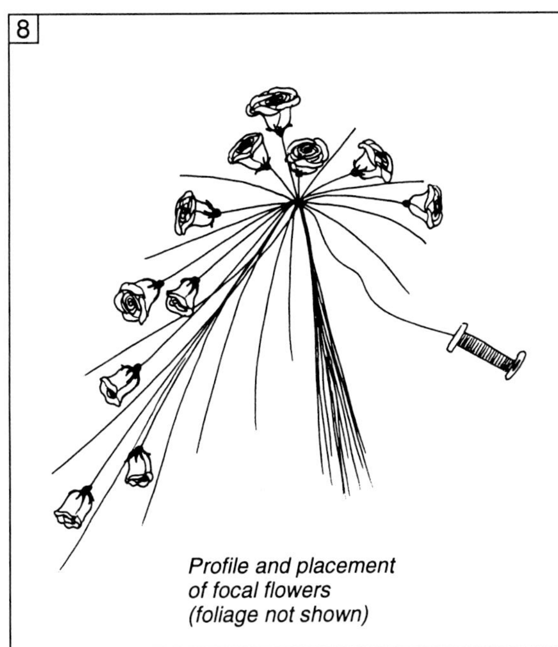

8

Profile and placement of focal flowers (foliage not shown)

9. Continue to fill in the design with the remaining flowers and foliage. Care should be taken to follow through all pattern lines and colour groupings. Some materials should be recessed deeply into the bouquet to provide visual depth and to conceal the binding point without having to add too much material.

9

10. Trim the handle to approximately 15–20 cm in length and bind with white binding tape. The use of white tape instead of green ensures that the handle ribbon does not look discoloured.
11. Bind the handle with narrow satin ribbon the same colour as you are using for the bow, being particularly careful with the binding over the end of the handle. Start binding at the top of the handle and work down. Fold and pleat the ribbon over the end of the handle and bind back up to the top. Tie off the binding ribbon.

    Finally, tie a bow on with two long ribbon tails at the top of the handle. Trim ribbon tails, once secured, to required length.

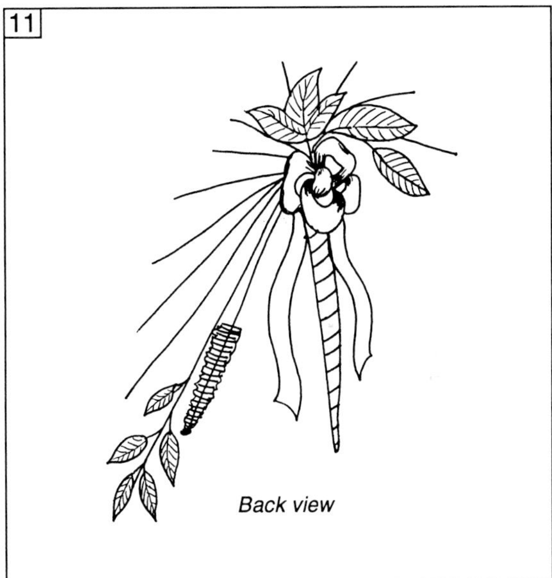

11

Back view

12. Make final adjustments of any materials that have moved during the construction.

Tip

Use natural units whenever possible to achieve a degree of movement within the design of a shower bouquet. As this style of bouquet tends to be quite large, there is a danger that it can become very stiff and solid.

Crescent Bouquet

Crescent bouquet

The crescent bouquet is another formal bouquet, but it is less popular than the shower. It is a symmetrical design and should therefore be carefully constructed so that both sides visually balance each other. The flowers should radiate out from a central point above the handle and form two matching curved cascades on each side. In order to balance the curving tails, the return end of the bouquet is raised slightly so as to almost resemble a fan shape in the centre of the design.

Smaller, lighter flowers are generally more suited to this style as they are easier to use within the confines of such a strong-shaped design. One of the easier ways to make this style is by constructing three separate units which when put together form the finished bouquet.

Flowers

Depending on the bouquet size all the usual flowers for wired bouquet work are suitable. The following are particularly useful.

Lily of the valley	Stephanotis
Cytisus	*Euphorbia fulgens*
Freesias	Spray carnations
Small lilac sprays	September flowers
Solidaster	Waxflowers

Foliage

Ruscus	Ivy
Cytisus	Rosemary
Nephrolepis	

Wired leaf units

Garrya leaves
Skimmia leaves
Euonymus leaves

Larger focal area leaves

Camellia
Synogonium
Ivy
Spathiphyllum

Method

1. All materials should be mounted and support wired if necessary in the usual way. Prepare equal quantities and lengths of materials for each section. An average curved section is approximately 20–25 cm long.
2. Construct the two sections by wiring the stems together to form a handle and then bending the materials over to form the tail and shape of the bouquet. Make sure that these two sections curve in opposite directions.

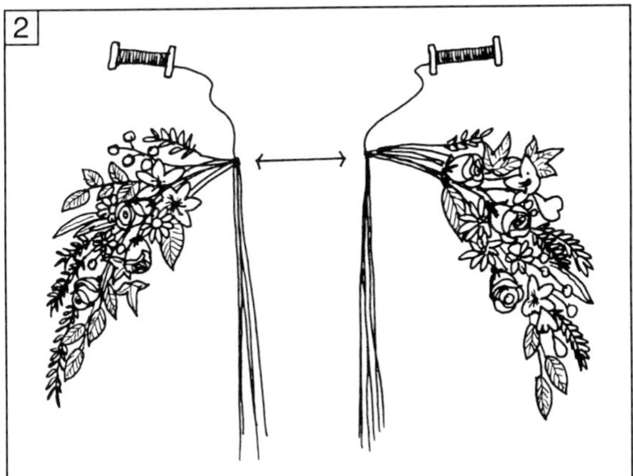

3. Make the third or central section which will form the top of the bouquet. Add enough material to be able to infill the area between the two curved sections.

4. Bind the two curved sections lightly together. The stems should be bound together at the same point and the flowers then curve outwards at right angles to each other.
5. The central unit can then be added to complete the overall design. If the three sections feel loose or will not stay in position, it is useful to take the binding wire down the length of the handle and up again for added security.
6. Add some large flowers and leaves if needed to form and strengthen the focal area at the front of the design. These can be added once the basic shape has been established, care being taken not to use too many and spoil the crescent shape.
7. Trim off the handle and bind with white tape. Bind with ribbon and finally finish off the back of the bouquet with a bow.

Tip

Bouquets can be greened up with foliage by a less skilled florist well in advance of the addition of flower material, thus saving valuable time.

Semi-crescent Bouquet

This style of bouquet is ideal for bridesmaids as well as the bride. It looks particularly effective if two bridesmaids carry bouquets which curve in opposite directions. The curved shape is best described as forming part of a circle. If the bouquet were placed on a circle, the line of the flowers would follow the curve exactly. Although quite different from a shower bouquet in its appearance, the same design principles should be applied during its construction, resulting in two-thirds of the length below the binding point and one-third above.

Suitable flowers and foliage
The same selection as for a crescent bouquet.

Semi-crescent bouquet

Method

1. All materials should be prepared and mount wired using as light a wire as possible.
2. Construct the lower half in the same way as a shower bouquet by holding the wired materials parallel with the body line and bending them down to form the handle and length of the bouquet. The materials must next be bent into a gentle curving shape. The most important thing to remember is to build up materials on the outside of the curve and use very little on the inside. This is followed through up to the binding point.

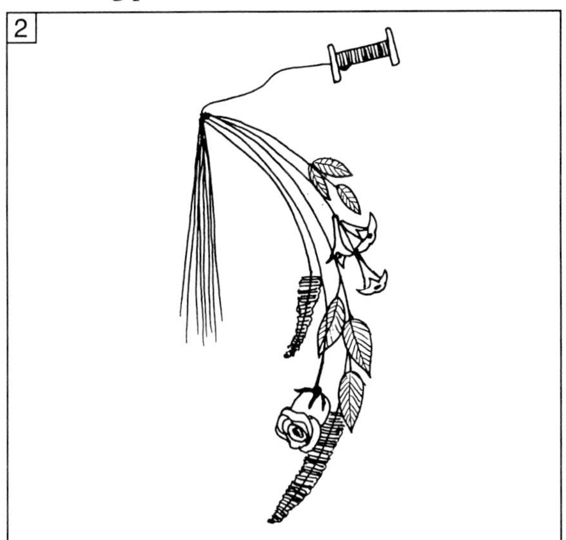

3. Add the focal flower directly above the binding point. This central area of the bouquet can be reinforced with one or two larger focal flowers to add visual strength and colour. This should be the widest point of the bouquet, although the curving shape is still maintained by longer material on the outside edge and shorter materials on the inside. The tallest focal flower of this point should not be more than 12–15 cm above the binding point. All materials in the bouquet should also appear to radiate out from this central area.

4. The return end can now be added to complete the flowing curve and should be in proportion to the length of the tail of the bouquet.
5. The handle can be trimmed to the required length, covered with white binding tape and then bound with a suitably coloured ribbon. Finally a bow is added at the top of the handle at the back of the bouquet for neatness.

USING FOAM HOLDERS

Foam holders have revolutionised the work of the florist in wedding design, enabling preparation well in advance of the actual day. Constructing a bouquet on a foam holder takes a quarter of the time that a wired bouquet requires and is therefore more economical, saving valuable time when the florist has a number of bouquets to prepare

Two kinds of foam holder are available, the main difference being that one contains wet foam and the other dry. Holders are angled or straight and look rather like a cone filled with ice cream. They are available in diameters of 5 or 7 cm.

The larger ones are suitable for large shower and semi-crescent bouquets or where more materials are required. The smaller ones are ideal for a small bridesmaid's posy or a presentation posy.

The wet foam holder allows the plant material to take up moisture into the stem, enabling the bouquet to be made up at least two days before it will be required, providing the materials used have been well conditioned and the completed bouquet is kept in the cold store.

The dry foam holder does not hold any moisture, but providing the materials used are well conditioned and the stems are sealed with glue prior to insertion into the foam, the materials will also last well if placed in the cold store after construction. Whether using wet or dry foam, avoid putting stems into foam and then taking them out. Plan exactly where each stem is to be placed before inserting it, as holes in the foam will weaken the structure and create instability (see colour section).

Method

Although the bouquet shape is the same as for wired work, the method of construction is different.

There is no need to support wire every piece of material being used although it is advisable to support wire focal and lateral flowers, which may be more vulnerable, and particularly flowers such as roses in hot, humid weather.

Place the holder in either a ready-made bouquet stand or a cheap alternative such as an empty wine bottle filled with sand. This allows for both hands to be free to construct the design.

Dry foam

Dip all stems into hot glue. This is easiest with a glue pot. Then push the stems firmly into the foam.

Wet foam

Lightly soak the foam according to the manufacturer's instructions. Cover the handle in a toning ribbon to complement the colour scheme being used. Some brand products with a covering over the plastic handle may not require a ribbon.

Mount all the plant material on a single leg mount of a suitable wire gauge. Push the mount into the foam, ensuring that the stem also goes in. The wire should protrude through the foam and be bent back to form a 'hairpin' which is then pushed back into the foam. This gives firm anchorage to the stem and ensures that it will not fall out or move around when the bouquet is handled.

For added security, stems being used in a wet foam holder may be glued as well as wired, but they should be inserted whilst the foam is still dry. In this case the foam is soaked after completion of the bouquet but before addition of the ribbon bow.

Foam holders (dry and wet)

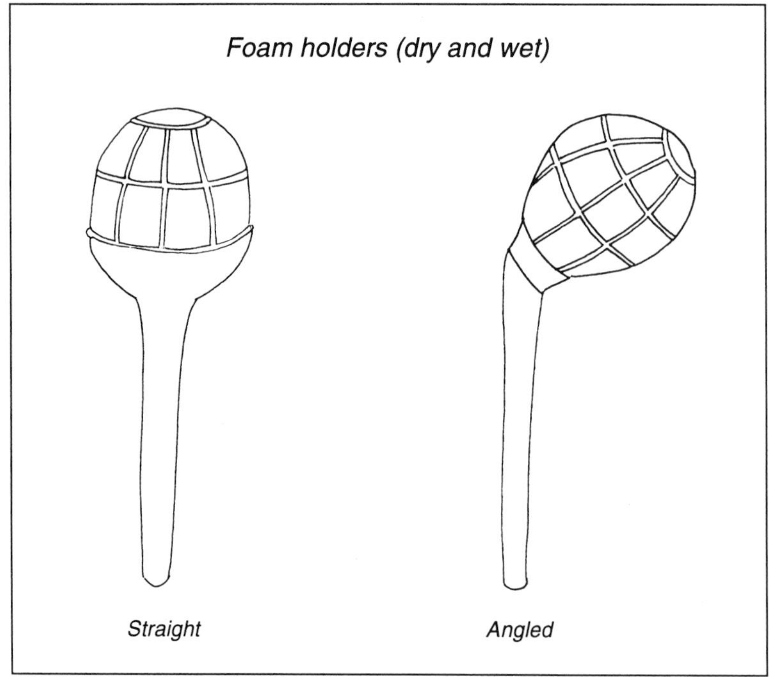

Straight *Angled*

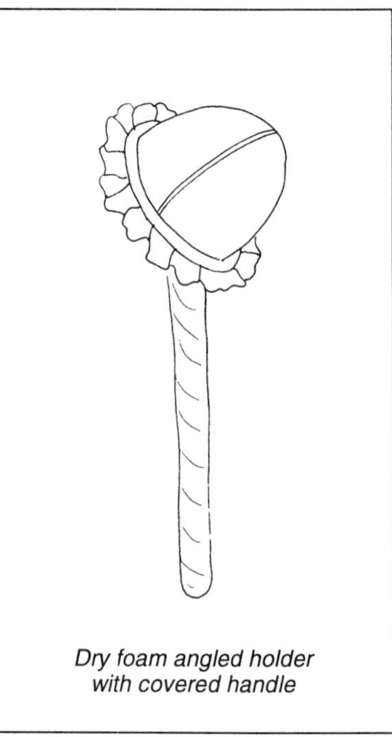

Dry foam angled holder with covered handle

For both wet and dry foam, the design required can be achieved by first creating an outline of plant material and then adding the focal point. The outline should be filled in, including pattern lines, grouping, recession and transition within it. As in any design using foam, the foam should not be visible. Larger leaves may be used well recessed around the focal area to help cover the foam and enhance the focal area.

As the bouquet will be viewed from all angles, remember to bring the sides and back placements down so that the material falls over the hand. The design should be attractive at the back, and a ribbon bow placed there in a toning colour is an important addition.

Spray the bouquet lightly when completed and place in the cold store in the stand used until required.

If a bouquet has been made in advance, before packing it should be checked for any material which may have wilted. Allow enough time to fix anything which may need attention.

Tip

Satin or fabric ribbon should always be used in wedding design. Polypropylene ribbon, which is waterproof, is suitable only for funeral work and packaging.

CAKE TOP ARRANGEMENTS

Although usually referred to as an 'arrangement', this item has been included in the wedding bouquet section as it usually forms a part of the main wedding order for the florist. Because of its size it requires careful thought and construction, and it should use similar flowers to those in the bridal bouquet. Indeed, as it gives the finishing touch to the cake, the workmanship should be of the same standard as for the bridal bouquet.

Cake top arrangements can be basically made in two ways, as a wired work or in foam, using a piece cut to size or an Iglu. The most popular shape is an all-round pointed or conical design. This can sit directly on the top tier of the cake in a very small dish or lid of some sort or it can be in a small vase. As these traditional vases are very thin and tapering, it is extremely difficult to arrange much at all in them, and they have a tendency to overbalance if filled with too many flowers. Plastic vases, which are mainly used nowadays, are really too light to put water or foam into safely. Glass or silver vases provide more stability but are of course more expensive.

If a more compact design is called for, a small flat jar lid serves very well as a container for a small piece of foam. The flowers will completely cover this so that it will not be seen when in position on the cake. Small, fine-stemmed flowers and foliage must be used to prevent the foam from breaking up. Try to repeat some of the flower types which have been used in the bouquets. Small flowers which have difficult stems such as stephanotis and hyacinths can be mounted on wire stems and taped before arranging.

The shape and construction of both flat and vase arrangements are really the same, the one difference being the preparation of the foam. For the flat design, a small trimmed cube of foam secured by a thin piece of tape or glued onto the lid before soaking is sufficient. For the vase, a piece of foam must be cut to form a plug which fits the neck and extends approximately 3–5 cm above the rim. The corners and edges of the foam should be lightly rounded off and then secured with a thin strip of tape onto the sides of the vase. The tape should not extend too far down the sides of the vase as this is difficult to cover with the flowers.

The methods described here are really only the basic designs. Cake decorations like bridal bouquets are many and varied, created to suit the individual style and decoration of the cake. Some can be as simple as just a few flower heads, petals or leaves laid or scattered over the cake. Others almost cover the cake, with fern and flowers cascading from the top tier down over the cake and onto the table.

Always check to see when the cake will be delivered to the reception venue. If the florist has to decorate the cake in situ, it will be necessary to arrange delivery in adequate time for this.

Tip

Spray arrangements lightly before placing on the cake. *Never* spray flowers in position on the cake as this could cause damage to the icing.

Flowers	
Freesias	Spray carnations
Spray roses	Stephanotis pips
Hyacinth pips	Small daisy-type chrysanthemums
Dendrobium orchids	Delphinium florets
Muscari	Solidaster
Gypsophila	Waxflowers
Statice	*Helleborus foetidus* bells
Mimosa	Small sprays of sedum
Ivy flowers and berries	
Small roses	

Foliage	
Ivy leaves	Senecio leaves
Euonymus leaves	Small leatherleaf sprays
Asparagus umbellatus and *sprengeri*	Small eucalyptus leaves
Soft ruscus sprays	Rosemary
Box sprays	
Myrtle sprays	

Cake Top Arrangement in Foam

Method

1. Trim pre-soaked foam to suitable size and shape and secure in the container with tape.

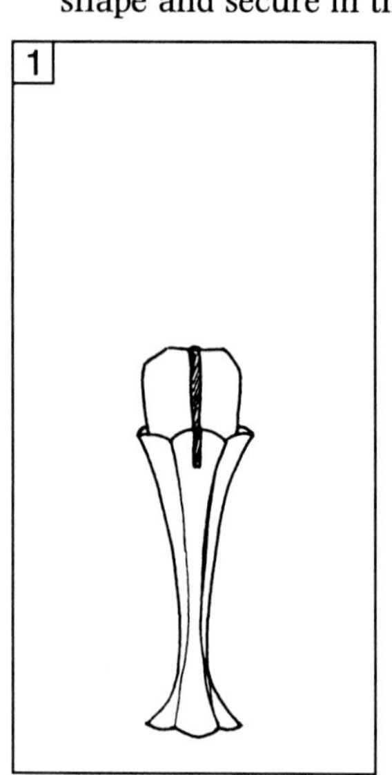

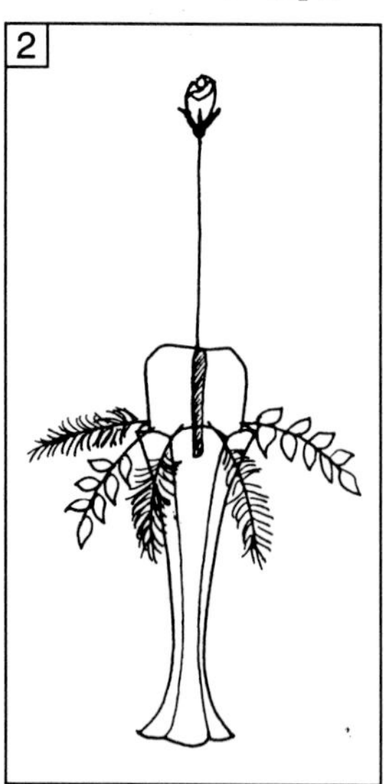

2. Inset the topmost flower or bud, ensuring it is straight when viewed from all sides. Place five or six pieces of material in a ring around the base of the foam. If using a vase, angle this material slightly downwards to disguise the vase rim.
3. Place the main focal flowers, grouping larger open flowers towards the centre of the design and small half-open flowers and buds towards the edges and top of the arrangement. These flowers should be positioned so as to be seen from all sides.

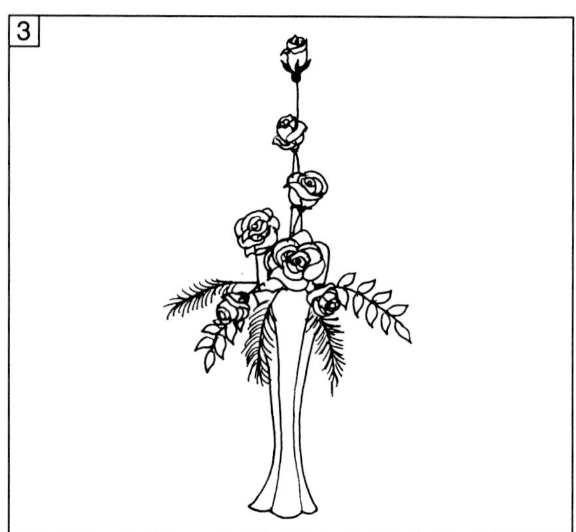

4. Infill the arrangement with more short pieces of foliage and secondary flowers, taking care to strengthen the top and edges of the design and to cover the foam.
5. Add the final small or choice flowers such as stephanotis, gypsophila or hyacinth pips to infill any weak areas and to add lightness to the design. The finished design should be a perfect arrangement in miniature: conical in shape with some trailing materials covering the edges of the vase.

Cake top arrangement in vase

Cake Top Arrangement in Foam Iglu

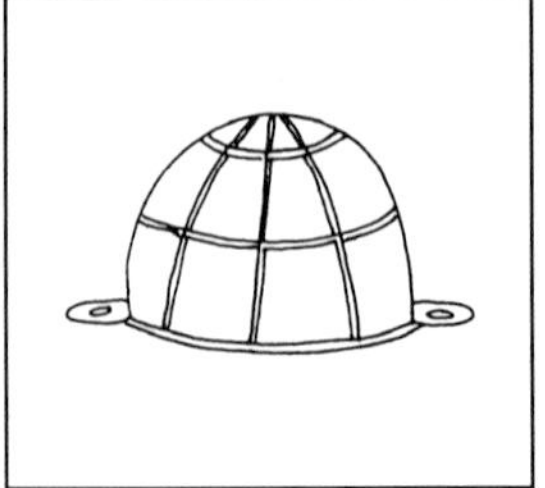

The Iglu is a plastic cage in the shape of an igloo, containing a piece of foam which is approximately 5 cm across in diameter and 5 cm high. (The two small holes on the 'wings' at the sides are to attach ribbon when using the Iglu as a base for a pew end.) It is an alternative to the foam base just described.

Method

1. Cover the base neatly with either foil or thin white plastic to protect the cake.
2. Soak the foam lightly according to the manufacturer's instructions.
3. Create the outline with the plant material and establish the height. The size and shape (square or round) will be determined by the cake.
4. Fill in with flowers and foliage, remembering to include pattern lines, transition and recession. Add bows to tone if relevant.

Wired cake top arrangement

Base of arrangement

Wired Cake Top Arrangement

If an arrangement in foam is unsuitable as a cake decoration, a wired design is a useful alternative. The finished arrangement looks very similar to the conical design previously described. This design requires no container whatsoever as all the materials are wired and taped together. The finished arrangement is very light and sits quite safely on the cake itself. The same rules as before apply for suitable flowers: they should be small, lightweight and blend with other bridal flowers.

Method

1. Wire and tape a selection of flowers and foliage of different sizes and re-assemble some into small units.
2. Attach 0.32 mm binding wire to the flower which will form the central tallest point of the design. The point at which the binding wire is attached will decide the overall height of the design. When the arrangement is finished, the binding point will be at the base of the design and rest on the cake top.

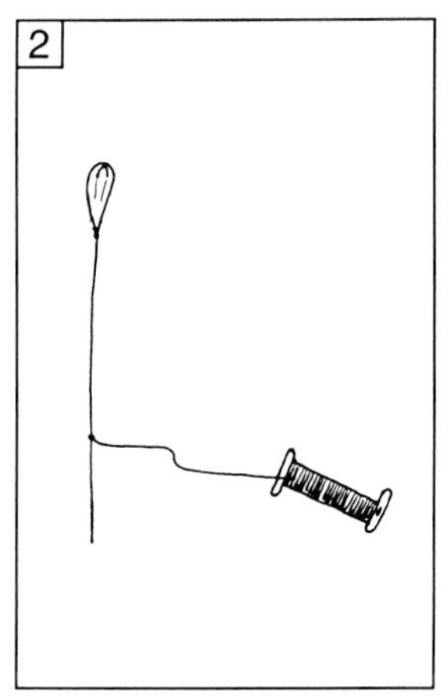

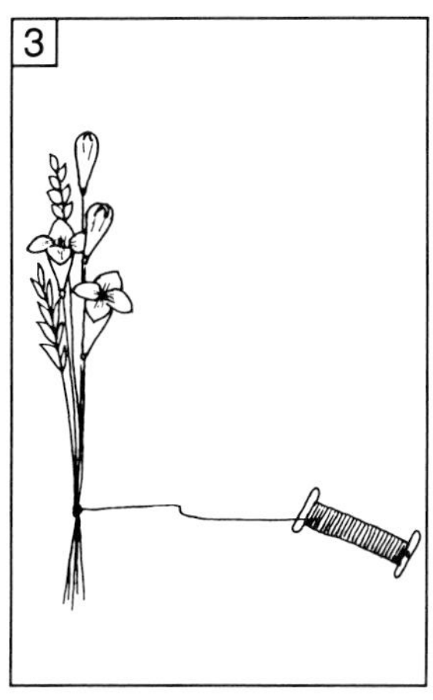

3. Bind in three or four more central pieces slightly lower than the first piece to strengthen the top of the design and to form a central core. The wire stems from these pieces should be long enough to provide a handle for the design.
4. Attach five or six foliage and bud units and bend them down at right angles to the central stem. These should now form a circular base to the arrangement. Ensure that the diameter of the base is in proportion to the height.

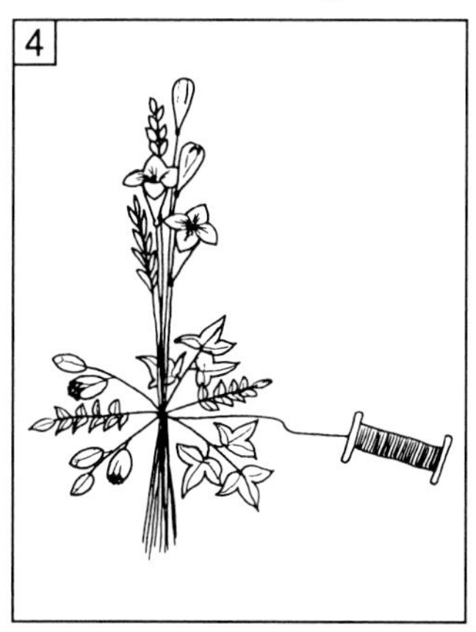

5. Add the larger focal or choice flowers through the design so as to be visible from all sides. Turn the arrangement as it is being constructed to maintain a balanced shape. Recess one or two larger flowers over the binding point to add depth and weight to the design.
6. Continue to bind in further material to infill and strengthen the overall shape. Turn the design during construction so that all wires are added straight and do not cross over each other. After a wired flower has been bound in straight, it can be bent into its final position.
7. Once the arrangement is finished, trim off the wire stems underneath to approximately 3–4 cm in length. Divide these wires into three or four equal sections and neatly bind each section or 'leg' of wires with white plastic tape. Ensure that the binding point itself is also covered. These small legs can be bent outwards to form feet for the arrangement to stand on, very much like the base of an artificial Christmas tree. They should not, however, extend or be visible beyond the outer edge of the arrangement. Some of the lower flowers and leaves can be pulled downwards so that the feet cannot be seen when the decoration stands on the cake.

CHAPTER 8

Funeral Design

TAKING A FUNERAL ORDER

When a customer comes to order flowers for a funeral, certain points should be considered.

- The customer will be upset, so it is preferable to speak in a quiet corner of the shop. This is not always possible, but do consider the customer's feelings.
- The customer will very likely be indecisive about the type of tribute required, so show a possible selection. Try to find out if the deceased had any favourite flowers or colours, or belonged to any organisation such as a gardening club. It will then be easier to suggest a suitable tribute.
- The customer, especially if a close relative, will probably have no idea how much they wish to spend, so a selection of tributes at different prices can be suggested.
- The selection guides of the relay organisations are very helpful but it is a good idea to have your own portfolio of work as well, which would include unusual designs.
- It is *very* important to take down all the relevant details on the order form:
  - The date of the funeral
  - The time of the funeral
  - The name and address of the undertaker
  - The name of the deceased in full.
    J Smith is not sufficient, as there may be a Mr John Smith and a Mrs Joan Smith at the same undertakers on the same day. Wrong or insufficient details can lead to mistakes being made.
  - The type of tribute, detailing flowers, price and colours required.
  - The customer's full name, address and telephone number.
- The card should be written by the customer if possible.

When making up any funeral tribute, there are a few points to keep in mind:

- Remember that the space between the top of the casket and the roof of the hearse is limited and in some cases no more than 25 cm.
- Always consult with the undertaker first if any tributes are to be placed on top of the casket for transportation.
- Tributes are not only viewed from above but will be seen at eye level if placed on top of the coffin, so always ensure that material covers the base completely.
- Spray the finished tribute lightly. Place the card in a clear cellophane envelope to protect the writing from moisture. Then attach the envelope to a plastic pick and push firmly into the foam in a suitable place.

Tip

Always keep strictly within the outline of any design as any unevenness will spoil the shape. This is particularly so when constructing animals or unusual shapes with foam where the shape has to be recognised easily.

THE SPRAY

Funeral sprays are probably the least expensive form of tribute because there is less preparation involved than in making most other designs. They are made on pre-soaked foam fastened with pot tape to a spray tray.

The three most popular and their diagrammatic shapes are as follows.

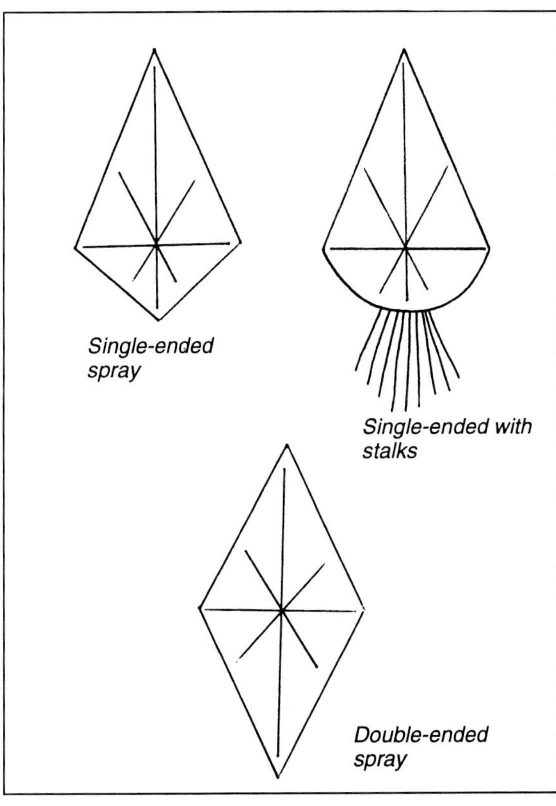

Suitable Flowers	
Irises	Liatris
Carnations	Lilies
Roses	Spray carnations
Gerbera	Mini gerbera
Alstroemeria	Larkspur
Anthuriums	Limonium
Spray chrysanthemums (double and single)	Gladioli
Tulips	Asters
Narcissi (buds)	Alchemilla

Most flowers are suitable except for really small ones.

Suitable Foliage	
Tsuga pine	Leatherleaf
Laurel	Euphorbia
Bay	Elaeagnus
Arbutus	Ruscus
Senecio	Cupressus
Eucalyptus	Portuguese laurel

Double-ended Spray

A large double-ended spray is called a casket arrangement as it is placed on top of the coffin. It should be two-thirds the size of the casket.

Flowers	Foliage
Gerbera	Laurel stems
Spray carnations	Leatherleaf stems
Lilies	Croton leaves
Waxflowers	Eucalyptus stems

Method

1. Attach half a block of pre-soaked foam to a spray tray with pot tape.

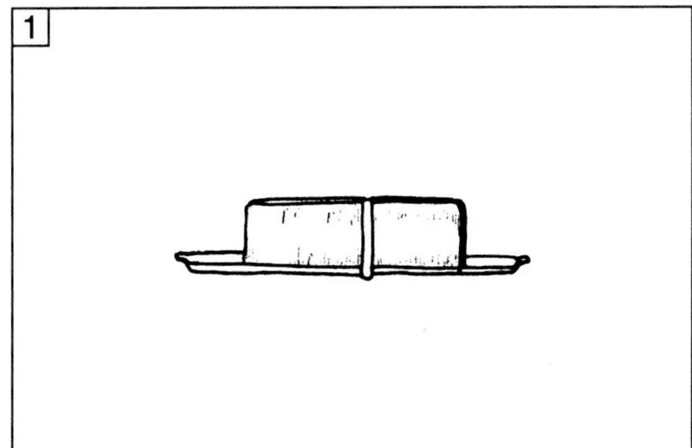

2. Insert a piece of laurel about 25 cm long at each end of the base. Next insert a piece 15 cm long on either side.
3. The rest of the laurel should be arranged to look as if it radiates out from the focal point, and should keep within a diamond shape outline.
4. Some of the laurel should be taken through the centre, along with a few pieces of leatherleaf. The foliage should be slightly elevated at the centre.

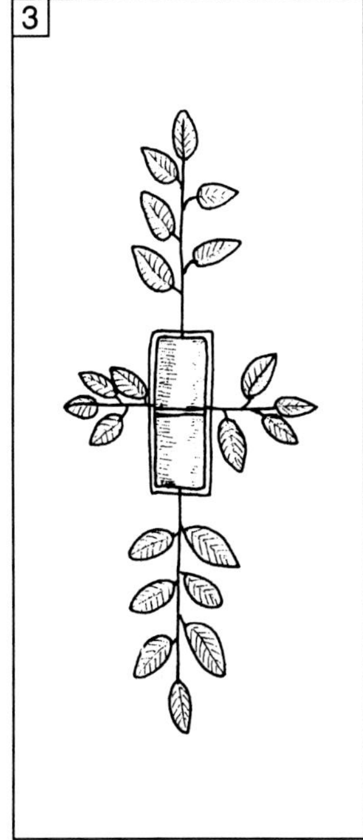

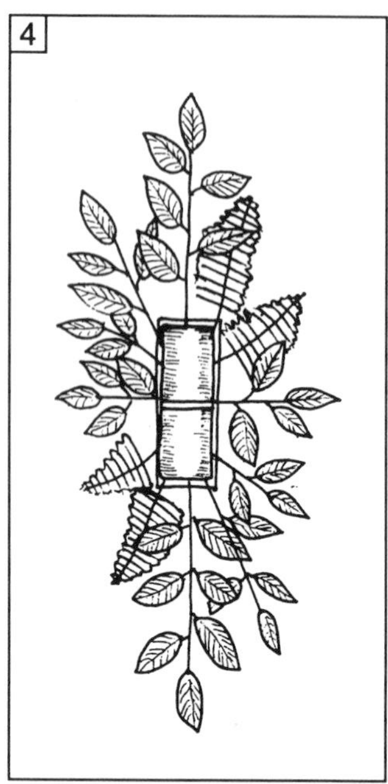

5. Take the gerbera through from one end to the other in a broken line, using a gerbera as the tallest focal flower. Follow the line through with the lilies, recessing the more open flowers in the focal area and using the buds on the outside. Place the croton leaves low down around the focal area.
6. Take the spray carnations through diagonally from one side down to the other, and arrange the waxflowers from top to bottom in an opposite diagonal. The gaps can be filled in with eucalyptus.

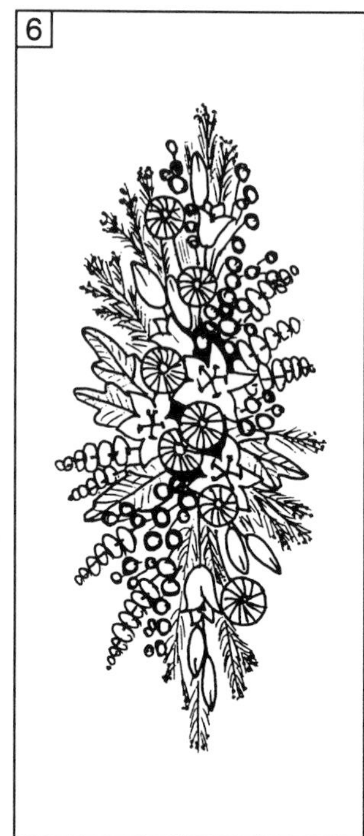

Double-ended spray

Single-ended spray

Single-ended Spray

The single-ended spray is made in the same way but the proportions are two-thirds to one-third as shown in the drawing.

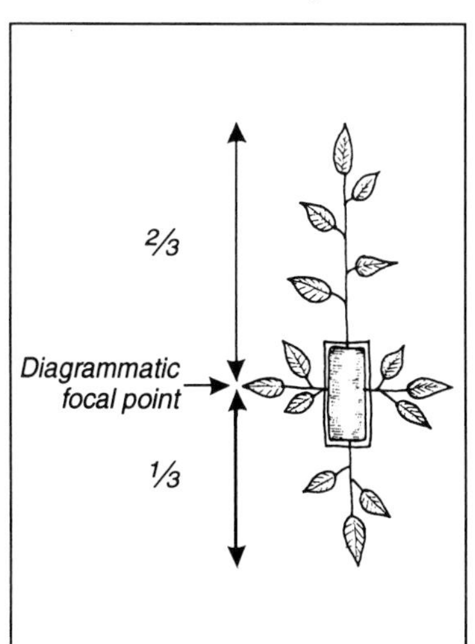

Spray with Stalks

Make the top half of the spray in exactly the same way, except for putting all the cut stalks aside for use later.

When the top part is completed, add a few short pieces of foliage to the bottom half to cover the foam. Clean the stalks and insert at the bottom, the proportions being two-thirds flowers and foliage and one-third stalks radiating out from the focal area.

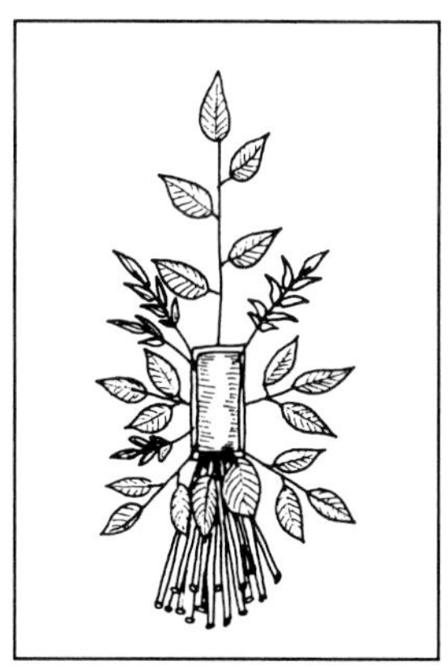

Single-ended spray with stalks

Tied Sheaf

See page 46.

BASED TRIBUTES

Most funeral tributes nowadays are made on a wet foam base, which has many advantages over mossing: it is cleaner to use, holds more moisture and necessitates very little wiring of plant material. Therefore the tribute can be completed quickly and can be made well in advance if stored in a cooler. This enables florists to plan work and take more orders than would be possible with mossed tributes.

Bases are available in various sizes, depending on what the customers require and how much they wish to spend. Some of the more unusual tributes may have to be made from designer sheet or constructed of moss on a wire frame. Designer sheet is a sheet of foam with a polystyrene base which can be cut into any shape to make unusual and 3-D designs. (See page 118.)

The foam base should be soaked according to the manufacturer's instructions. It is very important not to oversoak, as the foam will become heavy and waterlogged. Equally, undersoaking will leave dry patches and the plant material will not take up water and will thus wilt.

The foam base should be prepared by shaving the edge with a sharp knife to bevel it. This rounded base gives a better profile to the finished tribute, particularly if it is a heart, pillow, cushion or posy pad where a cushion effect is required.

If an artificial edging such as polypropylene ribbon is required, this should be attached to the foam prior to soaking. Any material used in continental design such as bark, slate, stones or anything artificial should also be applied to the dry foam with a glue gun, as the glue will not adhere to wet foam.

Bumps are used for attaching clusters or small sprays to base forms, and these should be fixed on prior to soaking. The bump may be a piece of foam cut to the required size, covered with fine nylon netting and then attached to the base with German or wire pins. Ready-made bumps with a screw on the base of the plastic case that can be screwed into the foam are also available.

Plant stems should be cut cleanly at an angle, preferably with a sharp knife, and then cleaned of foliage. Any foliage on the stem will make a larger hole in the foam than necessary so that the stem will not be secure and can fall out. Stems should be pushed well into the foam. This is very important because funeral tributes can receive very rough handling by the undertakers.

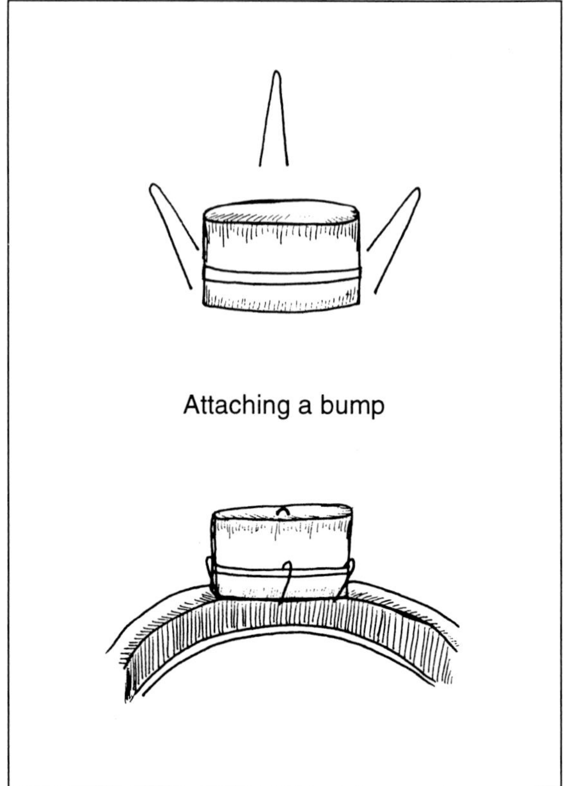

Attaching a bump

The focal flowers in the spray or cluster may need support wiring and anchoring as they are the most likely flowers to be knocked when the tribute is moved about. If the tribute is very large and heavy, the lateral flowers may also need anchoring with a double leg mount, the ends of which should be bent back before pushing into the foam so as to give added security.

Edging

This is the material placed on the edge of the tribute. Polypropylene ribbon is mostly used, as it is attractive and waterproof. Other materials may be foliage, bark, hessian, individual leaves, rope or fabric. The colour of the ribbon should tone in with the flowers and not dominate the tribute.

Ribbon edging is pleated with a stapler prior to attaching to the tribute. The pleats should be very neat and even. Their size will depend on that of the tribute: a small posy pad for a baby would require very small pleats of 2 cm per pleat, but a large cross for a coffin would require 4 cm.

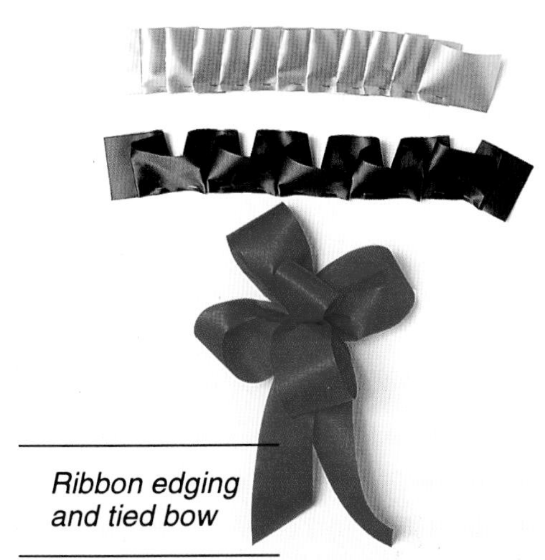
Ribbon edging and tied bow

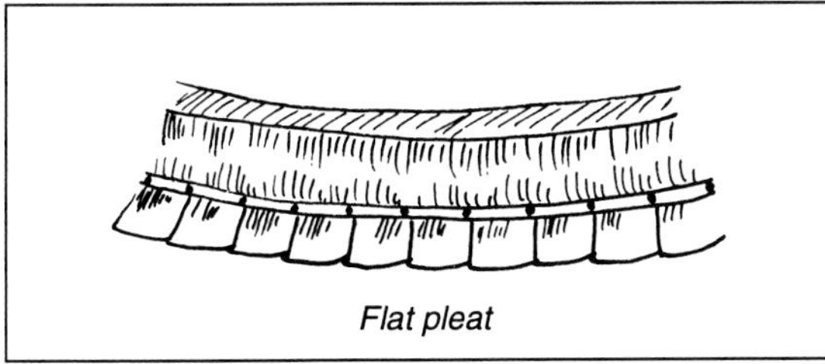
Flat pleat

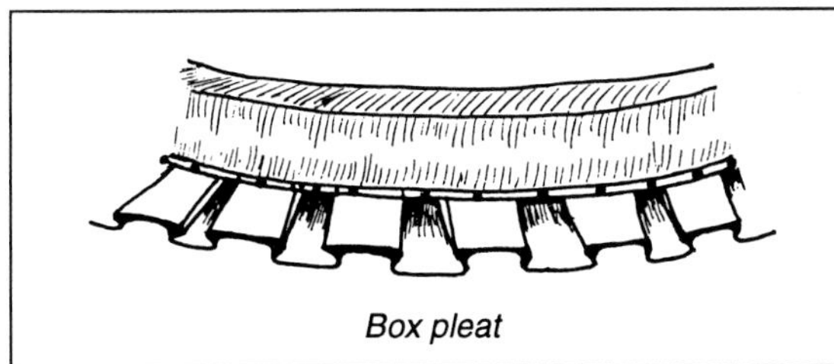
Box pleat

The pleats can be either flat (overlapped) or box and can be done with one or two ribbons. It looks very attractive to have two complementary ribbons to create a double edge, or to use lace or fine hessian over a plain ribbon. When pleating is placed at a point, as on a heart or pillow, the corner should be mitred. On a cross each end should be square. When using a fabric ribbon, a strip of plastic should be attached to the wet foam to stop the fabric acting as a wick and absorbing the moisture. This is a particular problem with hessian.

To ribbon edge a tribute which requires mitred points, each side should be edged individually, leaving enough ribbon tails at each end to join to form a point and then be stapled together.

To ribbon edge a cross, the sections on the sides

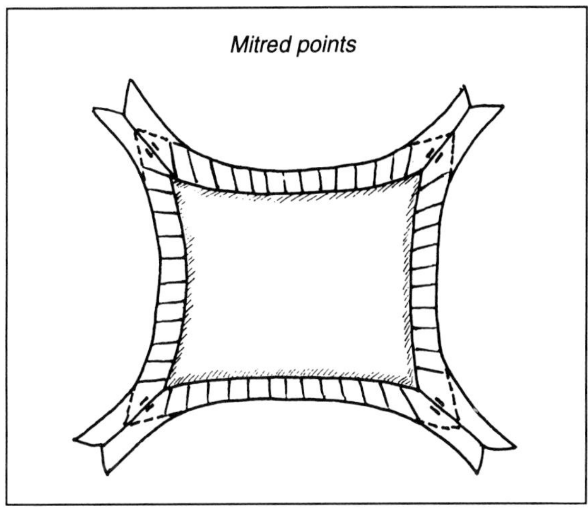
Mitred points

should be edged individually and then four sets of two pleats made to attach at each end on the cross (see page 106).

Various types of foliage edging can be used (see next page) and, as shown in the diagrams below, should be placed at an angle into the foam.

Single leaves such as ivy or camellia will need to be support wired and mounted prior to inserting into the tribute. However, sprigs of foliage do not need support wiring or mounting as the main stem will be strong enough on its own. The pot tape is not necessary for foliage edging.

Note that the foam base is soaked *before* foliage edging is inserted, whereas it is soaked *after* ribbon edging has been applied.

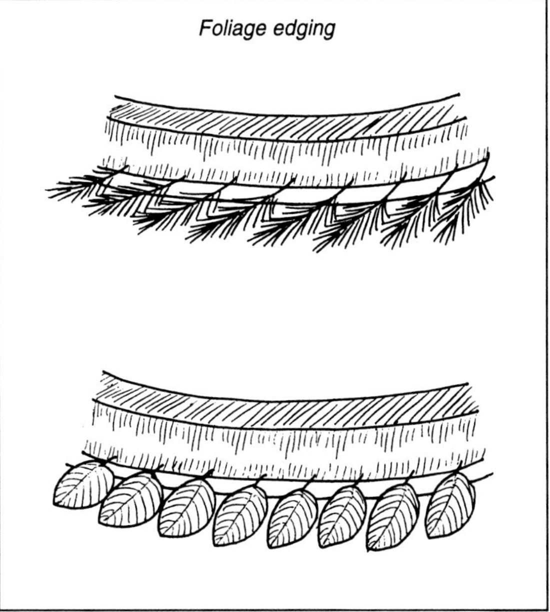
Foliage edging

Suitable foliage for edging	
Ivy	Cupressus
Camellia	Box
Laurel	Heather (when green)
Aucuba	

Basing

The term 'basing' refers to the complete covering of the frame with material such as flowers, foliage or moss. This material should be bonded: that is, there should be no gaps between the material, which should have an even, uncrowded appearance. It is important that the material follows the shape of the frame and does not alter its outline.

Suitable basing materials

Flowers	
Chrysanthemums, single and double	Lilac
Hydrangea heads	Trachelium
Sedum	*Achillea taygetea* 'Moonshine'
Roses	Sweet williams
Carnations	Daffodils
Violets	Stocks
Viburnum	Heather

Foliage	
Rubus tricolor	Conifers
Laurel	Ivy
Aucuba japonica	Box

Other materials	
Bun moss (different colours)	Fir cones
Reindeer moss	Poppy seedheads
	Berries

Tip

When buying double chrysanthemums for basing, ensure quality is good. Double chrysanthemums bond better than single ones and give better density to the finished work.

Spray

The spray or cluster is the flower and plant material which is placed onto the bump. There can be more than one spray, depending on the design. If there is only one, it should be one-third the size of the overall design. On a based wreath, heart, pillow or cushion, one large cluster can be made with a smaller one to complement it.

The flower material is generally choice, as it is intended to catch the customer's eye, and it is usually a mixture of three or four types of flower and two or three types of foliage. The suitable flower varieties are many and varied and depend on the style being created.

Suitable spray flowers	
Roses	Lily of the valley
Lilies	Irises
Gerbera	Sweet peas
Freesias	Bouvardia
Tulips	Anthuriums
Hyacinths	Anenomes
Ornithogalum	Agapanthus
Carnations	Gladioli
Liatris	Nerines
Orchids	

Profile

The finished tribute should have a rounded profile when viewed from the side or at eye level. This is very important, particularly if the tribute is placed on top of the coffin, because for part of the funeral service it will be viewed at eye level.

THE WREATH

The wreath is one of the most popular tributes, the shape implying continuity and eternity. It is also a very versatile tribute. The following styles of wreath are usually available from most florists: based, loose, section and cluster.

Based or Massed Wreath

Flowers for the base
Double spray chrysanthemums

Flowers for the spray	
Roses	Ixia
Spray roses	Waxflowers
Freesias	

Foliage for the spray	
Cyclamen leaves	Trails of *Rubus tricolor* (using underside of the leaves)
Senecio	
Trails of *Hedera helix* 'Glacier'	

Based wreath

Method

1. Prepare the ring foam base by shaving the outer and inner edges with a sharp knife to create a rounded profile except on a section of about 10 cm where the cluster bump will be attached.

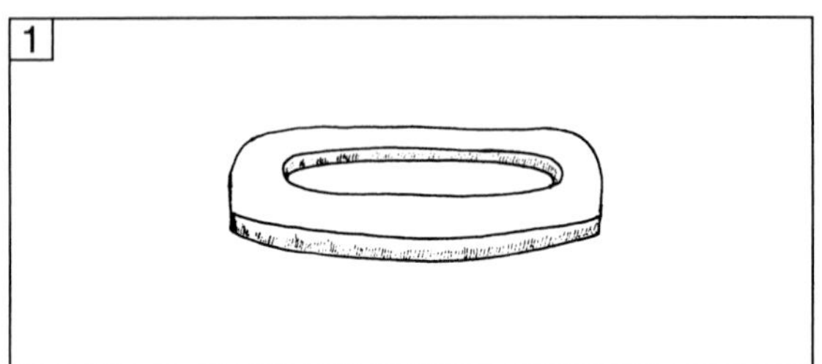

2. With steel pins, attach pot tape around the foam ring above the plastic base.

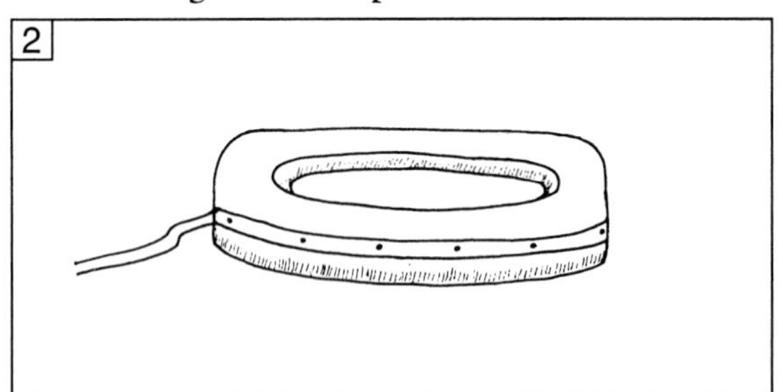

3. Staple ribbon and make box pleats of equal size. Continue until there is enough pleated ribbon to go round the inner and outer edge of the wreath and then attach with German pins, steel pins or a hot glue gun.
4. Attach the foam or ready-made bump for the spray. If using foam, cut it to size, cover with fine netting and put pot tape round it. Then secure with long German pins.

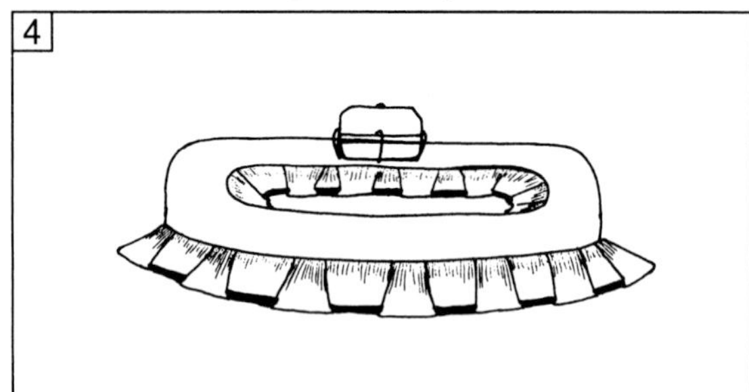

5. Soak foam.
6. Cut the spray chrysanthemums, leaving stems of approximately 5 cm. Then grade the heads into small, medium and large. Push the stems well into the foam so that they are secure. Small heads go on the inside of the ring, medium on the outside and large in the centre. Arrange them in such a way that the profile is rounded but the overall appearance is of one level, giving a bonded effect. The flowers should come down on both sides of the foam frame and overlap the ribbon edge.

7. Support wire some of the cluster's focal flowers. The rest can be used without any wiring. The form is similar to that of a corsage or small arrangement.
8. Make the outline with the ivy and small trails of rubus. Some of the leaves from the rubus can be used singly in the centre of the design with the cyclamen leaves. The roses can be placed in the centre of the design, which should be crescent shaped following the curve of the tribute. The roses should create a focal area, with the height created in the centre of the cluster.

   Next add the ixia through from one side to the other in a broken line. Take the freesias through following the line of ixia but going wider near the centre. Add the spray roses, recessing the larger heads towards the centre. The senecio can then be added through the focal area, and the waxflowers can fill any gaps.

   As with any design, transition should be taken into account, with larger heads in the focal area and smaller flower heads and buds on the outer edges.

Loose wreath

Loose Wreath

The loose or open wreath is an extremely popular choice. It is also known as a bin wreath. Often when flowers such as carnations and lilies are being conditioned, their stems are broken, and instead of throwing these flowers away they can be used in funeral work. Every florist has a bucket or bin of such odds and ends.

Loose construction uses flowers and foliage of one or more types which are not bonded tightly together as in a based tribute. Note that 'open' can also refer to a wreath or heart that is open in the middle.

Flowers	Foliage
Standard carnations Alstroemeria Gypsophila Spray chrysanthemums Freesias	Cupressus Box Arbutus

Method

1. Chamfer the edge of the ring foam base to give a rounded edge and soak the frame.
2. Insert the foliage at a slight angle to give a catherine wheel effect, making sure the foliage is placed at an angle down the side of the frame so as to cover the base. Foliage can be of one variety but it looks much nicer if there are at least two kinds and perhaps even three.

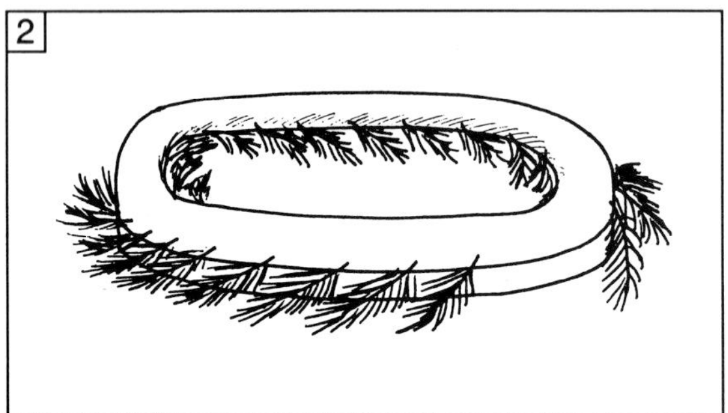

3. Having covered the base, start to add the flowers. The carnations should have the longest stems, and all the other flowers should be recessed at a lower level. Space the carnations equally round the base, and add the freesias in between them and on the outside.

Add the alstroemeria, which have been cut into single flowers, between the main flowers. The chrysanthemums should also be cut into single flowers and should be placed at random throughout the design.

4. Check at all angles that there are no gaps.

Section Wreath

As its name suggests, this tribute is divided into sections filled with a single type of flower. Any number of sections from three upwards can be made, depending on the size of the foam. This is an ideal group tribute to send from a group of people, usually close family.

It is similar to the loose wreath in having an even overall appearance.

Flower head sizes must be uniform. Colour choice is important as similar colours next to each other merge into themselves. Two colours used alternately look very effective. These can be a complementary colour harmony based on two colours, for example blue and orange. A monochromatic harmony using tints, tones and shades of one hue is also attractive.

Flowers	
Spray chrysanthemums	Solidago
Carnations	Viburnum
Spray carnations	Phlox
Irises	Narcissi (all varieties)
Dahlias	Lilies
Roses	Anemones
Gerbera	Freesias
Achillea	*Alchemilla mollis*
Tulips	Gypsophila
Zinnias	Statice
Scabious	Trachelium

Foliage	
Box	Viburnum
Senecio	Hebe
Leatherleaf	Euonymus

Method

1. If a ribbon edge is used, this should be pleated and attached using the same method as previously described. The base should then be marked into sections of equal size.
2. Prepare a complete section at a time, placing the flowers mostly on the same level.
3. Check that there are no gaps between the flowers or between the sections and make sure the material comes down over the edges so that the base cannot be seen.

Cluster Wreath

This wreath can be made in a traditional or continental style. It is another tribute which can be sent from a group of people and is particularly popular for a grandparent, each spray or cluster representing a grandchild. It is very effective when made of spring flowers or summer garden material. Three, four or five clusters can be used, depending on the size of the wreath frame. Each cluster is made of a single variety of flower.

Traditional style cluster wreath

Basing materials

Reindeer moss	Sedum
Bun moss	Double chrysanthemums

Flowers for the sprays

Tulips	Anemones
Narcissi	Spray chrysanthemums
Carnations	Freesias
Roses	Eustoma
Muscari	Sweet peas
Hyacinths	Ornithogalum
Irises	Nerines
Liatris	Spray roses
Mini gerbera	Scilla
Amaryllis	

Foliage

Leaves around sprays

Cyclamen	Bergenia
Ivy	Camellia
Rubus tricolor	*Alchemilla mollis*

Filler foliage for sprays

Hebe	Hard ruscus
Senecio	Leatherleaf

Continental style cluster wreath

Continental style cluster wreath

Method

1. Ribbon edge the tribute as previously described. The colour of the ribbon should tone in with the flowers and not dominate.
2. Place foam where the sprays are to be positioned and secure with tape and pins, or secure ready-made bumps with German pins. Soak the base.

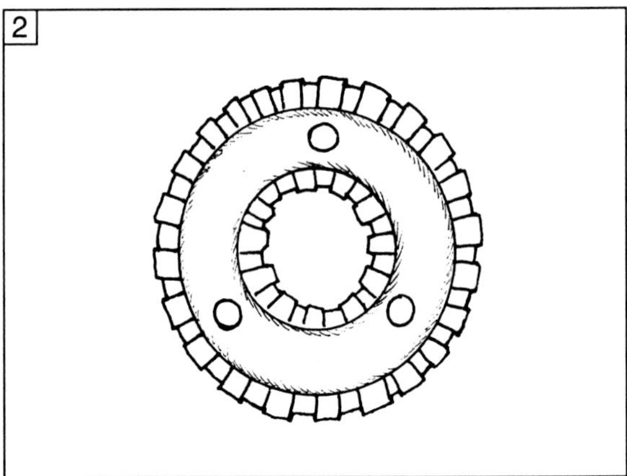

3. If using moss for basing, clean it and attach with German pins to give an even coverage between the clusters. If a flower base is being used, attach it in the same way as for the based wreath. It is also possible to use a foliage base.

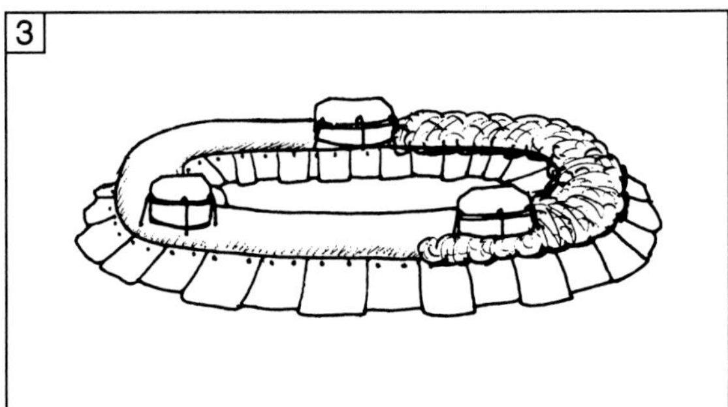

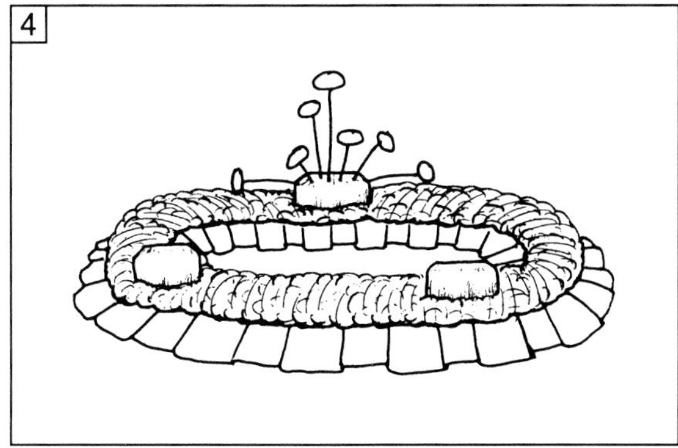

4. Make each cluster using one variety of flower material. The larger heads should be recessed and the smaller flowers and buds used in the height and outline. Each cluster should look like a small individual arrangement. Place larger leaves around the base of the cluster.

THE CROSS

Based Cross

The cross is one of the more formal tributes. It can have a military or religious interpretation, and it is very suitable for a family tribute to be placed on the coffin. The based cross lends itself to having one or more clusters – the central cluster at the axis and smaller clusters along the main stem of the cross. Alternatively these clusters can be linked together with materials such as bear grass or ribbon.

Tip

Always use small flower heads when the outline of a tribute has to be readily identifiable.

Based cross

Flowers for the base	
Spray chrysanthemums	Sedum
Hydrangeas	Violets in bunches
Roses	*Viburnum tinus*
Carnations	

Other basing materials	
Laurel	Ivy
Aucuba	Reindeer moss
Camellia	Bun moss

Flowers for the spray	
Lilies	Cymbidium and dendrobium orchids
Roses	Spray chrysanthemums
Gerbera	Waxflowers
Carnation blooms	Trachelium
Spray carnations	Solidago
Liatris	Nerines
Freesias	Asters
Gladioli	Anthuriums
Irises	Agapanthus
Tulips	
Delphiniums	

Foliage for the spray	
Ivy leaves and trails	Rubus leaves and trails
Nephrolepis fern	Dracaena
Box	Aucuba
Pittosporum	Senecio
Eucalyptus	
Syngonium leaves	

Method

1. Prepare the cross foam base by rounding off its edges. Take some pot tape along the area adjoining the plastic or polystyrene base and pin every few inches to secure.

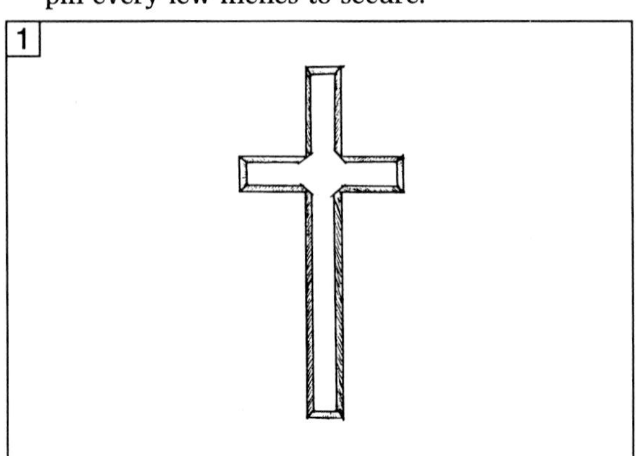

2. Box pleat the ribbon edge. To ensure that the ends are squared, the ribbon edging should be made in 12 separate pieces that are joined at the corners. These should be attached either with German or steel pins or with a glue gun. There should be one pleat length beyond the end of each arm of the cross and at the top and bottom.
3. Attach foam or a bump at the centre of the cross. For a large cross it is a good idea to place a smaller second spray two-thirds down.

4. Cut spray chrysanthemum stems to a length of approximately 5 cm and grade the heads into large and medium (use any small heads in small arrangements). Insert the medium heads along the sides of the cross, barely overlapping the ribbon edge. Insert the larger heads straight down the middle of each section of the cross and then fill with the rest of the chrysanthemums until the whole base is covered except for the spray area(s).

5. Construct the spray(s). Spray material should make up no more than one-third of the total area of the cross. The spray can be symmetrical or asymmetrical in design.

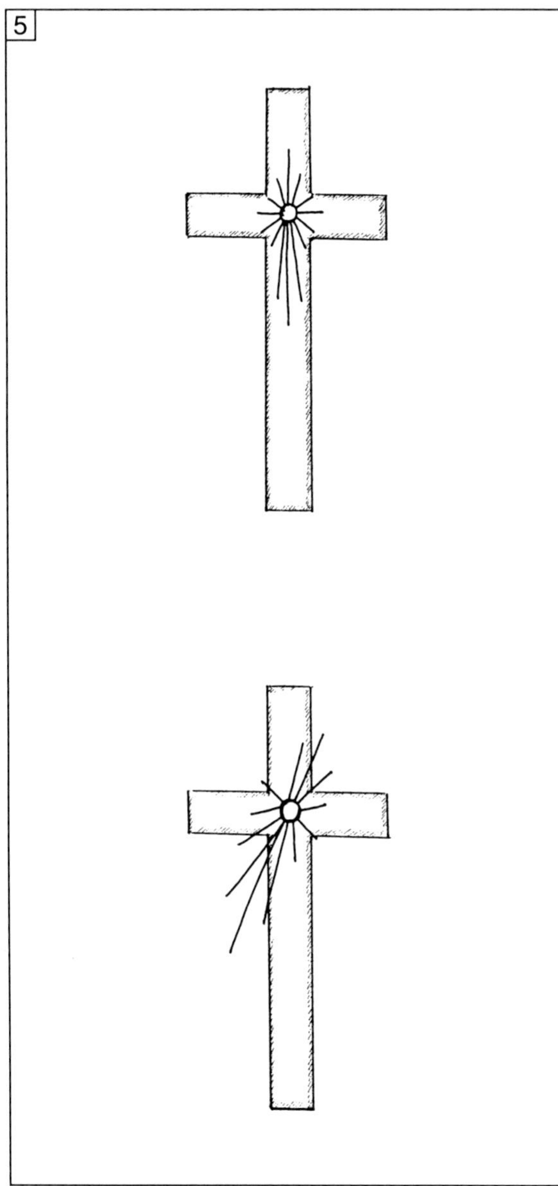

6. For a coffin cross, the focal flowers in the spray(s) will need to be large. A good selection would be lilies, gerbera, freesias, spray chrysanthemums and roses. At least three varieties of foliage should be used, with larger leaves for the focal area, for example, *Hedera canariensis* or aucuba, and then perhaps some dracaena leaves or ivy trails and filler foliage such as senecio or hebe.

First make the outline of the large spray with ivy trails and create lines of foliage within the outline. Take the larger leaves through the centre and reinforce the focal area. The senecio can be arranged through the centre from one side to the other.

Using one type of flower at a time, start at the top with the freesias and take them down to the bottom and then from one side to the other, following the ivy trails. The lilies can be arranged through the centre from side to side, using the buds on the outer edges and larger flowers through the centre. Take the gerbera through from top to bottom, using one as the main focal flower. The roses can be taken through following the line of gerbera but extending beyond at the top and bottom.

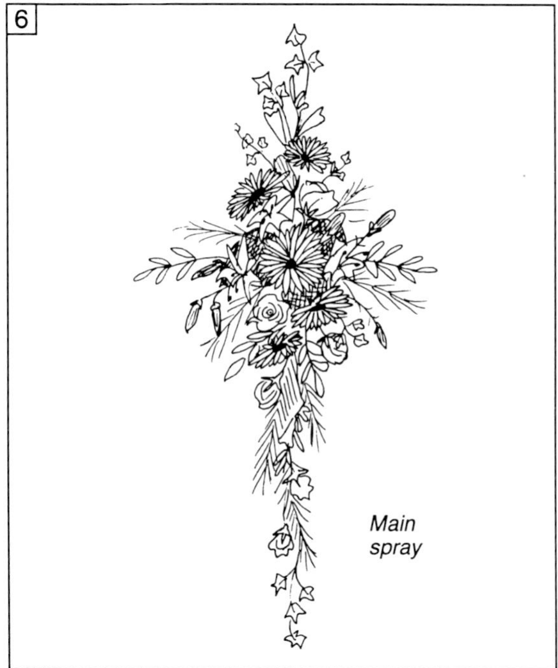

7. One gerbera, two roses and some foliage should be used for the small cluster toward the bottom of the cross.

8. Add a small bow in the same colour as the ribbon edge to visually link the two sprays.

Loose Cross

A loose cross can be placed on the coffin or it can be a small individual tribute. It is made in a similar way to the loose wreath and is sometimes referred to as an open cross.

Flowers	
Roses	Dahlias
Carnation blooms	Sweet williams
Spray carnations	Gypsophila
Irises	Daffodils
Gerbera	'Soleil d'Or' narcissi
Asters	Tulips
Alstroemeria	Alchemilla
Spray chrysanthemums	Statice

Foliage	
Cupressus (all kinds)	Ivy
Leatherleaf	Ming fern
Senecio	*Viburnum tinus*
Laurel	Tree heather

Method

1. The cross may be ribbon edged in the same way as described. Alternatively it may be edged with mixed foliage or one single type of foliage. If a foliage edge is made, it must follow the shape of the base and have clearly defined square ends.

1

2. The foam base should be lightly covered in foliage. A few pieces of reindeer moss can be pinned at random throughout to add some interest.
3. Place irises down the centre and across the arms. Place spray carnations at a lower level between the irises and at the sides, coming out at an angle. Place 'Soleil d'Or' narcissi between the spray carnations. Then add spray chrysanthemums at random all over the cross to fill in any gaps.

3

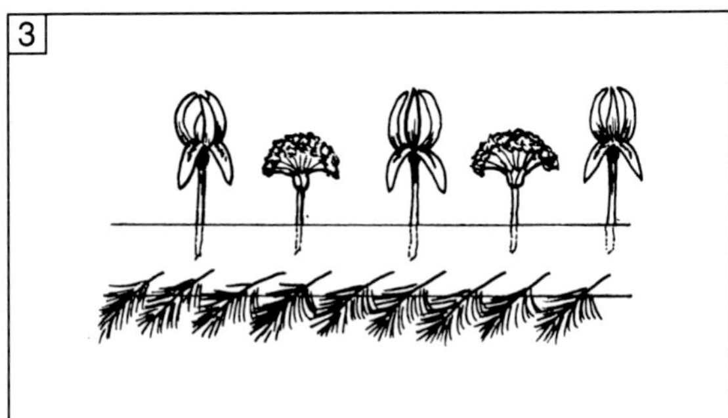
3

CHAPLET

The chaplet shape represents victory and achievement and is used at sporting events in the form of a complete foliage chaplet. In funeral work it is suitable as a tribute to represent the achievement of a politician or a military person.

A based chaplet can be made with a flower base with foliage or ribbon edging, with a foliage base or with a moss base. It looks very effective with a spray attached in any of the positions shown.

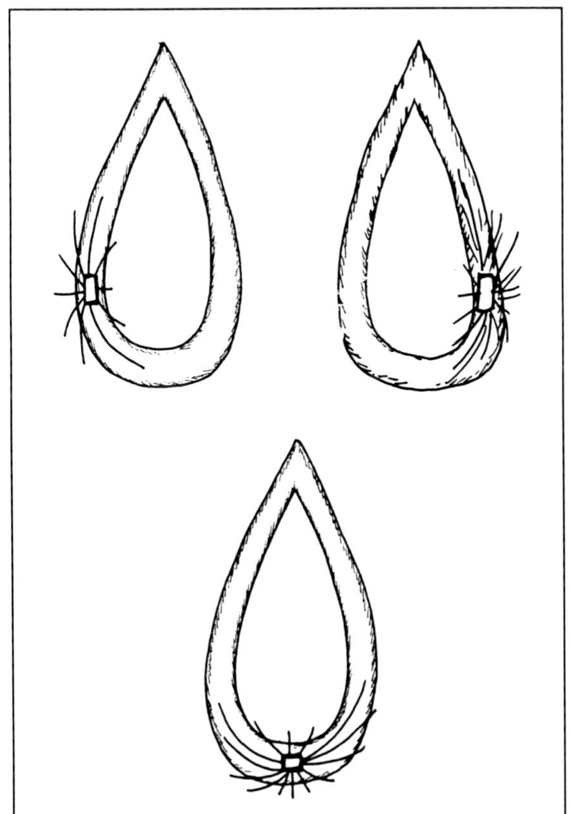

An open chaplet is made in exactly the same way as the loose cross, using similar types of flowers.

Based Chaplet

Foliage for the base	
Laurel	*Hedera canariensis*
Aucuba japonica	Camellia

Flowers for the spray	
Mini gerbera	Lily heads (open)
Freesias	Spray carnations

Foliage for the spray	
Box	Variegated ivy trails
Cyclamen leaves	Chlorophytum leaves

Laurel chaplet

Method

1. Prepare the chaplet base and foam or a bump.

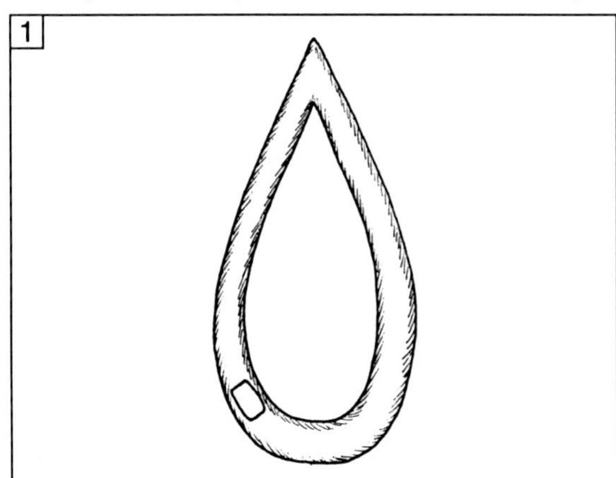

2. About 80–100 leaves will be needed for the base, depending on size. Make sure they are all perfect and clean. Wipe with damp cotton wool if necessary. Grade them into three sizes: large, medium and small. Then cut off the base of the leaves, including the stalk.

3. Attach the leaves to the frame with short German pins or hairpins made with 0.71 mm wire. Insert the pin two-thirds down from the tip of the leaf.

   Start by placing a small leaf at the point of the frame. Place the next one slightly at an angle and then one at either side of the second placement. Leaves should overlap so that the pins cannot be seen and should be angled to create a rounded profile covering the base of the frame. As you progress down from the point, use bigger leaves so that the widest part of the frame has the largest ones. It is important to keep to the shape of the frame.

   Once the bump is reached, go back to the point and complete the other side, working in the same way down to the bump.

   After both sides are completed, some large leaves can be placed to form a whorl around the bump.

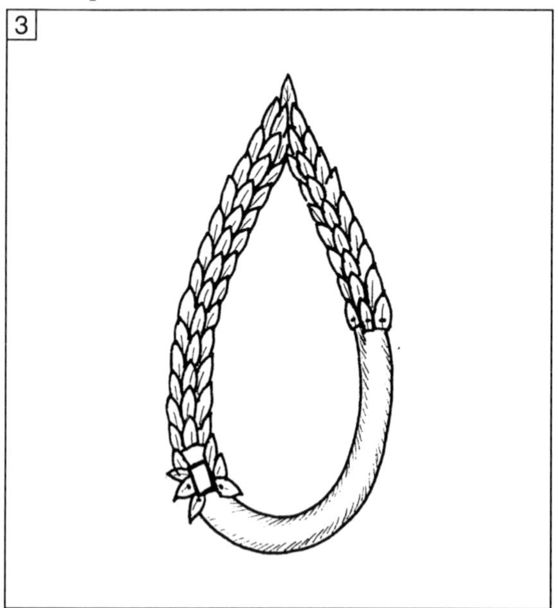

4. Start the cluster by placing the chlorophytum leaves on either side of the bump. They will need to be mounted with 0.56 mm green wire as they have no stem. Next place the ivy trails through the design, keeping the cluster as a crescent shape. The cyclamen leaves can be placed near the centre of the cluster.

   The mini gerbera should be internally supported with 0.71 mm wire to prevent bending. Arrange them through the design, using more in the focal area.

   Place the lily heads in the focal area, one higher and the others recessed into the design. Place the freesias through from one side to the other, using the more open flowers recessed and in the focal area. A staggered line of spray carnations can be taken through from top to bottom.

   Use the box to fill in any gaps.
5. Spray the based leaves lightly with leaf shine.

THE HEART

Based Cushion Heart

This tribute is very suitable for a close relative, the shape speaking for itself.

Flowers for the base	
Hydrangea heads	*Viburnum tinus*
Sedum	Sweet williams
Double spray chrysanthemums	Trachelium
Violets	Statice
Carnations	Lilac

Flowers for the spray	
Roses	Asters
Ornithogalum	Anemones
Freesias	Bridal gladioli
Dendrobium, cattleya and cymbidium orchids	Gypsophila
Lilies	Narcissi 'Paper White' and 'Soleil d'Or'
Sweet peas	Nerines
Spray carnations	Spray roses
Eustoma	Lily of the valley
Waxflowers	

Foliage for the spray	
Hedera helix	Ming fern
Leatherleaf	

Method

1. Prepare the heart-shaped foam base.
2. The ribbon edge can be made in various ways: using a single 5 cm polypropylene ribbon; using

Based cushion heart

two ribbons together, showing both colours; or using lace or punchinello over a darker ribbon.

If two ribbons or ribbon and lace are being used, staple them together. Then box pleat the ribbon in two sections, measuring as you go against the base and leaving 7.5 cm of ribbon plain at the ends. The pleats should be even and no more than 5 cm wide. The pleating should be attached with steel pins or glued directly on to the base.

Start by attaching the ribbon at the point of the heart, leaving a straight piece unpinned. The end of the pleating should be exactly in line with the tip of the point. Take the pleating 5–7.5 cm down into the cleavage and cut off at

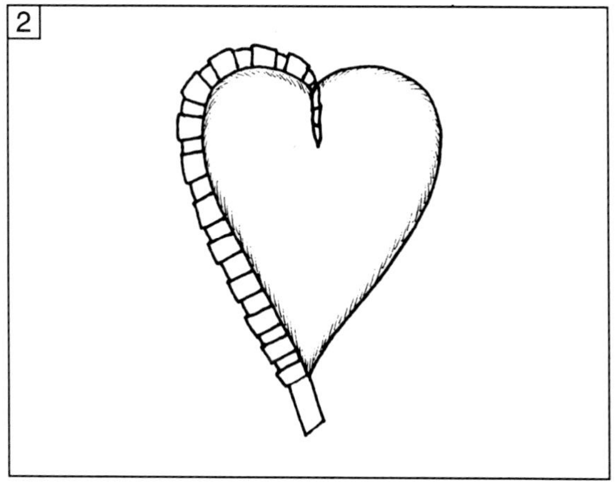

an angle any remaining ribbon. At this point the ribbon should be standing proud from the base.

Attach the other side in the same way, ensuring that the two pleats are exactly in line with each other at the tip. Trim the two tails and staple together to form a mitred point.

3. Attach foam or a bump in the centre of either the left or right lobe of the heart.

4. If using hydrangea flowers, break them up into little bunches and pin on the base with small German pins or hairpins made with 0.71 mm wire. The aim is to get an even coverage. The base should have a rounded profile with the two lobes raised more in the middle.

   Flower heads such as spray chrysanthemums and roses should be graded into small, medium and large and the flowers at the tip should be in line with the flowers at the cleavage. Place the larger and taller heads towards the centre and the smaller heads at the sides so as to clearly define the outline of the tribute.

5. Make up the cluster as a diagonal design and position it in the centre of one lobe of the heart. To link the cluster to the edging it is a good idea to add a bow in the same ribbon but split to a narrower width to be in proportion to the spray.

   There is often a secondary spray. If so, the two sprays can be linked with the same ribbon as used for the edging.

Tip

With a based cushion heart, care should be taken to ensure the main cluster is placed in the centre of the lobe and not to the side, where it will look as if it is falling off the edge. The lobes should also be raised in the middle.

Loose Heart

This is prepared like the loose wreath except that taller flowers must be placed in the centres of the lobes to give a domed effect as in the based cushion heart.

Flowers	
Carnation blooms	Roses
Spray carnations	Alstroemeria
Roses	Narcissi 'Paper White' and 'Soleil d'Or'
Gypsophila	Irises
Scabious	Sweet peas
Muscari	Freesias
Snowdrops	Spray chrysanthemums
Lily of the vallley	Solidago
Violets	*Alchemilla mollis*
Anemones	

Foliage	
Hebe	Viburnum
Senecio	Ming fern
Box	Eucalyptus

Open Heart

As an alternative to a solid heart, an outline heart can be made up as a based or a loose tribute. The loose open heart can look particularly pretty when made with a base of small mixed foliage topped with spring flowers such as muscari, narcissi, miniature irises and freesias.

Open heart

Based Posy Pad

Probably one of the most popular based designs, this tribute is particularly suitable for a small child or baby. It is made on a posy pad foam base. It can also be made in foam on a dish as a small all-round arrangement.

Materials for the base	
Spray chrysanthemums	Hydrangea heads
Roses	Bun moss
Carnations	Reindeer moss
Violets	

Flowers for the spray	
Spray roses	Freesias
Rose blooms	Spray carnations

Foliage for the spray	
Hebe	Eucalyptus
Viburnum tinus	Ivy
Senecio	Arbutus
Cyclamen leaves	Box
Leatherleaf	Ming fern

Method

1. Make the ribbon edge a continuous length and attach with steel pins into the pot tape or glue it on. The edge can also be made of foliage such as ivy leaves.
2. Attach a piece of foam or a pre-made bump in the centre in the usual way.
3. Prepare the base flowers by cutting stems to 5 cm. Small heads should be placed around the edge overlapping the edging just slightly. Work towards the centre using larger heads, and taper stems so that the profile has a cushioned effect.
4. The shape of the spray can be either round or diagonal. Create an outline with the foliage in the shape required, arranging camellia leaves near the centre. These will need to be mounted on 0.71 mm wire if there is too little stem.

   Take the freesias through from one side to the other, using buds on the outside and more open flowers recessed around the focal area. Arrange the roses through the centre, recessing two or three more open flowers around the focal area and using a rose for the focal flower. Some of the more vulnerable roses should be support wired with 0.71 mm wire. Take the spray carnations in the opposite direction. Use spray roses, broken down, to fill any gaps.

Based posy pad

Funeral Posy

This is a small simple design arranged in foam. It resembles a circular table arrangement but should be made a little more compact and should not look too much like a flower arrangement. The design is circular and slightly domed. Smaller informal flowers are best suited to this style.

The flowers are arranged either in a pre-soaked foam cylinder or a cut and trimmed piece of foam. The container can be any type of flat plastic dish and the foam should be securely taped into this.

The construction techniques are exactly the same as for a circular table centre arrangement (see pages 34 and 138).

This design is particularly suitable as a tribute from children, perhaps to a grandparent, incorporating a few favourite flowes from the deceased's garden. Sweet-smelling flowers are a nice addition.

Flowers	
Freesias	Mimosa
Spray roses	Bouvardia
Small spray chrysanthemums	Scilla
	Hellebores
'Paper White' and 'Soleil d'Or' narcissi	Dianthus
	Asters
Muscari	Gypsophila
Anemones	Alstroemeria
Hyacinths	

Foliage	
Leatherleaf	Small eucalyptus
Pittosporum	Asparagus fern
Euonymus	Box
Ruscus	

Funeral posy

Cushion and Pillow Tributes

These are very similar tributes. The cushion is squarer than the pillow but both shapes speak for themselves.

Flowers for edging	
Hebe	Scindapsus
Leatherleaf	Camellia
Cyclamen	*Aucuba japonica*
Croton	*Hedera canariensis*

Materials for the base	
Double spray chrysanthemums	Hydrangeas
Roses	Violets
Sweet williams	Carnations
Sedum	Reindeer moss
	Bun moss

Flowers for the spray	
Roses	Single spray chrysanthemums
Asters	Freesias

Foliage for the spray	
Hebe	*Hedera canariensis*
Leatherleaf	

Based cushion

Based pillow

Method

1. Construct ribbon edge. Measure the four sides and make four lengths of box pleats leaving 7.5 cm plain ribbon at each end. Attach the pleats in the usual way. The pleats must be in line at each point. The ends are then turned in and stapled together. The excess is cut away to give a mitred point at each corner.

   Foliage can also be used for the edging. This should be either pinned on or mounted as appropriate.
2. Attach the foam or bump in the usual way. This may be in the centre or to one side.

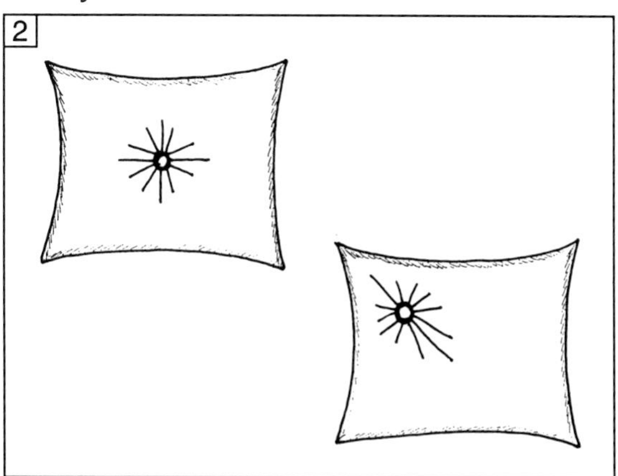

3. Prepare the flowers for basing in the usual way by grading the flower heads into small, medium and large and cut stems to 5 cm. The larger flowers will need longer stems of approximately 7–8 cm to give extra height to create a cushioned effect. Attach them as for a based wreath.
4. Construct the spray in the usual way, remembering to group the flowers, recessing some of the larger flowers and using buds on the outside.
5. A small spray may be added and linked to the main cluster with either matching ribbon or a piece of foliage such as ivy. Remember that in this case the main spray should be slightly less than one-third of the overall size to make allowance for the extra spray.

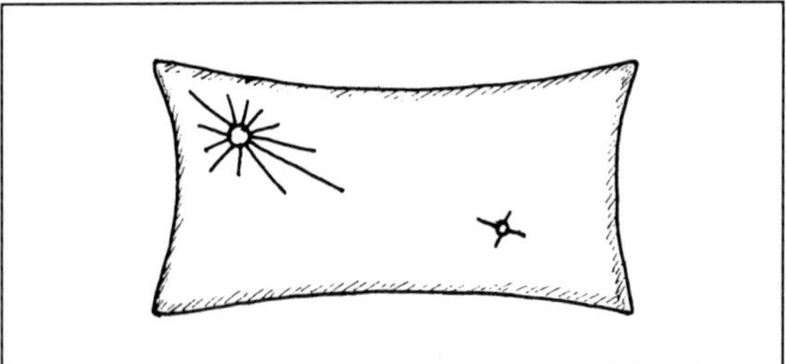

Personalised Tributes

These are tributes which are made up of letters such as MUM, NAN, DAD, etc. in foam on a plastic stand which displays the tribute at an angle.

Basing material as previously mentioned is suitable. The edging can be made with pleated polypropylene ribbon or with foliage.

It is usual to have two sprays, one slightly larger than the other, designed inside the outline of the letters. The spray flowers need to be small: roses, freesias, spray carnations, spray chrysanthemums, etc.

Method

1. Attach the foam or pre-made bump on the first letter and on the last letter with either glue or pot tape.
2. Soak the base and then add an edging of cupressus. Follow the line of each letter.
3. Attach the basing flowers in the same way as previously described for a based wreath, using large, medium and small flower heads. Place the small heads on the inside of the letter. Complete one letter at a time.
4. Construct the main spray in the usual way and then make the smaller spray. The two sprays can be linked with some ribbon.

Sympathy Basket

This is also known as a cremation basket, as it is often chosen when the deceased is cremated and the flowers are then sent on to a hospital or old people's home. Because of the lack of space, flowers sent to crematoriums are often there for only a short time before being removed, so a tribute which can be used elsewhere and give other people pleasure is quite suitable. The basket should be either rectangular or oval and have a flat base so that it can be placed on the coffin during the service.

A personalised tribute

Sympathy basket

The term 'sympathy basket' may also refer to a basket of flowers suitable for sending to relatives of the deceased as a gift showing sympathy. This kind of basket may be any shape, as it is intended to be placed in the home.

Most flowers of medium and small size are suitable for this design, but the customer may well wish to choose specific flowers and colours.

Flowers	
Carnation blooms	Freesias
Spray carnations	Spray roses
Spray chrysanthemums	Mini gerbera
Bridal gladioli	Anemones
Ixia	Eustoma
Alstroemeria	All spring flowers
Limonium	Sweet peas
Asters	*Alchemilla mollis*
Roses	

Foliage	
Box	Senecio
Eucalyptus	Arbutus
Leatherleaf	Privet
Hard ruscus	Ivy (individual leaves and trails)
Ming fern	
Viburnum	

Method

1. Secure foam in basket as previously described (see page 37).
2. Create an outline with the foliage similar to the shape of a double-ended spray. The foliage should lie at an angle over the basket so that when viewed on the coffin the plant material is trailing down.

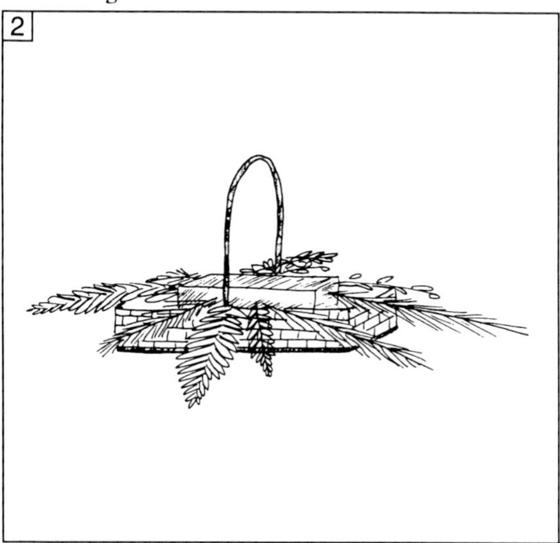

3. The widest point of the design will be on both sides of the basket at the same point as the handles.
4. Group the flower material through the design using small buds at the outer edges and recessing the larger choice flowers in the centre below the handle, leaving enough space between the top flower and the handle to enable the basket to be carried.

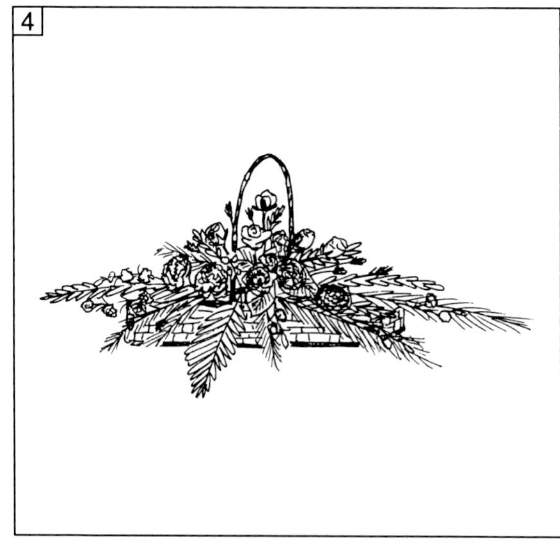

SIZES OF FOAM BASES AVAILABLE

Wreath ring
203 mm (8″)
254 mm (10″)
305 mm (12″)
356 mm (14″)
406 mm (16″)
432 mm (17″)
508 mm (20″)
610 mm (24″)

Heart
305 mm (12″)
381 mm (15″)
457 mm (18″)
533 mm (21″)

Pillow
254 × 381 mm (10″ × 15″)
305 × 457 mm (12″ × 18″)
356 × 533 mm (14″ × 21″)

Double ring
432 mm (17″)
508 mm (20″)

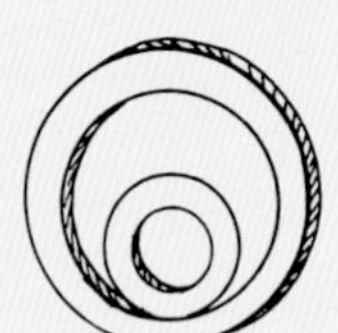

Open heart
381 mm (15″)

Cushion
305 × 305 mm (12″ × 12″)
381 × 381 mm (15″ × 15″)
457 × 457 mm (18″ × 18″)

Cross
457 mm (18″)
610 mm (24″)
864 mm (34″)
1220 mm (48″)
1524 mm (60″)
1830 mm (72″)
Extensions are available
to increase the sizes.

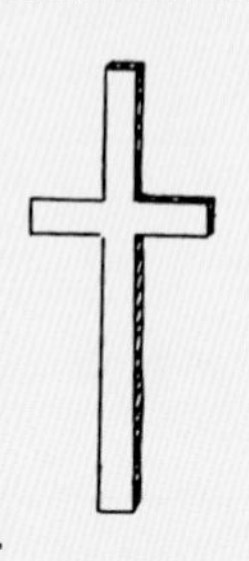

Double heart
381 mm (15″)

Garland (extendible)
2000 mm (78″)

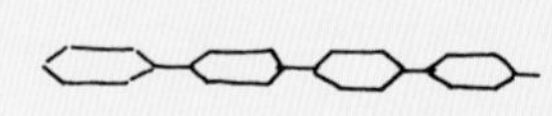

Chaplet
457 mm (18″)
533 mm (21″)

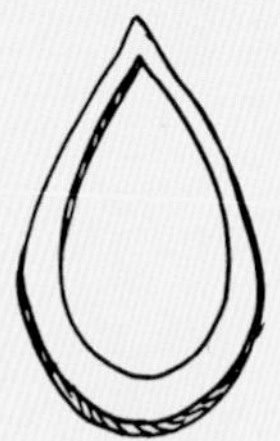

Designer sheet
610 × 305 mm (24″ × 12″)
610 × 610 mm (24″ × 24″)
610 × 1220 mm (24″ × 48″)

Le-Bump
Small, medium and large

Posy pad
127 mm (5″) also available with handle
178 mm (7″)
203 mm (8″)
254 mm (10″)
305 mm (12″)
356 mm (14″)
406 mm (16″)

Letters and numbers
305 mm (12″) letters A–Z
305 mm (12″) numbers 0–29

Letters are attached with Velcro pads to an angled support frame which can be lengthened with a letter extension kit or connecting bars.

Unusual Frames

Anchor
610 mm (24″)
813 mm (32″)

Horseshoe
330 × 330 mm (13″ × 13″)

Teddy
483 mm (19″)
584 mm (23″)
813 mm (32″)

Car
864 × 381 mm (34″ × 15″)

Motorbike
762 × 457 mm (30″ × 18″)

Train
864 × 406 mm (34″ × 16″)

Gates of heaven
508 × 457 mm (20″ × 18″)

Open book or bible on a stand
610 × 305 mm (24″ × 12″)

Vacant chair
584 × 228 mm (23″ × 9″)

Guitar
966 mm (38″)

Rabbit
584 mm (23″)
813 mm (32″)

Only a small selection of the range of foam bases is shown. Each wholesaler carries a wide range of stock in different shapes and sizes. For personalised designs, such as club emblems, animals or symbols, designer sheet foam may be used. This is available in several sizes and consists of a sheet of water-absorbent foam attached to a polystyrene backing. It can be cut and shaped. Foam blocks may be glued on to the designer sheet or glued together to create a three-dimensional effect and then be shaped to the chosen design.

CHAPTER 9

Outside Decorating

Most of the floral designs which are used to decorate a marquee for a wedding are also suitable for decorations at parties, corporate events, promotional displays and conferences. Whether in a marquee, hall or hotel, the basic structure and design of the display remains the same. For instance, pedestal arrangements, table centre arrangements, buffet table displays, topiary trees and flower tubs are all widely used for these types of events. In many cases a stronger colour theme would be called for than would be used for a wedding, and also a plainer and more streamlined style is best for business events rather than the traditional 'frothy' look so often associated with weddings. The size of the displays should always be taken into consideration depending on the surrounding space and the way in which the room or hall will be used.

Obviously for certain business events and conferences care should be taken not to overdress the room with flowers and plants. The displays should certainly be eye-catching, have impact and be distinctive but at the same time should not be too intrusive or overpowering.

Outside decorating can offer challenging work to the florist. The key to success is to plan ahead and be well prepared.

CHECKLIST FOR OUTSIDE DECORATING

- If the venue is in a town or city, find out in advance what the parking facilities are.
- Find out whether the venue is locked and, if so, who holds the key.
- Check whether a church service or any other function is scheduled on the day that the work is to be carried out.
- A security pass may be needed, so ensure that all the staff have the necessary passes.
- Find out if water is available.

EQUIPMENT REQUIRED

Scissors	Hammer/nails
Knife	Step ladder
String	Glue gun and sticks
Secateurs	Dust sheets
Pot tape (white and green)	Bin liners
Wire netting	Dust pan and brush
Reel wire (fine and thick)	Stiff broom
A selection of stub wires	Plasters
Box of pins	Cloth
Sellotape	Towel
Double-sided sticky tape	Water mister (full)
Plastic tape	Tabard
Staplers and staples	Kitchen roll
Staple gun and staples	Extension lead

CHURCH FLOWERS

Decorating a church for a wedding requires forward planning to ensure that all runs smoothly on the day. Like any decorating job, as much preparation work as possible should be carried out beforehand. Working in churches does, however, present certain practical problems to the florist which with a little forethought can be avoided, thus reducing the waste of valuable time on the day.

One aspect of church decorating work which is always overlooked is the amount of time it can take just to carry everything you need – buckets of flowers, boxes of foliage, pedestals, foam, etc. – into the church. This should be borne in mind when pricing the job. All too often an awareness of this dawns suddenly when for the umpteenth time you are struggling up the church path with awkward flowers which constantly keep falling out of their buckets.

Always try to arrange a visit to the church as early as possible to meet the bride and to discuss any ideas. If you are in the building itself, it is much easier to decide what is needed and to discuss how to achieve the best effect with the client.

Certain information needs to be checked during this visit which could affect the style of decorating and the preparation of a detailed estimate for the work. Listed below are several factors which, if dealt with in advance, will certainly make the work easier and leave tempers and reputation intact!

- Is the church kept locked and, if so, where is the key kept? Arrange in advance of any work to collect and return the key.
- Find out the name of the vicar and check that flower displays are allowed in all the positions you have discussed with the client. In some churches the altar is kept free of flowers at all times and there are restrictions on the vases used there. Flowers on or in the font and on pew ends are also sometimes discouraged.
- If the altar is to be decorated, check with the local flower rota (usually posted on the church notice board in the porch) and arrange to take responsibility for the altar flowers for the date of the wedding whenever possible.
- Check positions of light switches. It might seem a small point but it can become very important when decorating for a winter or an evening wedding. Light switches are invariably hidden behind a curtain or are in a corner of the vestry or, in some cases, halfway up the church away from the main door!
- Is there a water supply? Few churches have running water. A rainwater tank around the back of the church is usually the only water available. It is much easier to take your own and this can be done in the buckets of flowers and foliage to be used for the arrangements.
- If pew end arrangements are desired, check that the aisle is of sufficient width to take them and look closely at the pew ends to see if it is possible to attach them securely. Count the number required.
- Look in the vestry or store cupboards to see if there are any pedestal stands or vases that you can utilise. This saves time and space in transportation, and since most wedding flowers are left at the church after the ceremony, it eliminates a journey back to the church to collect any containers you have supplied.
- Ensure that the church is free of any other events or services on the day of decorating.
- If windowsills are to be decorated, check to see whether they are level and deep enough to take an arrangement. Many are sloping and can only be decorated by using an angled wooden block or shelf attached to the windowsill.
- Take a tape to measure the length of any garlands required around pillars or doorways.

Pew Ends

Decorated pew ends can add the final finishing touch to a church for a wedding by providing a focus along the aisle, which in a large church can be quite important. Likewise if a church is being decorated on a tight budget, pew end arrangements can give the impression of a church full of flowers more so than perhaps windowsill arrangements.

The style of pew end arrangements can vary enormously depending on the theme of the wedding but generally they all tend to be an elongated 'teardrop' of flowers and foliage, wider at the top and tapering down to a finer base. Ribbon bows can be incorporated at either the top or the bottom of the design.

Pew end

The practical considerations of a pew end can limit the design possibilities. The finished arrangement must be very flat so as not to pose a hazard for people walking along the aisle!

Some unusual effects can be created with a bit of imagination. Small bunches of corn or oats tied with a length of ivy or hessian ribbon with perhaps a few white daisy chrysanthemums or cornflowers added would be perfect for a farming wedding. Natural 'picked' bunches of evergreens such as yew, bay and box tied with a velvet ribbon and hung onto the ends of the pews for a winter wedding, perhaps with a few gilded fir cones or nuts added for interest, provide a cheap decoration. For a summer wedding nothing looks better than clusters of fat cabbage roses, mock orange blossom or sweet peas.

The easiest way to make a traditional pew end in foam is to use a specially made tray with a handle for hanging, sometimes referred to within the trade as a shovel. This describes it fairly accurately: the piece of foam, about a quarter of a standard block, is tapered into the tray, and either green or brown string or fine ribbon is passed through a hole in the handle for hanging. Foam taped into an O-bowl with a hole made through its edge for hanging can also be used.

Two important points to remember when suggesting pew ends for a wedding:

- Make sure that the actual pew end is suitable to hang an arrangement on: old carved or shaped pews are ideal; modern flat-topped pews are not.
- Make sure the aisle is wide enough to take arrangements each side and still allow room for two people to walk down it side by side!

Tip

Pew ends can be made in advance to save time and then just hung in position at the church. Always make sure the finished designs have had time to drain off any excess water before hanging!

Method

1. Secure the foam in the plastic tray with pot tape. These trays usually hold about a quarter of a standard-size block. Tie a length of string or fine ribbon through the top of the handle ready for hanging.

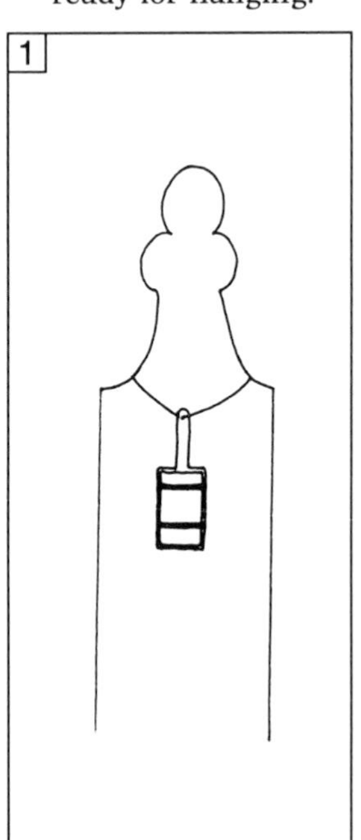

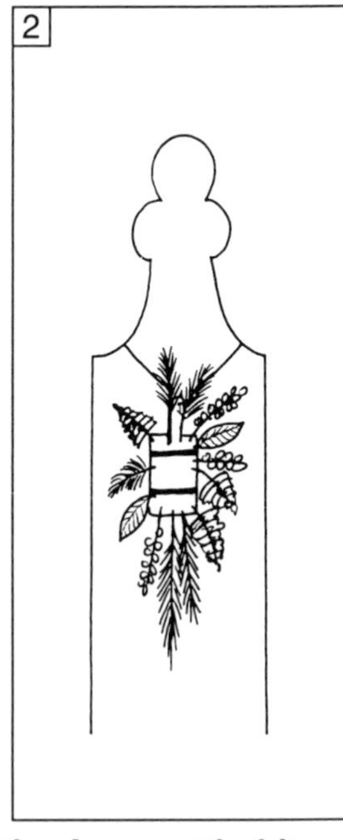

2. Form the outline of the design with foliage, remembering that the finished design should not extend above the top of the pew or beyond its width. An elongated teardrop shape is usually the most effective.

3. Add some of the smaller flowers and buds such as spray carnations, chrysanthemums or gypsophila into the outline.

4. Place the line of focal flowers along the length of the design, ensuring that the largest or top flower does not extend too far out from the design.

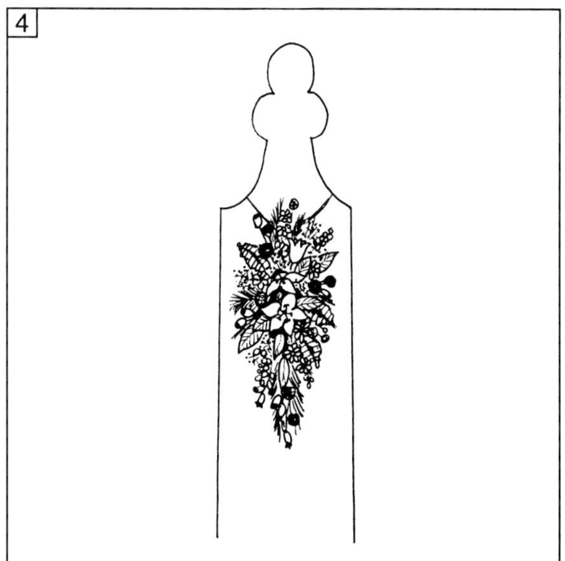

5. Continue to infill the design using the remaining materials. Use some of the outline foliage and flowers in the centre of the design to avoid a 'collar'-like effect of edging materials. Even with such a flat design as this, care should be taken to achieve some recession of materials to prevent the finished designs looking solid.

6. A ribbon bow with long tails can be added at the top or the bottom of the finished arrangement. Fix a wire stem to the bow and simply push into the foam as you would a flower.

Altar Flowers

Flowers for the altar in a church can present a particular problem to the florist because of the restrictions of altar vases! In most churches it is required that you use the existing altar vases – usually brass and very narrow for foam or, in fact, for many flowers. One solution is to use materials with fine flexible stems such as spray carnations, gypsophila, some of the smaller types of lily and bridal gladioli. Selecting materials such as these not only allows more flowers to be fitted into the vase but also gives a fuller, more generous effect than just a few straight stems standing to attention.

If there is room the only mechanics possible would be chicken wire. In most cases the foliage used will have to support the flowers in the vase. Foliages such as pittosporum and eucalyptus are ideal and should be placed in the vase first and the flowers carefully threaded through. If arrangements in foam are allowed to decorate an altar, shallow plastic bowls can be used with foam taped in. A pair of symmetrical or, more effectively, asymmetrical arrangements look best.

One important thing to remember is that altar flowers are only seen from a great distance away, so smaller fussy flowers and darker receding colours tend to disappear leaving only the larger and lighter coloured flowers visible. If the wrong colours are used, perfectly shaped arrangements viewed from the bottom of the aisle will lose all sense of design and shape.

Whatever colour scheme has been chosen, try to use the lighter, more reflective shades within the scheme rather than the darker hues. White, of course, always looks suitable.

Windowsill Arrangements

It is not always necessary to decorate every window in a church. For instance, if there are three windows each side of the aisle, only the middle ones might be decorated if a pair of pedestal arrangements are placed at the chancel steps. Alternatively, if the pedestals are omitted, the first and third windowsills could be decorated leaving the middle ones empty. Spreading the flowers around the church evenly can give the impression of more flowers than have actually been used.

Church windows generally tend to be very tall, quite wide and often with very narrow sills. In some of them the rules of proportion governing an arrangement will be altered slightly. The height of the design needs to be increased perhaps more than its width, and the depth of the arrangement will be very narrow. Within these constrictions one must try to achieve a degree of balance both visual and actual so that the arrangements do not appear flat.

The style of an arrangement for a window depends on several factors, such as the size, depth and height of the windowsill. Some designs however are more suited to this situation than others – for example, the symmetrical triangle, asymmetrical triangle, European upright style or the low cascading/waterfall effect which is particularly suited to very high sills.

Containers can be cheap plastic ones such as spray trays or bowls. Generous amounts of foam need to be used to provide weight at the base of the arrangement and prevent it from tilting forwards. Decorative china or terracotta vases, urns or bowls look particularly effective, as well as large baskets allowing a more interesting and innovative style of arrangement.

For the best results windowsill designs should be arranged in situ. A ready-made design rarely looks comfortable on the windowsill because an arrangement done on a workbench is viewed from above and looks totally different when seen from below in a window.

During the construction of a design in the

Arrangement in church window

church the arrangement should be viewed from a distance several times. Bold bulky flowers such as dahlias, gerbera, large lilies, gladioli and tulips are very useful in these designs, as are spray chrysanthemums, solidaster, September flowers, sedum and branches of blossom which fill in the arrangement quickly without making it too heavy or fussy.

Backlight from the windows can be one of the most difficult problems to contend with. Sunlight behind an arrangement will render all the carefully chosen colours and shapes of the flowers virtually invisible, turning the design into a silhouette. One way to partially counteract this is to use large, solid backing foliage, which will reduce the amount of light coming through the design. Laurel, conifer and other large-leaved evergreens are ideal, but must not be allowed to overshadow the arrangement and make it appear heavy.

Font Decorations

Decorating a font is one of the more challenging areas of a church to deal with. Check beforehand that flowers are allowed in or on the font itself. The position of the font within the church, usually at the bottom of the aisle, makes it an ideal focal point for the congregation upon entering and leaving the church, and it thus forms an important part of a decorating scheme.

The size of the font is usually such that unless the flowers are of a substantial size, they can look insignificant. One of the more common ways to deal with this is to completely fill the top of the font with flowers and foliage, which will give the effect of a 'top' to the whole structure. A design of this kind does, however, require a lot of materials to be effective and therefore can become quite costly. A good idea is to use a lot of foliage such as beech, viburnum and privet, or lilac and prunus blossoms as 'padding' and fewer well-chosen impact flowers such as gerbera, and large 'Casablanca' or longiflorum lilies.

This style of arrangement requires a large container and several blocks of foam. A washing-up bowl that will easily take four or five blocks of foam is ideal. The container and foam should be placed in the well of the font, the foam extending just above the rim. This allows some trailing material to cascade over the edges. The overall arrangement should be roughly conical in shape rising up to a high point in the centre which looks in proportion with the font itself.

Some fonts still retain their elaborate wooden covers, the majority of which are richly decorated with carvings and sometimes coloured paint and gilding. To place flowers on these would be difficult and not particularly effective. The only addition could be, for example, some natural ivy trails, or light foliage garlands might be draped or bound around the cover. These can be extended down and around the plinth of the font to link up with an arrangement at the base or on the floor. A lot of fonts have one or two stone steps around the base, and these lend themselves very well to arrangements, which can be in spray trays concealed by the foliage in the arrangement.

Although, as mentioned, large obvious flowers are ideal for this type of display, some stunning effects can be created with tiny flowers such as gypsophila, or even common sheep's parsley. The key to success with these finer flowers is massive quantity. The top of a font filled with a cloud of gypsophila or a cascade of the delicately arching sprays of September flowers can look wonderful. As in most things, simplicity is often the best idea.

Porches

In terms of floral decorations the porch is one of the most important areas of the church as most people arriving for a wedding get their first impression here.

Porch decorations often consist of only one or two token arrangements placed on the window-sills or a pedestal arrangement used to hide the notice board rather than for any welcoming effect. Sometimes, because of space, this is all that is practical but there are other possibilities, some of which can create beautiful effects without too much extra work. Listed below are a few ideas.

Arches and Doorways

To create a really grand entrance a decorated arch or door takes some beating. It is so eye-catching that it is the only form of decoration needed in a porch. However, it is very time-consuming and this should be remembered when pricing the work.

The most difficult part of this work can be the actual fixing of the garland base to the arch or door frame. Fortunately a lot of church doors already have small nails, hooks or carvings to which the garland base can be tied. Light garlands can be supported by drawing pins or tacks; Blu-tack and strong adhesive tape are not suitable.

There are two methods of making a garland. The first, constructed in a foam base, gives a much fuller effect when finished and because of the moist foam allows a much greater choice of materials. Because of the garland's considerable weight it must be secured firmly by tying onto nails or hooks.

The second method is wired. This is lighter in weight, which is an advantage when hanging. It can also be partially prepared beforehand, but it results in a lighter, thinner effect and the flowers and foliage must be carefully chosen for their lasting qualities.

Foam garland

1. Buy a ready-made garland base or make your own by cutting up blocks of foam into equal sized lengths, covering with thin plastic or foil and tying them together into the required length. It is not necessary that each piece of foam touches the other, as space between will allow greater flexibility when hanging around a curve or over an arch.

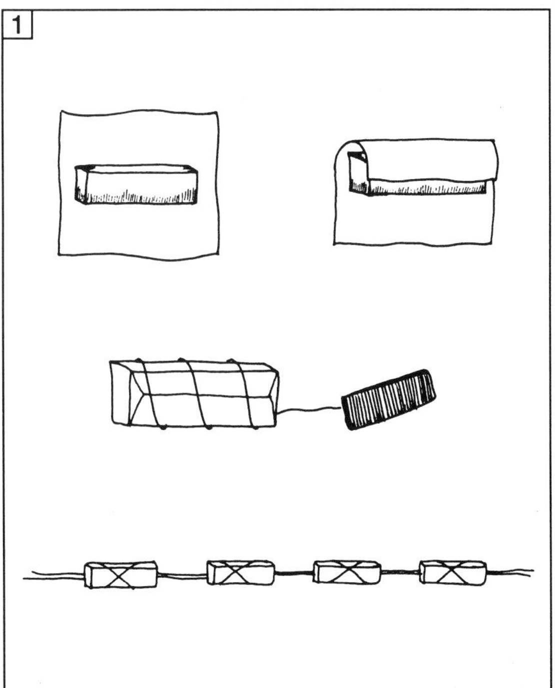

2. Lightly soak the foam, being careful not to over-soak; drain for a few minutes and fix securely to the door or archway. The length of the garland is purely a matter of personal choice. It can extend to ground level either side of the door, completely framing it, or can cover just the top half of the arch. This second

method looks effective if two matching tubs of flowers or topiary trees are placed each side of the door underneath the garland. All flowers and foliage should have been well conditioned beforehand; an overnight drink is best. A pair of strong steps is essential for this type of work and another pair of hands if possible.

2

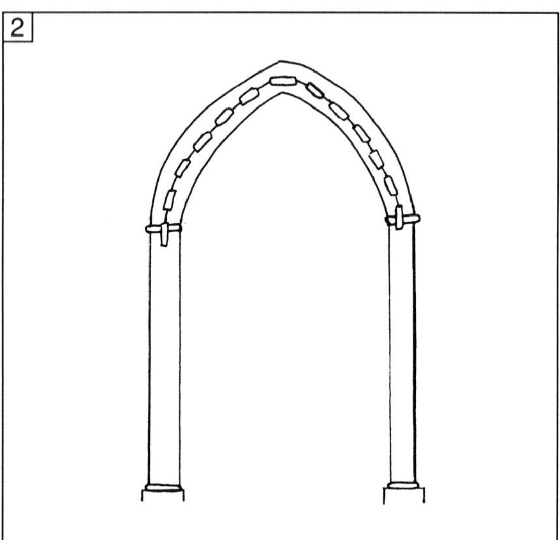

3. Start at exactly the halfway point at the top of the garland. The materials should appear to flow in opposite directions from this point down each side of the doorway. Start by inserting stems in the foam to form an outline of mixed foliage. Keep the width even along the garland's length with stems pushed into the foam at a downward angle. Shorter pieces of foliage can be used to cover the top of the foam. Continue until one side of the arch has been lightly covered with foliage and leaves and then add the chosen flowers. Repeat random groupings of one flower type or colour to provide interest and give a more natural appearance to the garland.

Some of the flowers might need support wiring, especially those with thin or weak stems. Heavier items such as fir cones or fruit should always be wired before use.

3

4

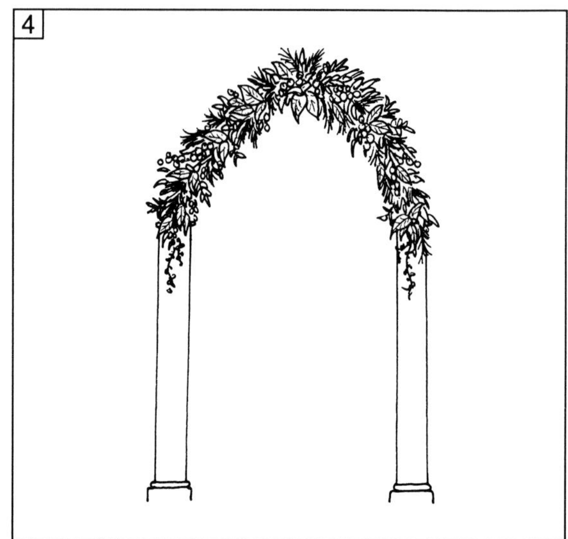

4. Construct the second half in exactly the same way. A ribbon or hessian bow can be added at the top and at each end to give the impression that it is tied onto the wall. To further increase this illusion it is also very attractive to weave lengths of ribbon through the design so that it appears to bind some of the materials together. Short lengths of ribbon can be used for this, fixed at each end with a single wire leg mount. This looks particularly good when used on a garland of mostly foliage or evergreen, perhaps for a Christmas wedding using a conifer foliage base, gilded fir cones and velvet ribbon.

Wired garland

The base of a wired garland can be made a day or two in advance, providing mature evergreen foliage is used and the base is stored in a cool place in a plastic bag.

Select foliage such as conifer, in particular thuja and cupressus, or box, tree ivy, eucalyptus and euonymus. These have very tough leaves and stems which do not wilt and remain fresh-looking without water for several days.

Method

1. Cut all foliage to be used into small sprays of approximately 6–8 cm in length and lay out on a table top in groups by type.

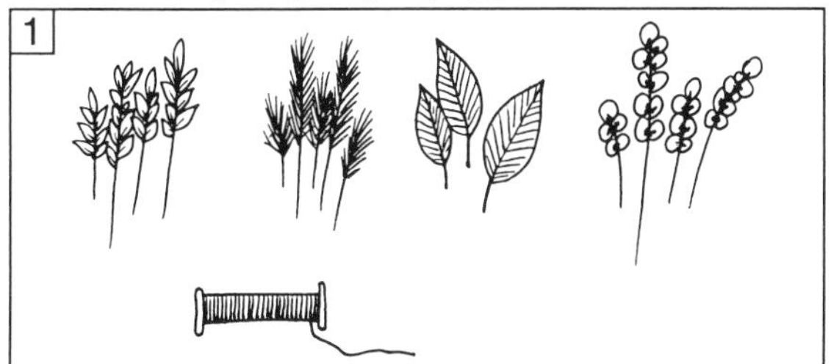

2. Attach a 0.56 mm black or green binding wire to the first piece of foliage leaving an end of wire beyond the foliage. This can be used to help fix the finished garland to the door. The garland is made by wiring each piece of foliage onto the stem end of the previous piece.

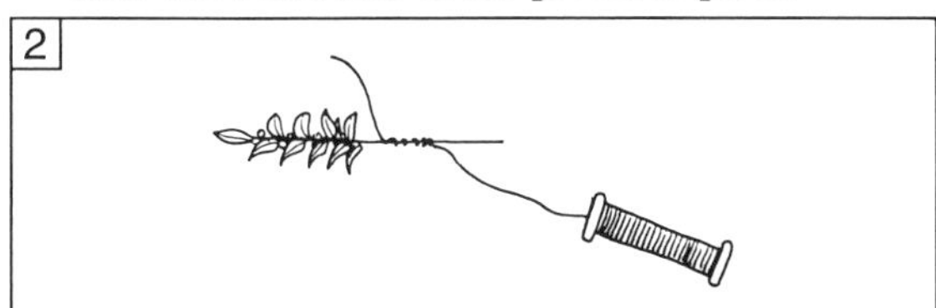

3. Each spray of foliage should overlap the last piece by approximately one-third of its length, the stem from the previous piece providing the anchor for wiring for the next. Care should be taken to make sure that all foliage overlaps and that there are no weak points or gaps in the binding.

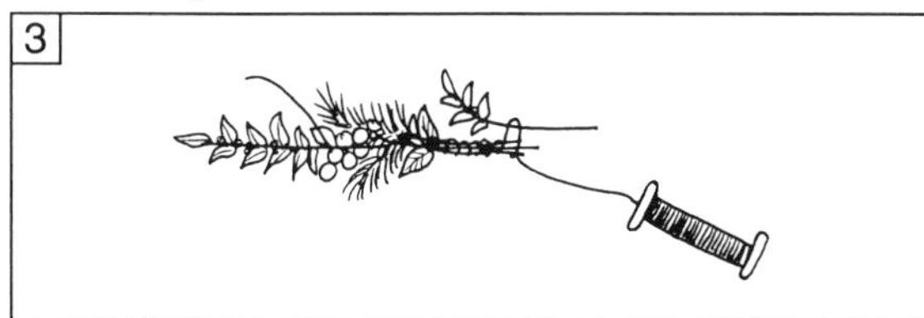

4. Overlapping each piece gives the finished effect of a full continuous length of foliage without any stems being visible. Complete the garland by binding the wire firmly onto the last stem, leaving a length of wire for fixing, the same as when the garland was started.

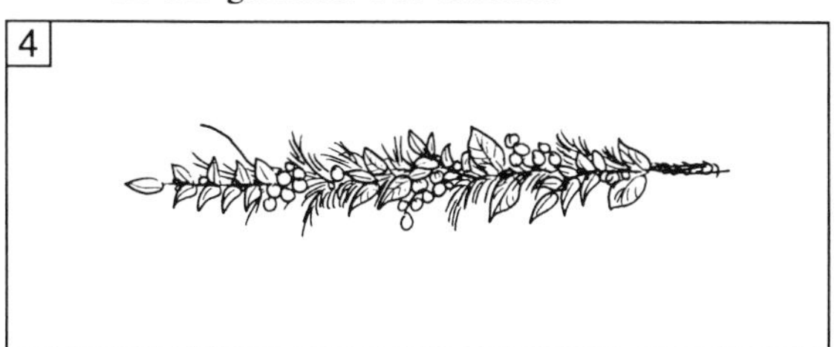

5. If using mixed foliage, space the different kinds evenly throughout rather than putting in large blocks of one type. The easiest way to add the flowers to this type of garland is after it has been hung up, as this ensures that they can be positioned for maximum effect. They can, of course, be bound in as the garland is made but only if it is constructed a few hours before use. All flowers and additional materials should be wired on 0.56 mm single leg mount wires. The wire stem is simply pushed through the foliage base and carefully bent over at the back. This is enough to secure the flower heads. If fruit or cones are included, a heavier wire such as a 0.71 mm should be used and more care taken to make sure these items are secured firmly.

   Long-lasting flowers are best such as spray chrysanthemums, spray carnations, carnation blooms, roses, tulips, statice, gypsophila, hydrangeas and achillea. Flowers with a linear or spiked shape such as gladioli, irises, liatris and antirrhinums are not suitable as they would project too far out of the garland and spoil the effect.

   The wired garland is particularly flexible and is suited to a number of uses such as outlining doorways, windows and mantelpieces and running as a decorative swag along tables.

Flower Tubs

Tubs of flowers or plants outside the porch door or either side of the inner church door provide a quick, large and very effective decoration.

Choose good-quality plastic patio tubs or terracotta pots. They need not be watertight as it is unnecessary to fill them completely with water or foam. A smaller bucket or plastic bowl can be placed inside the larger tub. The space between the two containers can be packed with moss or even newspaper for added stability.

Depending on the size of the tub, two or three blocks of foam can be stacked on top of each other to extend above the rim of the container by approximately 10–15 cm. It can then be secured with pot tape. Using a dense foliage such as box or bay, start to build up the rough structure and outline by placing the tallest piece of foliage in first. This should be roughly twice the height of the container, although this may vary depending on the design of the tub. The finished effect should resemble a tub of flowers growing naturally, so a defined 'arrangement' style would be too contrived. Instead try to form a domed or rounded shape. Having established the height, place further pieces of foliage around the rim of the container. These should be approximately half the length of the tallest piece and should be inserted into the foam at a slightly downward angle to cover the rim of the tub. Loosely infill with more foliage so that the general shape is formed and the foam partially covered. Larger individual leaves such as hosta or bergenia can be added slightly recessed in order to give visual weight to the design and provide contrast to the smaller types of foliage.

All types of flower are suitable for these designs, provided they have a good stem length. To achieve the best effect, however, the choice of flowers should be limited to three or four types at the most. A typical combination providing a good contrast of flower shape and size would be Asiatic lilies, solidaster, gerbera and alstroemeria. Tubs of a single flower look particularly effective, resembling a pot of naturally growing flowers more than a mixture would. Always make sure that you use enough of one type of flower to create an effect and wherever possible you should use flowers at different stages of development – buds and half-open, as well as fully open blooms. Daffodils, tulips, lilies, irises, dahlias and alstroemeria are always more effective when used in this way.

MARQUEE DECORATIONS

Decorating a marquee for a wedding party or promotional event presents the florist with a challenging and enjoyable task. As marquees are temporary structures, they somehow seem far better suited to more extravagant and abundant displays than would be normal in a hotel or similar building.

To be asked to decorate a marquee for a party or ball can seem an ideal job. Ideas for the chosen theme or overall look should be written down as soon as possible and then looked at very carefully in order to assess the practicalities of actually being able to carry them out. Some ideas which might seem perfect could just as easily turn the job into a nightmare if they are difficult to construct within the time scale available, the structural limitations of the marquee or the restrictions of transportation and availability of materials. Although the basic types of floral decorations and displays generally used in marquees are very similar to those for any outside decorating job, such as pedestals, topiary trees, pots and tubs of flowers, garlands and flower baskets, they lend themselves to a much more imaginative treatment. In addition to these, table arrangements of different sizes and styles are important whether for grand buffet table centrepieces, top tables for banquets or weddings, or small posy styles for individual guest tables.

Decorations for marquee posts are the one type of display which is particular to this area of floristry. They can vary from bunches of evergreen foliage tied onto the poles with ribbon and large flower balls hanging from light brackets to very large flower clusters up to 2 m in length attached to either side of the post itself.

As with church decorating it is worth taking the time before starting the job to get exact details about the marquee. Again, this will save a lot of time on the day.

Displays can also be hung from the top rail of the wall of a metal-framed marquee. These can be made in exactly the same way as a pew end (see page 121) but on a larger scale.

Listed below is some information needed before work can start.

- Will the marquee be lined with decorative material and if so what colour? Most marquees are lined with ruched or pleated nylon that comes in a variety of pastel colours, usually wide stripes of cream and an alternating soft colour such as pale green, pink or peach. Navy blue and even red are also available.
- Will the marquee be traditional post and canvas or erected on a metal frame? If the latter, this will exclude decoration of the posts as framed marquees generally do not have central supports. If they do have them, however, the roof height is considerably lower than in the traditional types and this will influence the use of flowers on the posts.
- On which day before the event will the marquee be erected and how soon after will it be dismantled?
- Check to see if heaters are to be used and their positions. This will affect the placement of some floral displays.
- Obtain the name and telephone number of the caterers to find out the number and size of tables and the length of buffet table or top table. If garlands or elaborate arrangements are to be used on the tables, these will need to

be clothed before the arrangements can be made and positioned. This needs to be pre-arranged with the caterers.

- If using post decorations check to confirm the method of attaching them to the posts, whether by hooks or nails into the wood or by hanging from bracket lights off the posts.

Pedestal arrangements are particularly vulnerable in these situations and are best kept to the corners or flanking the entrance doors. The floors of marquees can be very uneven so it is worth taking along some squares or circles of painted plywood to provide a stable base for pedestal arrangements.

Hanging Spheres

Hanging spheres of flowers provide a dramatic and eye-catching feature in a marquee. They can either be hung at intervals along the length of the marquee roof or suspended from protruding light brackets which are attached to the central support posts. If they are to be hung along the centre of the roof, the marquee contractors must be consulted to arrange a means of hanging them by hooks or ropes and pulleys.

The flowers and foliage needed for this type of design are those which will cover the foam and create the shape quickly. They should have thin yet firm stems and good lasting qualities.

Flowers	
Lilac	Spray carnations
Philadelphus	Standard carnations
Escallonia	Spray chrysanthemums
Prunus	September flowers
Forsythia	Solidaster
Cytisus	Alstroemeria
Viburnum opulus	Irises
Euphorbia	Gerbera
Lilies	Trachelium

Foliage	
Soft ruscus	Beech
Eucalyptus	Viburnum
Privet	Ivy
Senecio	Box

Marquee decorations

Method

1. Choose plastic-coated wire hanging baskets of suitable size, available from any good garden centre. These should be filled with pre-soaked foam up to the rim. Baskets can be lined with thin plastic such as a bin liner to prevent water dripping, but it can be difficult to push soft- or fine-stemmed materials through the plastic. If the sphere is made well in advance of the event and allowed to drain, water seepage should not be a problem.

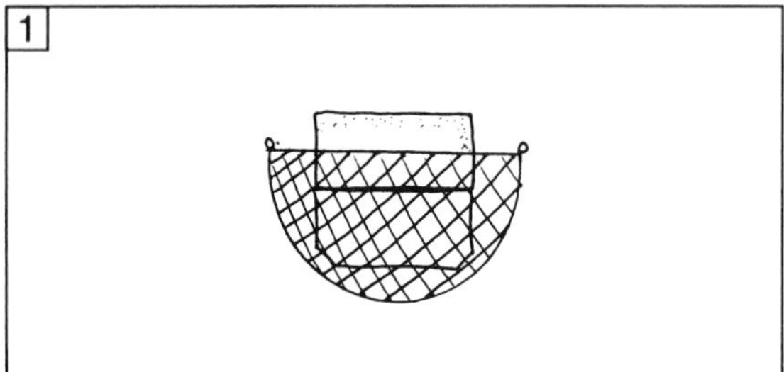

2. Constructing the sphere whilst balancing on top of a pair of steps can be a difficult, not to say frustrating job, the main problem being that the sphere rotates every time you insert a flower or piece of foliage. One idea is to construct as much of the design as possible before hanging it up. This can be done by placing the foam-filled basket in the top of a bucket, thus allowing both hands free to work. It is possible to finish about two-thirds of the sphere in this way, leaving only a small area on the underside to complete after it has been hung.
3. Start the sphere by placing the topmost piece of foliage and the widest pieces in position. The widest point across the sphere should be approximately level with the rim of the basket. Continue to cover the foam with more foliage to form the circular shape.

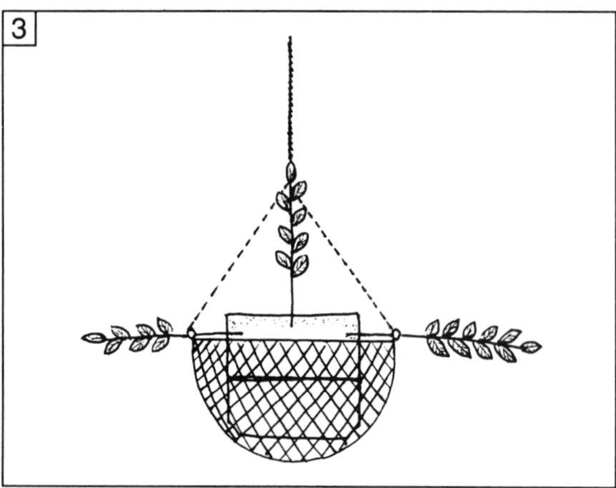

4. Add the flowers, remembering to use fewer on the top of the sphere and more of the choicer types around the edges and underneath. When the finished design is hung up the top will not be seen as much as the underside.

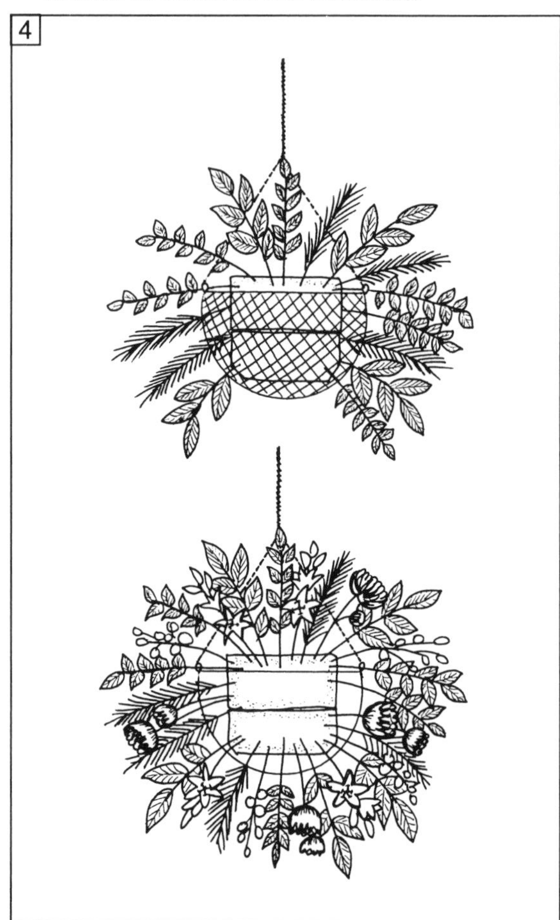

5. Clusters of ribbons of varying length can be added at the bottom of the design. This is especially effective for parties.

Tent Pole Decorations

Another way to decorate marquee posts is to attach a block of foam to each side of the post and create a large circular cluster of flowers and foliage which completely encircles the post. This very popular method is widely used at weddings, providing an impressive and eye-catching display high up in the marquee well out of harm's way.

It does have certain disadvantages, the least of which is the way in which the foam is attached to the posts, and of course the whole display must be made in situ, which necessitates working on top of a stepladder. This can be a tedious job for one

Tent pole decoration

person, requiring many journeys up and down for materials, so it is always recommended to have an extra person available to pass up flowers and foliage as needed. The displays are made in two halves, which must join at the sides so as to appear whole. The height at which to attach the displays varies depending on the finished size, but as a general rule they need to be approximately 3–3.5 m above ground level. Remember that the foam block will be at the centre of the display with possibly 60–90 cm of material hanging down from it. Because this should not be so low as to create a hazard, the positioning of the foam blocks is very important. It is usual to decorate every post in a marquee, and they can range from one or two up to five or six in number. When more than one post is decorated, care must be taken to ensure that all finished displays are equal in size and are level with each other!

Flowers	
Alstroemeria	Larkspur
Spray chrysanthemums	Dahlias
Standard carnations	Asters
Spray carnations	Solidago
Tulips	Alchemilla
Gerbera	Gypsophila
Irises	Prunus
Peonies	Cytisus
Stocks	Lilac
Lilies	Philadelphus
Statice	

Foliage	
Ivy	Lime
Laurel	Ruscus
Privet	Eucalyptus
Aucuba	Viburnum
Green and copper beech	

Method

1. Securely tape two pre-soaked blocks of foam onto two plastic spray trays.
2. Using nylon string, tie the blocks and trays up like a parcel, crossing the string at the back and bringing the two loose ends up to one end of the tray; knot them tightly. Leave two long pieces of string after tying the knot.
3. Locate the pulley ropes, which run the length of the posts. If the posts have been covered in material there is usually a seam of Velcro which can easily be opened where the foam is to be positioned. Tie the first block of foam to the pulley rope as tight as possible; then tie the second. As there is only one seam in the material down one side of the post, one of the foam trays will have to be hung on a slightly longer string to enable it to be twisted around to the other tray on the opposite side of the post.
4. Once the foam has been fixed, attach pot tape around the post above the trays and bind the tape around the two trays and post several times. It is important to ensure the trays are in the correct position before doing this. Bind as tightly as possible to clamp the trays to the post; work down the length of the trays until the last section of tape encircles the post underneath the trays.

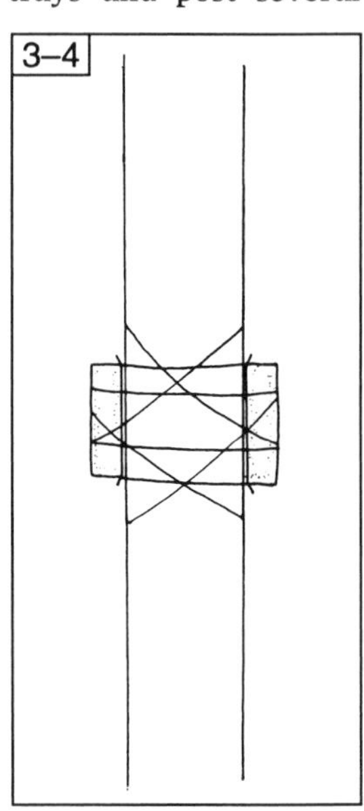

5. Insert the top and bottom pieces of foliage and the two widest side pieces; continue to infill between these four pieces to roughly form an oval shape. All materials at the sides should be angled backwards as far as possible so that when the second half of the display is made, the two halves join and appear to be one complete arrangement around the post.

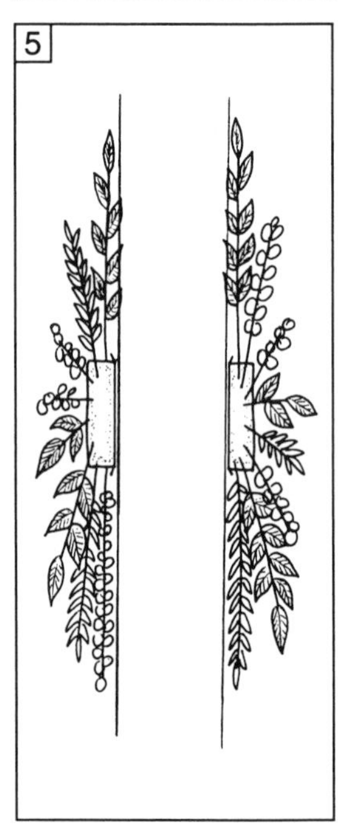

6. Shorter pieces of foliage should be added to cover the foam block. Remember that these displays are viewed from ground level so enough material must be angled downwards to avoid any gaps. It is easy to

forget this when working at eye level and to use most of the flowers in the top half and leave the lower section looking sparsely filled from the ground.

6

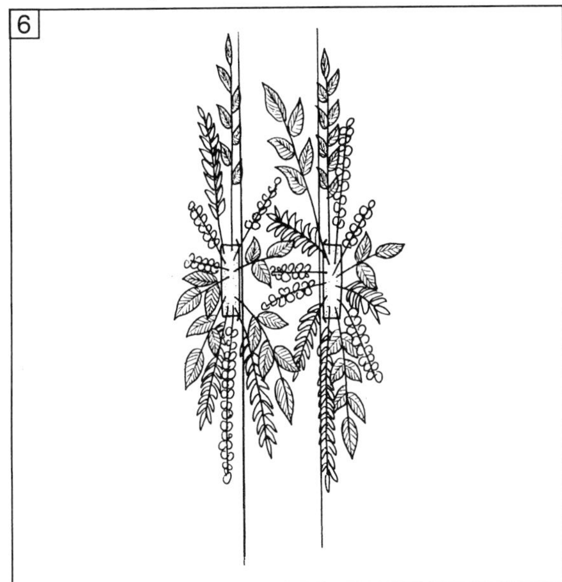

7. Add the flowers, ensuring an even distribution over the whole design. Start working at the edges of the design and work towards the centre, finishing off with shorter larger blooms clustered towards the centre.

   If gypsophila, September flowers and limonium are being used, add these at the very end. This will not only save these fine materials from being damaged during the construction but will reduce the amount needed and show them off to greater effect.
8. Finally, thoroughly spray the arrangement with water to maintain the freshness of the flowers for as long as possible. It is a good idea to leave these designs for the last decorating job so that they have less time to dry out.

TOPIARY

Topiary or plant material that has been clipped and trimmed into decorative shape is one of the oldest forms of ornamental plant use. The ideal plants for this treatment are dense-leaved evergreens such as box, bay, privet and certain types of conifer. The shapes which can be created are endless, ranging from simple geometric forms to animals, birds, even complete chess sets laid out as if ready for a game.

The amount of time and care needed to achieve these results is, however, reflected in the considerable price of even the simplest ball or cone-shaped bush.

The use of imitation or made-up topiary of cut foliage has thus become very popular as a form of decoration for weddings and parties over the last few years. It is cheaper and easier to transport, as it is made on site; it also offers a wide range of flower and foliage combinations.

The use of topiary today, particularly in floristry work, is mostly confined to geometric shapes such as spheres, pyramids, cones, obelisks and rectangular- or square-shaped bushes. However and wherever it is used, topiary will instantly provide a formal, structured look for an event or function. For this reason much should be made of the placement of individual pieces to emphasise the symmetry and formality of the decoration. Pairs of conical bushes flanking a doorway, an avenue of obelisk bays, or matching groups of graduated lollipop trees can provide such a strong visual impact that very little else in the way of decoration is needed.

Traditionally, topiary bushes used for interior or temporary decoration were grown in containers allowing them to be moved around to create new or different effects. These containers were usually either wooden, such as half barrels or square Versailles tubs, or stone and terracotta ornamental pots. Such was the success of these combinations of shaped plant and container that they have remained unchanged and have become accepted as almost classic forms of garden floral art. A lollipop bay tree in a white-painted Versailles tub or a pyramid of box in a swagged and moulded terracotta pot is instantly recognisable as somehow being 'right'.

Made-up topiary work consists of the basic tree or bush shape, usually a lollipop which is formed from foliage inserted into foam. The basic shape is then 'dressed up' with flowers, fruit or ribbon bows added into the foliage base. The work can also be made up entirely of flowers. For example, a mixed ball of gypsophila, spray carnations, spray chrysanthemums or lilies looks particularly effective supported on a natural wooden stem and placed in a decorative container.

As with all large pieces of work, materials with long-lasting qualities should be chosen. Foliage should always be mature and flowers should have firm stems. All materials must be conditioned for several hours before use.

There are companies which specialise in topiary hire and ornamental trees in containers. They will deliver to the site and collect. It is important to remember to build this additional cost into your pricing structure. The use of real topiary alongside cut flower displays can create a total look.

Flowers	
Single spray chrysanthemums	Achillea
Gypsophila	Waxflowers
Alchemilla mollis	Alstroemeria
Sweet peas	Roses

Foliage	
Box	Soft ruscus
Bay	*Eucalyptus gunnii*
Viburnum tinus	Bush ivy
Conifers such as Douglas fir and *Cupressus macrocarpa*	

Materials for a floor-standing display
Suitably sized outer decorative pot or container, preferably wood or terracotta
Smaller inner container, such as a plastic flower pot, large enough to counterbalance the weight of the finished tree
A fairly straight length of natural branch
Cement mixture
Two or three blocks of wet foam or a foam sphere
Pot tape
Wire netting
String
Lichen or bun moss, stones, bark

Method

1. Cut the branch to the required stem length of the topiary tree, allowing for the depth of the plastic flower pot. An average length would be approximately 80–100 cm.
2. Place the branch upright in the centre of the plastic plant pot and fill with cement mixture. This needs to be done several days in advance so that the stem is securely fixed in the cement before use.

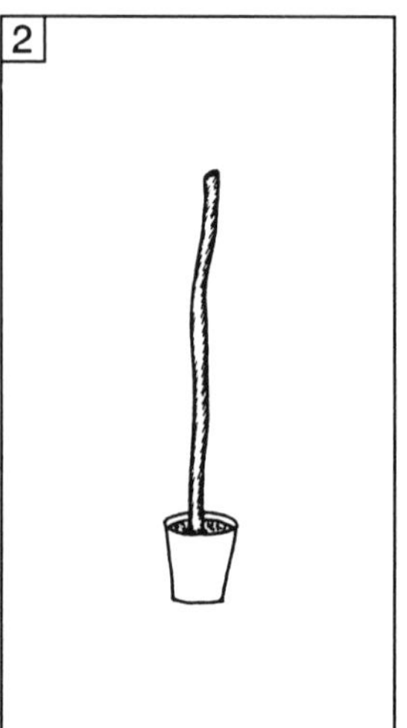

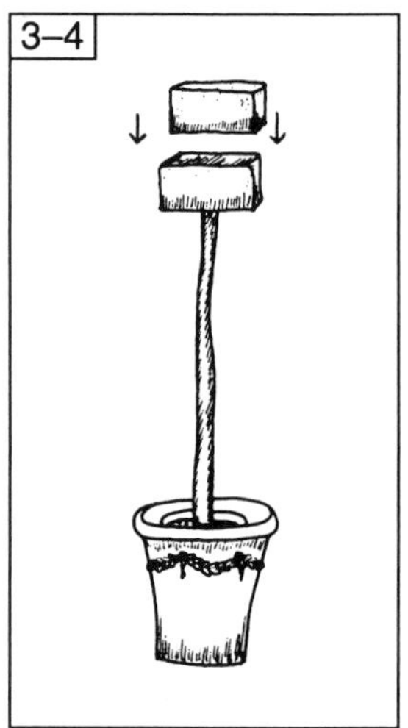

3. Place the cement-filled pot and branch inside the decorative pot. Firmly pack the space between the two pots with moss.
4. Push a block of pre-soaked foam onto the top of the wooden stem. Take care to ensure that the foam does not split in half. The stem should be pushed in to about half the thickness of the foam. Place the second block of foam on top of the first and trim off the corners to form a rough sphere.
5. Secure the blocks of foam by binding them together with the string and tie off firmly.
6. Enclose the foam with the wire netting, carefully bending the edges under the foam, and tie securely to the stem.
7. Insert four pieces of foliage, each about a quarter of the overall stem length, at the top and bottom of the sphere and on both sides. These are the guide points for the sphere. Continue to use the foliage to cover the foam until a well-rounded shape has been formed.

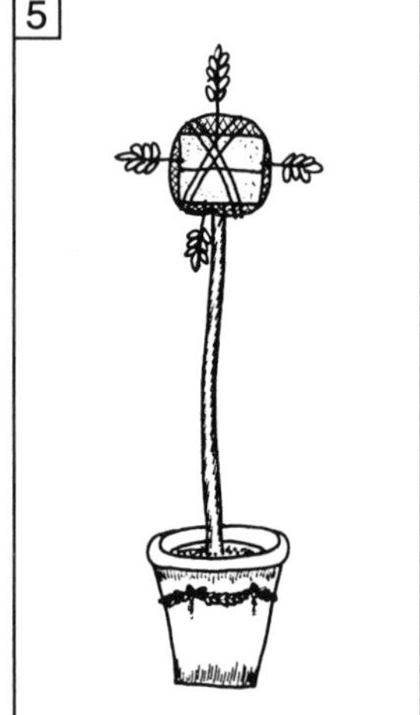

8. It may be necessary to lightly trim the foliage to tidy the outline if a very formal look is required.
9. Once the 'ball' of foliage has been made, the flowers or other decorations can be added. Insert flowers directly into the foam, making

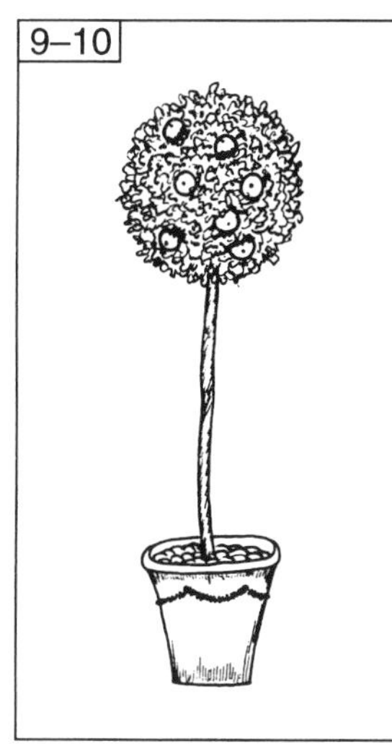
9–10

sure that they are evenly spread over the entire shape. Fruits, cones and bows should be support wired with 0.71 mm or 0.90 mm wires.

10. Once the tree is finished, the surface of the pot can be finished off with a decorative covering such as bun moss, lichen, pebbles or bark chippings.

TABLE ARRANGEMENTS

Buffet Table

A buffet table usually calls for a centrepiece display. This can be of food: a specially decorated dish, perhaps a whole salmon, an elaborate pudding or a collection of different fruits. Quite often a floral display is used, which gives a really festive look to the table.

Displays of this type look wonderful when combined with fruit and can range from a simple basket of apples decorated with ivy and daisy chrysanthemum heads to lavish arrangements of exotic fruit and flowers which resemble Dutch still-life paintings of the sixteenth and seventeenth centuries.

Whatever the display, it is important to check with the caterers to find out how much table space can be used and to determine the overall dimensions of the arrangement. Buffet tables placed against a wall can be seen from only one side, whereas both sides will be visible on tables in the middle of a room.

All sorts of combinations of materials can be used depending on the type of occasion. A lunch party or midday wedding would be appropriate for a display using baskets of flowers and fruit in fresh clean colours, whereas an evening dinner or banquet requires something a little more formal. The flowers might be arranged more traditionally in a classical urn, perhaps with a swathe of damask or brocade material providing a base for randomly grouped fruit and flower heads. Fir cones, dried grasses such as pampas, and peacock feathers all add an unexpected touch to an arrangement and turn an ordinary display into something a little more exciting. As arrangements of this type are mainly used for festive occasions, they provide an opportunity for the florist to demonstrate some more flamboyant ideas!

The basic shape of most displays of this type is the symmetrical triangle. It is well suited to a front-facing table design and can be easily adapted to include two or three separate arrangements or groups of flowers or fruits, all of which can be loosely contained within an imaginary triangle. Arrangements which are to be viewed from all sides are loosely based on the idea of two triangles placed back to back.

Arrangements that will be seen from both sides of a table need not always be long, low designs. A dramatic effect can be achieved by constructing a taller design using a traditional urn or vase as the container. An arrangement with an overall height of perhaps a metre creates an impressive centrepiece for a suitably sized table.

An altogether more informal look is easily created by laying foliage and flowers along the length of the table between the dishes of food. A centre arrangement in wet foam from which long pieces of foliage extend along the table can be created, or two or three smaller designs can be placed at intervals and linked with foliage and flower heads laid directly onto the tablecloth. A very old traditional idea for dressing up a table, this can look stunning (see colour section). However, some points are worth remembering:

- Plant material used with or near food must be clean and in good condition.
- Avoid using flowers or foliage that may cause allergic reactions either from their scent or sap.
- It is not a good idea to use ornamental berries or seeds as part of these decorations for obvious reasons!
- Remove the stamens from lilies to avoid staining the cloth and also do not use plants such as narcissi that bleed sap from their stems when cut.
- This type of display can be put together only at the very last minute, quite often after the table has been laid out with food. Because the majority of plant material will not be in water it needs to be very well conditioned before use.
- As table arrangements are always seen at close quarters, they must be finished off to a high standard of workmanship.

Guest Table

The most widely used tables for weddings and parties are generally circular and seat eight to ten people. Round posy arrangements are ideal for these and depending on the number of place settings can be quite large. For evening or winter events a candle looks particularly attractive as a centrepiece. To vary the design and create different effects, fruit, nuts, fir cones, moss and a variety of other natural materials can all be used in addition to flowers. (See also page 34.)

Round baskets filled with moss and fruits with just a few well-chosen flowers such as roses or lilies and a group of perhaps three candles in the middle can create a different and very effective centrepiece.

Another idea is to make miniature topiary trees of 30–50 cm in overall height in small terracotta pots. The tops of the trees can be made from reindeer or bun moss pinned onto a foam sphere and decorated with gilded acorns or small fruits such as clementines or crab apples. Fruit, nuts and even vegetables associate very well with table decorations, and wherever possible should be used in abundance to provide a lavish or opulent effect.

Posy arrangements will form a large part of a decorating job, and twenty to thirty tables to decorate is not uncommon (see photograph on page 131). Although posy arrangements are quick and relatively cheap to make, such a number, or even as few as ten or twelve arrangements, can be very time-consuming, so it is always advisable to make them in advance rather than spending time on the day. Being low and fairly compact, arrangements of this type can easily be packed into large flower boxes and will travel without suffering any damage. If candles are used it is a good idea to remove them during transportation, not only to avoid breakages but to stop them shaking loose in the foam during the journey. A good-sized table arrangement can be made by using a plastic saucer and a cylinder of foam.

Tip

Table arrangements are always seen at close quarters so must be finished off to a high standard of workmanship.

Flowers	
Single spray chrysanthemums	Alstroemeria
Spray carnations	Mimosa
Lilies	Solidaster
Roses	Gypsophila
Freesias	September flowers
Tulips	Eustoma
	Statice

Foliage	
Leatherleaf fern	Lighter types of conifer such as thuja
Eucalyptus	Bush ivy
Pittosporum	
Soft ruscus	

Method

1. Securely tape the foam cylinder into the saucer. If using a candle in the design ensure that the tape cuts across the foam to one side of the centre and not exactly in the middle. This will allow the candle to be positioned in the centre of the arrangement and not be obstructed by the foam tape.

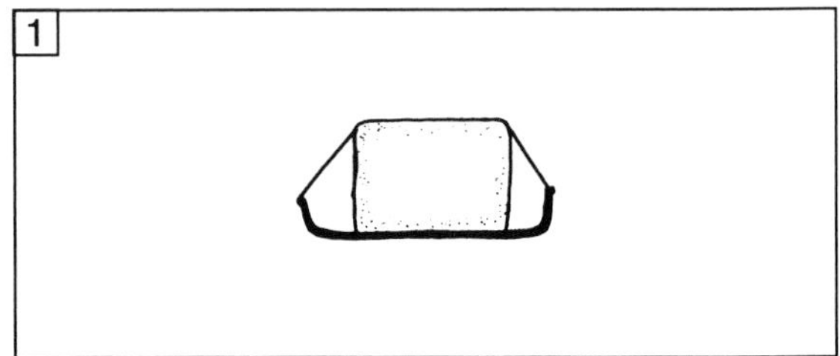

2. Form a circular outline of mixed foliage to the required size.

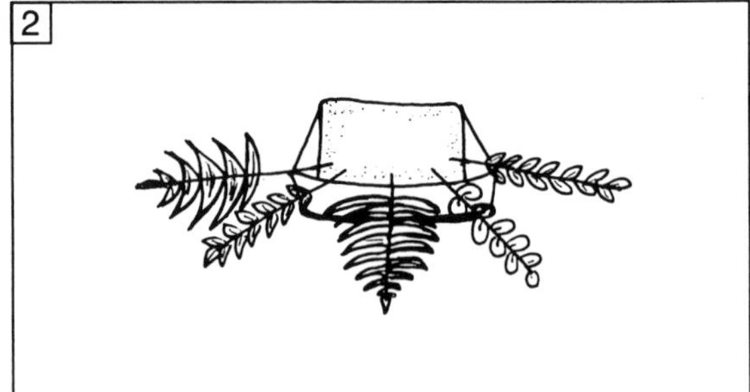

3. Position the candle or a flower in the centre of the foam to determine the maximum height of the arrangement.
4. Lightly cover the foam with mixed foliage to form a conical shape.

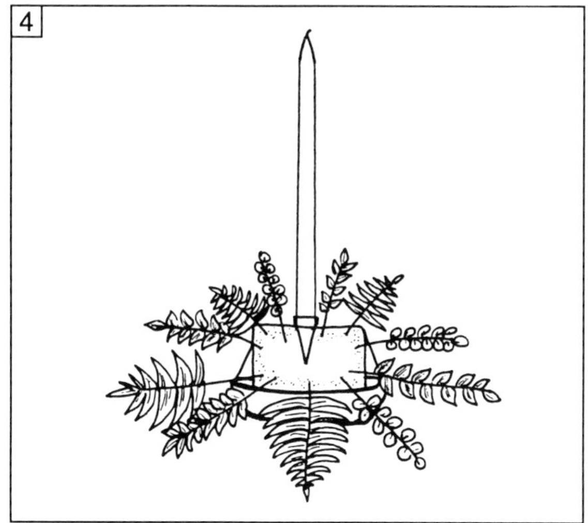

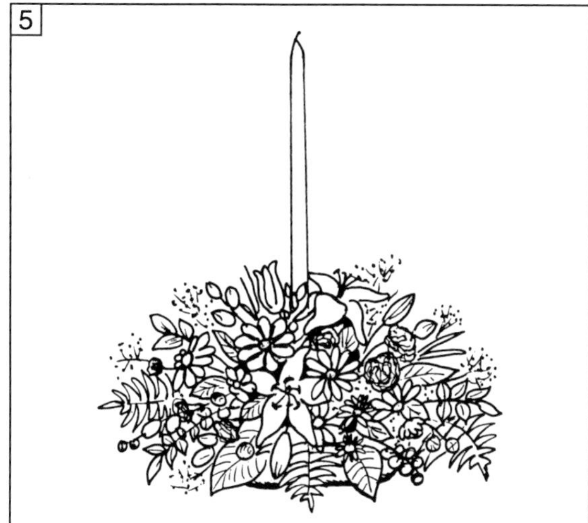

5. Add flowers, making sure that they are spread evenly over the whole arrangement. Place the flowers in the foam at various heights to create recession and variations within the design. A range of flower sizes and shapes and the use of flower buds will help to make sure that the arrangement does not become too heavy and turn into a 'pudding'. Turn the design several times to ensure that material is evenly distributed on all sides.

Top Table

Decorations for a top table at either a wedding or a conference are similar in style, the main requirements being that they are low enough for people seated at the table to see over them and that they are not too wide.

Usually only one side of a top table is used for seating so the flowers can be placed along the front edge and allowed to cascade over the front. A central arrangement is always placed in front of the principal guests and slightly smaller arrangements are positioned at intervals along the table as required. These can be linked with foliage for a more elaborate finish or by foliage garlands hung along the front of the cloth.

A variation on this idea is to construct a continuous arrangement along the whole length of the table using long spray trays. This arrangement works very well if made in the continental style of grouping flowers and foliage together in a more natural way. Other materials such as moss, fruit, nuts, fir cones and seed heads will add extra interest and the addition of groups of candles of varying heights finishes off a very distinctive display.

One point worth remembering is that quite often the arrangement is constructed in place on the tablecloth. Extra care must be taken to make sure that the cloth is not marked by water or green stains from the flowers. To make a central arrangement a complete block of soaked foam can be used securely taped into a plastic spray tray. It is a good idea to let excess water drain out of the foam before using, as spray trays do not have much room to collect any water and this can spill over onto the cloth. The advantage of using something as shallow as a tray allows stems to be placed into the foam at a downward angle to create a cascading effect over the front of the table.

Method

1. Tape a block of foam onto a spray tray and place in position at the front of the table about 3 cm from the edge.
2. Place the longest pieces of foliage at each end of the foam. These should rest on the table top itself. Insert a short piece of foliage at the back and three or four longer pieces at the front to

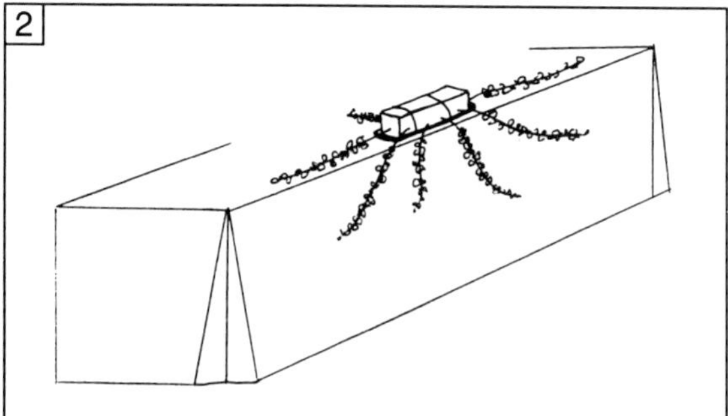

hang down over the cloth. It is much easier to achieve this effect if naturally trailing foliage such as ivy trails, asparagus fern or smilax is used. Place a short piece of foliage on the top of the foam to establish the maximum height. The dimensions of the arrangement have now been decided.

3. Arrange the main line of choice flowers through the design. An effective placement is to form a diagonal line from back to front using one of the flowers as the topmost point of the arrangement and grouping several blooms around the centre of the design. Flowers such as lilies, roses and carnations are particularly suitable for this.

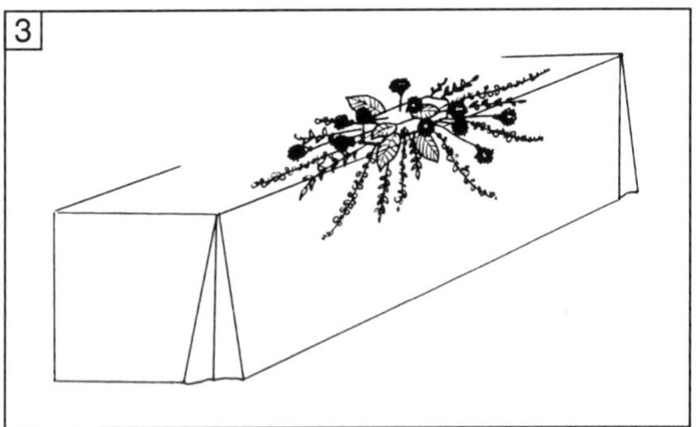

4. Infill the outline of the arrangement with further foliage and some larger leaves around the central area. Small flowers and buds can also be used so as not to create a solid edge of foliage.
5. A secondary line of one type of flower or of a colour can be formed from one end of the arrangement to the other. Pattern lines or groups of material should not be too regular or severe in their appearance. Being rather more broken or random gives a pleasing effect.

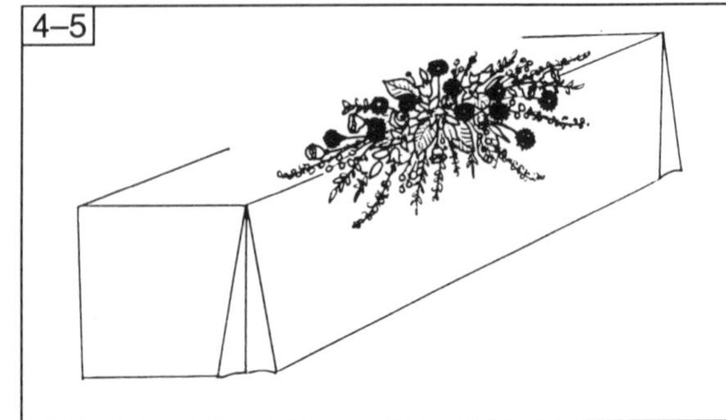

6. Complete the arrangement by infilling with more foliage and flowers so that the overall shape is strengthened and the foam covered. Remember to include some flowers in the trailing section over the edge of the table. So often this consists of only foliage, all the flower material having been used on the top of the table, leading to a lack of unity in the design.

Flowers used for decorating a top table need to be distinctive and bold to provide the necessary impact required of these arrangements. This is not to say that smaller flowers cannot be used, but they should be included to provide a contrast to the larger blooms, rather than forming the bulk of the materials. Lilies, gerbera and fully blown roses, hydrangeas, cosmos and open tulips, especially the lily-flowered and parrot types, all give a special look to arrangements of this type.

Top table arrangement

PEDESTAL ARRANGEMENTS

Pedestal arrangements are perhaps some of the largest individual pieces of work a florist will be asked to make. They can range from a short 1.2 or 1.5 m display to arrangements of over 2.4 to 3 m in height with a width of 1.2 or 1.5 m. A pedestal arrangement is defined as any floral display raised or elevated on a plinth or stand. Although this means that the pedestal itself is included in the dimensions, the arrangement on its own is still quite large.

The surroundings will, of course, determine the overall size of the display and once this has been assessed the type of pedestal stand can be chosen. Metal stands with a built-in foam tray or a flat top for a vase to stand on are the most widely used. Most are telescopic and can be adjusted to various heights. This is also a bonus when transporting them, as they take up a lot less room than stands of fixed height. One drawback, however, is that they tend to be rather lightweight and are not really suitable for a very large arrangement of 2.5 m in height. The sheer volume and weight of material in a display of this size could make them overbalance.

Wooden tripod plant stands or antique torchères look wonderful when topped with a full traditional arrangement and generally offer a greater height than most other stands. They are expensive and not really suitable for transporting from job to job, especially valuable antique ones. When used for a special occasion or party in a private home they look perfect and tend to harmonise more with the surroundings than, say, a wrought iron or plastic one would.

Plastic column-style pedestals are available but these tend to be a bit on the short side and need to be weighted inside with sand or cement to make them stable. Reinforced cardboard cylinder columns offer a wide range of heights and widths and can be bought finished in various effects such as marble and wood, or covered in hessian. They can also be painted and are often supplied unfinished so that the customer can apply the desired colour or paint effect. One big advantage is that they are relatively lightweight to handle yet remarkably stable and will stack comfortably inside each other for storage or transport.

Containers for pedestal arrangements need to be of a generous size to accommodate several blocks of foam. They fall roughly into two groups: those that will be visible and form a part of the overall display and those which will be completely hidden by the arrangement. The latter are usually wide bowl types but those which are seen can range from traditional urn and vase shapes to large ornate bowls or pots.

It is often difficult to find flower containers of these shapes of sufficient size. To overcome this problem it is worth looking at the range of garden or patio pots and urns sold in any good garden centre. They do not necessarily have to be waterproof as they can be lined with a cheaper plastic container. These make excellent formal containers and the plastic ones can be painted or distressed to resemble terracotta, lead or stone. Real terracotta and concrete containers provide a wide range of shapes but must be lined with either plastic or an inner container as they tend to be porous. The weight of these when filled with wet foam is an added problem.

For arrangements where the container will not be seen, plastic washing-up bowls, small buckets and larger plastic 'bulb bowls' are all useful, cheap and – if need be – disposable.

A large classical urn placed on a wooden or column pedestal is ideal for creating a formal classic arrangement.

To create a dramatic theatrical effect or simply to disguise an ugly container, swathes of cheap lining material or muslin draped around the container and falling around the column to the floor can look wonderful.

The design of a pedestal arrangement is usually based on the basic symmetrical triangular shape. This will need to be greatly enlarged and the proportion slightly distorted such as increasing the width at the base of the design to allow more material to cascade down over the rim of the container and the pedestal stand itself. The top can also be widened so as not to create too sharp a point but a fuller, more rounded display. Whatever the variations, the basic structure and techniques are exactly the same as when creating the standard triangular arrangement. Asymmetrical arrangements can look especially effective, especially when used in pairs. Again the design principles are the same as for a small arrangement, the height and width perhaps being exaggerated and increased to balance the overall finished size.

Because of the overall size of pedestal displays, a great deal of material has to be contained within a relatively small area of foam. It is thus essential that adequate and secure mechanics are used.

Few individual flowers are large enough to act as the focal point, so even with big flower such as dahlias, chrysanthemum blooms and lilies it is more effective to group several together and perhaps strengthen the grouping with some large leaves such as hosta or bergenia.

Flower types must be chosen carefully to provide the maximum effect from as few stems as possible. Spray chrysanthemums, dahlias, large lilies and branches of blossoms such as cherry, lilac and forsythia are far more effective than smaller single flowers such as freesias, spray carnations or bouvardia.

Arrangements of this size need a great deal of foliage to form the outline and for infilling. Foliage should always be well conditioned and whenever possible only mature leaves should be used. There is a limited range of commercially grown foliage available, and most of it is small.

When using branches and sprays of foliage, always try to position them within an arrangement in the way in which they grow. Branches such as beech and lime have a downward curving shape to the stems and are most effective when placed at the sides and base of a pedestal display where the natural curve is shown to best advantage. If a branch such as this is placed upright to provide height at the back of an arrangement, it will look awkward and constrained as the leaves will either appear upside down or at least at an uncomfortable angle. A straight growing branch, perhaps with some careful pruning to improve its shape, height and strength, can be added to the back of the arrangement with a more natural effect.

Most large displays in churches or marquees are not seen in detail, more as an overall effect at a distance. Therefore the materials used are best kept bold and simple. Small fussy flowers and variegated foliages will disappear within the design and only fragment the display when viewed from a distance.

Outline foliage	
Beech, green or copper	Douglas fir
Lime	Laurel
Hornbeam	Silver poplar
Birch	Privet
Tsuga pine	Portuguese laurel

Infill foliage	
Choisya ternata	Soft ruscus
Senecio greyi	*Eucalyptus gunnii*
Mahonia aquifolium	Conifer, chamaecyparis and thuja types
Elaeagnus ebbingei	
Bush ivy	

Trailing foliage	
Rubus tricolor	*Vinca major*
Hedera helix	Soft ruscus

Individual or accent leaves	
Hosta sieboldiana and other larger varieties	*Hedera colchica* 'Dentata Aurea'
Bergenia cordifolia	New Zealand flax
Cynara scolymus	*Acanthus spinosus*

Method

1. Ensure that adequate foam is used for the size of the display. It should extend at least 15–20 cm above the rim of the container and should be securely taped into the container. The container can in turn be taped to the top of the pedestal for added strength.

2. Avoid using too much material with thick stems.
3. Always use the edges and back of the foam first, leaving the central area open for as long as possible, and work towards the centre to finish. It is much easier to place the longer outer material first to ensure all of it is firmly pushed into the foam than to fill in the centre first.
4. Establish the overall shape of the design as soon as possible before adding choicer or detail flowers.
5. Try to see where the stems enter the foam. Flowers can be damaged and broken if they are pushed onto other stems already in the foam. To avoid the foam breaking up or the display falling over, it is a good idea to support the arrangement with one hand whilst inserting stems into the foam, especially larger and woody ones.

CHAPTER 10

Continental Design

There is a particular style in the United Kingdom which we usually refer to as 'continental'. In fact it is not strictly continental but a variation on a mixture of European styles. There is a lot of confusion between modern styles and the so-called 'continental' style.

Within Europe the styles are very varied. 'Dutch' floristry is quite different from 'German' floristry, which in turn is different from 'French' floristry, but all European styles are linked in a way unlike traditional British work.

The European style tends to favour strong contrasting colour harmony or monochromatic colour harmony using colour much more obviously as a design feature than in the British Isles. Flower and plant material is more obviously grouped rather than displayed in the pattern lines of English work. Unusual materials such as vegetables, fruit, dried materials and fabric are common in European floristry on a daily basis whereas in this country we tend to see them only on 'designer' or competition work and stick chiefly to flowers in our shops.

Texture is another design element which features very strongly in European work, and materials are used in unusual ways to give strong contrasts in textures – the underside of a leaf might be displayed, or flower stalks be tied with electrical tape.

The continental colour wheel has three primary colours but green is treated as if it were a primary colour, thus enabling the designer to use foliage and natural 'green' material as a dominant element of the design. The use of colour is more eye-catching yet subtle, and weighting of colour is very relevant to the design because colour affects the balance, particularly when a strong colour is used with a weak colour. The eye will be drawn to the stronger colour first, and this can greatly affect the impact of the design if strong colour is used to one side only.

The choice of materials is unlimited and the European style lends itself to experimentation, but remember that the finished product should be appealing to the customer and should be saleable.

There are two recognised styles that have been adopted in this country: the classic style, which has one focal area, and the modern style, which has many focal or dominant, eye-catching areas. Derived from these two main styles are the following types of design.

See the photographs on page 104 showing continental design used in funeral work.

Continental style arrangement

Continental style posy pad

Biedermeyer (classic)

This is a round design of posies, bouquets and arrangements very similar to our English Victorian posy but treated in a freer manner. The material may be arranged in concentric circles and finished with a foliage edge. It can be a pyramid shape with spirals of flowers closely arranged. Material such as bear grass, ivy or amaranthus can cascade or trail out of the design.

Linear

This design is based on the use of lines and the spaces between. Materials are specifically chosen to give a linear effect, whether curved or straight.

The design can be made in a variety of containers as long as the materials chosen are in proportion to the size of container. If a dish is used, foam will be necessary to provide support for the stems. If a large vase or jug is used, chicken wire may be needed to provide support for the stems unless the design is arranged in situ, in which case no support medium at all may be required (see colour section).

The plant material chosen should have a combination of curved and straight stems to achieve a good linear effect. An example of plant material for a large vase might be as follows:

3 stems *Phormium tenax*	20 stems bear grass
5 stems trailing ivy	2 gerbera
2 *Fatsia japonica* leaves	3 lilies

Some trails of clematis stems (without leaves or flowers)

These could be arranged as shown in the drawing below, making sure that there is plenty of space between the lines and that the curves give movement and rhythm.

Parallel (modern)

This has probably been adopted more than any other continental style in this country. It has tremendous appeal and is very versatile.

It is ideal for church work where windows, steps and the base of a font can be decorated using a lot of foliage. It is useful in hotel foyers and for table centres, where fruit and candles can be included. It looks very good on a foam posy pad or wreath ring for a Christmas arrangement. It is also effective in decorating catwalks and staging.

It can be made to any size and looks very good in a 'vegetative' form. The parallel style is made up of vertical, horizontal and diagonal placements, and the stems, like parallel lines, should be equidistant at all points.

The most important difference between the parallel and any other style is that the stems do not radiate out from a central point but are placed as if growing, and the design incorporates more than one focal area of dominance. Blocking and grouping of materials is a technique used to give colour impact. There is often a base or groundwork of plant material with material placed above the groundwork, using the space in between as part of the design. The groundwork should have rhythm and movement connecting the upright/vertical placements to establish harmony and balance.

The plant materials suitable for parallel designs are many and varied and could include stones, moss, cut stems, fungi, fruit, vegetables, all kinds of moss and dried seed heads.

There are usually three main groups of plant material in the design. These are placed vertically and are referred to as the main group, neighbour and near neighbour. The main group is the most dominant, the neighbour slightly less and the near neighbour the least. The weighting of the groups will either depend on the number of stems used or be entirely visual.

The plant material placed horizontally is at the base of the design. Leaves may be layered or stepped. Small flowers or foliage can be bunched together or plant material placed vertically on very short stems to form a groundwork giving a patchwork effect.

Containers are shallow and filled with foam. If the plant material is being used horizontally, the foam should extend well above the rim of the container to ensure that stems can be easily inserted. If only vertical material is being used, the foam does not need to rise above the rim as this can restrict the design.

If the stems of the main group are very heavy, it is a good idea to put a larger piece of foam in the area where that placement will be to support the extra weight. Alternatively, a grade of foam giving greater support can be used.

The following design is suitable for a coffee table and will be viewed from above and seen from all sides. The container should be shallow, but can be round, square or rectangular. The design given is in a monochromatic colour harmony.

Flowers

- 7 purple liatris for the main group
- 3 pale-pink lilies for the neighbour
- 2 dark-pink gerbera for the near neighbour

Materials for the groundwork

- 6 *Begonia rex* leaves
- 8 pieces of sedum
- 5 fir cones
- 5 *Hedera canariensis* leaves and trails
- 3 small bergenia leaves
- 5 cyclamen leaves
- 5 pieces of leatherleaf
- 10 dark-mauve carnations
- Selection of bun moss

Method

1. Put the liatris closely together in a vertical placement to form the main group. These will be the tallest group with the most impact. Next take the lilies and place to the right of the main group to form the neighbour group. The gerbera should be placed slightly to the back to form the near neighbour.

2. Start the groundwork by pinning bun moss around the base of the liatris to form a carpet effect from one side of the container to the other.

   Cut the carnations short (about 15 cm) and place vertically around the lilies slightly higher than the bun moss but with plenty of space between their tops and the liatris heads. There should be no gaps between any of the groundwork plant material. Support wire the fir cones and push into the foam around the base of the liatris on top of the bun moss.

3. Cut the sedum short and place around the base of the gerbera through from one side of the design to the other. Place three *Begonia rex* leaves on one side of the bun moss and two on the opposite side of the liatris in a layered effect. Place the leatherleaf horizontally to the right-hand side of the lilies. Insert the hedera trails below the bun moss in a horizontal position on one side of the design. Place the *Hedera canariensis* leaves next to each other below the carnations on the opposite side from the hedera trails. Step the five cyclamen leaves around the base of the leatherleaf.

Experimental (fantasy)

In this style almost anything goes and the florist is free to express him or herself without much restriction, although for any design to be pleasing and acceptable to the eye, the basic principles and design elements should be adhered to. However, in experimental design these principles and elements are stretched to the very limit.

It is not a style that is always practical for the commercial florist, but providing the materials used are accessing water and the finished product is transportable, then it is possible.

SUITABLE MATERIALS FOR EUROPEAN STYLES

Flowers	
Lilies (all varieties)	Orchids (cattleya, cymbidium, dendrobium)
Anthuriums	Clivia
Agapanthus	Waxflowers
Tuberose	Roses
Tulips	Anemones
Irises	Achillea
Amaranthus	Larkspur
Aconitums	Carnations
Lisianthus	Limonium
Delphiniums	Bouvardia
Gerbera	Brodiaea
Dill	Kangaroo paw
Sedum	Solidago
Dahlias	Peonies
Echinops	Ixia
Hypericum	Alliums
Heather	Stocks
Heliconia	Hydrangeas
Strelitzia	
Ranunculus	

Foliage	
Phormium tenax	Mixed fern
Hosta	Safari pack (foliage and mixed protea)
Senecio	Arbutus
Croton	Fir (all kinds)
Cordyline	Beech
Cyperus	Ivy (all kinds)
Cycas	Box
Bear grass	Myrtle
Euonymus	*Fatsia japonica*
Eucalyptus	Clematis
Bergenia	Contorted hazel and willow
Leatherleaf fern	Cornus
Nephrolepis	Vines
Camellia	
Blue pine	

Other materials	
Bun and Spanish moss	Fabric
Vegetables (cabbage, peppers, mushrooms, aubergines, etc.)	Cones
Coloured wire	Mixed seed heads (lotus, poppy)
	Flower stems

Virtually any kind of material can be used in European design, the choice depending on the style being created. If a parallel design is being made, straight stems should be chosen for the vertical placements and materials such as escallonia or ivy trails for the horizontal placements.

If a classic style is chosen, materials that have a natural curve should be used.

TERMS IN EUROPEAN WORK

Bunching Making material up into bunches and securing with wire or string to use as groundwork. This is particularly suitable for small flowers such as violets, snowdrops, forget-me-nots or similar plant material which will not go easily into foam as a single stem.

Continental style arrangement

Bundling Tying a number of stems together for ornamental effect. This can be done with any kind of tying medium, e.g. electrical tape in bright colours, raffia, string, coloured wire, ribbon or even strips of fabric.

Caging Using material to create a 'caged' effect around the main design. This technique can be applied to funeral, wedding designs, arrangements and hand-tied. Using a range of materials such as vine, bear grass, willow, coloured wires, etc. loops, latticing and more formal enclosure of the design can be achieved (see colour section).

Decorative Use of plant material in any way that the arranger wishes, whether it appears unnatural or not.

Groundwork/Basework This is used particularly in parallel design and gives a carpet effect under the main vertical placements. Variations in textures and height of the materials used form hills and valleys and pattern lines throughout the design. The groundwork should also have a colour link with the upright placements so as to create interest.

Layering Placing leaves or material closely together and overlapping, as on a laurel base or a foam sphere covered in leaves so as to give a flat finish.

Open work Using the space between groups created by the position of flowers in relation to their neighbour groups. Enhances the design by giving impact to its main focal area(s).

Stepping Placing materials like steps, with one below the other and space between each. This can be done vertically and horizontally.

Textures or blocking Grouping plant material of the same type and colour tightly together, so as to create impact. Materials can be of any height. This is used mostly for groundwork but also refers to any use of material in groups of one type.

Continental style bouquet

Vegetative Arranging seasonal flowers exactly as they grow outside. Summer flowers should not be used with winter material. Groundcover plants such as *Rubus tricolor* and hedera are positioned horizontally as they grow, whereas spring flowers are placed vertically. To achieve a correct vegetative design, the florist must be familiar with the seasons and with the way the plant material grows.

CHAPTER 11

Preserved and Artificial Material

DRIED FLOWERS AND MATERIALS

Over the past few years the range of dried flowers, seed heads, grasses and preserved material available to the florist has been improved and increased to provide an almost bewildering assortment of materials to choose from.

Dried flowers within the home were once confined to a vase of dusty pampas grass or faded helichrysum showing little or no thought in the creation of any sort of designed arrangement. Today, however, thanks to the improved range of materials available, dried flower displays are used in all parts of the home from the kitchen to the bedroom, ranging from country-style baskets, swags and garlands to scented rings and dramatic modernistic arrangements.

Dried flowers are also becoming increasingly popular as an alternative to fresh ones for wedding bouquets and headdresses. The fact that they can be kept for many years after the wedding is an advantage.

The methods of drying and preserving are of little importance to the florist, as few if any can afford the time and space to carry out this work. Dried flowers are so readily available and competitively priced that it makes sense to buy them ready for use. There are many specialist nurseries and growers in this country which produce and dry all sorts of materials. The range includes all the old favourites such as helichrysum, statice and achillea, as well as many other garden flowers like peonies, roses, alchemilla and gypsophila.

In recent years the general fashion for country garden flowers has led people to experiment with drying many more garden plants than previously, and a surprisingly large number of ordinary herbaceous and annual garden flowers respond very well to air drying and retain their colour and shape for many years.

A wide range of tropical or exotic materials now readily available from all over the world includes lotus seed heads, palm fronds and seeds, cones, protea and grasses. A lot of dried grasses and flowers are dyed after drying to increase the colour range. Many of these colours tend to look rather harsh and artificial but if used carefully and with other natural materials they can enhance a colour scheme by adding elements of colour otherwise not available.

One of the biggest drawbacks of using dried flowers is the lack of suitable foliage to include in an arrangement. Preserved foliage is available, but the general lack of fresh green material can sometimes make a dried arrangement look dull and lifeless. This can be partly overcome by the use of things like coloured sea lavender or mosses such as bun moss or lichen to cover the mechanics of a design and to provide the necessary 'padding' within an arrangement, rather than using more flowers to infill, which can result in an overcrowded design.

Dried materials associate particularly well with wicker and basketware containers, perhaps because of their similar country or rustic appearance. Some of the easiest designs to produce are simple mixed country-style baskets of flowers, seed heads and grasses, which can be used in almost any home setting. Other natural materials such as wood and terracotta also look particularly effective when used with dried flowers.

With this in mind the following information serves only as a general description of the various methods of drying and is not a how-to-do-it guide. Likewise the range of materials suitable for preserving is so great that it would be almost impossible to list them all. Those that are mentioned illustrate the wide range, and of particular interest are the garden flowers which, apart from being used within the trade as fresh flowers, can also be dried.

Tip

To keep dried flower arrangements looking fresh and dust free, clean them occasionally by blowing with a hairdryer set on the coolest setting.

Air Drying

Air drying is perhaps the easiest and most widely used method commercially. Flowers are hung upside down in loose bunches for a period of time depending on the flower type. The end result is a slightly desiccated form of the original flower still retaining the colour and overall shape. The preserved flower becomes quite brittle and should be handled with care to avoid damage.

Flowers dried in this way should be picked at the peak of development. If picked too late, they will shed their petals during the drying process. The so-called 'everlasting' flowers such as helichrysum, statice, acroclinium, etc. must be harvested just before the flower reaches full maturity, as they continue to open during drying. Flowers with papery petals respond well to air drying and this is demonstrated very well by feeling the texture of a fresh helichrysum bloom. Even when still on the plant, the flower has a dry papery feel to it and it is one of the easiest flowers to dry. Whatever material is being preserved, it should be harvested on a dry day when there is no moisture on the flower.

The process should be as fast as possible to reduce the risk of moulds attacking the bunches whilst they are drying. A dark, warm, dry, well-ventilated room or shed is ideal for this process. Special drying rooms are used at commercial dried flower nurseries. The flowers are harvested and hung on racks as quickly as possible and then wheeled into the drying rooms, where the atmosphere is carefully monitored to control the humidity levels in the air. Large quantities of materials can be dried within a short space of time in this way; also a greater range of flowers can be preserved, including roses, peonies and even dahlias.

Suitable materials	
Grasses	Fungi
Seed heads	Foliage (various)
Fir cones	Moss

Suitable flowers	
Achillea	Larkspur
Aconitum	Matricaria
Gypsophila	Sedum
Limonium	Hydrangeas
Peonies	Callistemon
Roses	Salix caprea (pussy willow)
Alchemilla	Celosia
Delphiniums	Zinnias
Mimosa	Eryngium
Statice	Lavender
Echinops	Astilbe
Molucella	Everlasting flowers
Dahlias	
Cornflowers	

Using Desiccants

Desiccants are useful for drying unusual and unexpected flowers which do not respond to air drying. Narcissi, camellias, violas and primroses are preserved beautifully by this method and can then be used as a point of interest among other dried materials in an arrangement, or better still as part of a display to be kept under a glass dome. This idea, which protects the flowers from dust and moisture, has once again become fashionable. The heyday of these glass-covered displays was the Victorian era, which saw large still-life compositions of fruit, flowers, leaves, birds and butterflies, many of which are still around today. The idea can easily be re-created using a mixture of air-dried and desiccant-dried flowers. Glass domes and bases are available from most good floristry wholesalers.

Different types of desiccants can be used with varying degrees of effectiveness. The commonest are silica gel crystals, borax powder and fine silver sand. A layer of drying material is spread to approximately half the depth of a container with a lid, such as a shoe box or biscuit tin. The chosen flower heads are placed onto the desiccant. The flowers should be in perfect condition, completely dry and free from any imperfections such as bruising or insect damage. Several flowers can be placed in one container but should not touch. It is best to use flowers of the same type or size in the same container so that they all dry at the same rate.

The desiccant is carefully sifted over the flower, ensuring that it goes between every petal and thus supports the shape of the flower before finally covering it with desiccant. Depending on the type of flower, drying can take anything from one to several weeks. Because of their structure, primrose, violet and freesia blooms do not take as long to dry as an orchid or daffodil. The surrounding desiccant draws the moisture from the flower, leaving it completely dry and papery to touch. Carefully remove the flower from the desiccant and with a soft paintbrush dust any remaining powder from the bloom. There might be a slight darkening of colour, particularly in red and blue flowers.

PRESSED FLOWERS

The art of pressed flowers is perhaps not particularly relevant to today's commercial floristry trade. However, there are still uses for this time-consuming method which are worth mentioning.

Only thin or very fine flowers, petals and leaves are suitable for pressing. Thicker leaves and flowers which have fleshy petals or blooms are not so successful because of the higher water content within the flower. The materials chosen should be free of any dampness and not marked or damaged in any way.

Remove the stems from any flowers which are to be used so that the heads can be flat. Clusters of flowers and buds should be separated and pressed individually and if need be re-assembled for the picture. Pieces of stem are very useful when making a picture and it is worth pressing a selection of these in different thicknesses and shapes. Form and shape are very important when constructing a pressed flower picture and this should be remembered when choosing foliage and leaves for preserving. The shape and outline of many ferns and leaves which are serrated or divided look far more effective within a picture than larger, heavier leaves.

The traditional method of pressing flowers is to place them between sheets of blotting paper within the pages of a large, heavy book. This is still perhaps the easiest way, although only small amounts of materials can be pressed at a time. Once the flowers have been placed in the book, it is a good idea to put several other books on top to increase the pressure.

The time of preserving will vary depending on the thickness of the flowers. It will usually take not more than two weeks for small flowers and leaves and anything up to four weeks for larger specimens. Because of this it is not a good idea to mix large and small flowers together on the same sheet for pressing. The preserved flowers will be very thin and papery and should be carefully stored between sheets of tissue paper in another book until used.

Purpose-made flower presses are available and although more costly than the book and blotting paper method they allow far more materials to be preserved at one time. With either method there will always be some loss of flower colour or discoloration. Again, blues and reds will darken, and pale colours, whites, creams and yellows will take on a brownish tint. This is not unattractive and only adds to the faded and muted effect of this type of work.

Obviously any material preserved in this way will end up very flat and can only be used in making pictures and collages. Pressed flowers and leaves can also be used to decorate boxes/books and containers by gluing them onto the object and then applying a coat of clear varnish.

True pressed flower pictures can be made using any type of picture frame and glass. Choose a suitably coloured piece of card or material-covered board as a background for the picture. Materials such as hessian, cotton and velvet provide interesting textures on which to display the flower. It is best to avoid shiny or glazed materials like satin or brocade. Arrange the picture first before gluing anything into position. This will allow the design to be altered or repositioned without any damage to the flower. Then, using a pair of tweezers to hold the flowers, carefully apply the smallest spot of any fast-drying household glue to fix the flower in place.

Frames that have a much deeper space between the back of the frame and the glass than ordinary picture frames are available from floristry wholesalers. Because of the greater depth under the glass, flowers, seed heads, nuts and cones can be combined with pressed leaves and flowers to create a more three-dimensional design. When the picture has been completed the back of the frame should be completely sealed with tape. Providing the picture is hung away from direct sunlight and in a dry atmosphere, it should last indefinitely.

Suitable flowers	
Violas	Primroses
Polyanthus	Freesias
Violets	Narcissi
Passiflora	Jasmine
Bougainvillea	Primula auricula
Clematis	Rose petals
Mimosa	Delphiniums
Pelargonium	Roses

Suitable foliage	
Bracken fern	Adiantum
Nephrolepis	maidenhair fern)
Boston fern)	Pelargonium
Acer	Clematis
Jasmine	Mimosa
Leatherleaf	Ivy

PRESERVED FOLIAGE

Pressed leaves are not suitable to include within a display, as they are far too delicate. Air drying foliage only results in a 'dead' look, the leaves becoming wrinkled and brittle. Preserving foliage with a mixture of glycerine and water, on the other hand, provides a useful range of materials which still retain their shape and flexibility. This method results in a very different finish from that of other drying processes, in which the materials become dry and somewhat brittle. Glycerine-preserved foliages do not break or shed their leaves but retain a softer, more pliable texture. This is retained long after the preserving process is complete, and leaves preserved in this way can be easily mixed with other dried materials for some very attractive effects.

Materials must be reasonably tough. Only mature leaves should be used, as young, soft growth will not preserve. Because of this, the majority of foliage used tends to be evergreens. Choose foliage at the peak of maturity, usually around mid or late summer. Pick sprays and branches of foliage of a manageable size.

Mix one part glycerine to two parts of boiling water and allow to cool. Trim the base of the stems and remove any leaves from the lower part of the stems. Stand loosely packed bunches of the foliage in jars containing approximately 5–10 cm of the liquid. The process can take several weeks to complete, especially for larger foliage. During this time the jars should be placed in a well-ventilated room away from direct sunlight or heat and checked regularly to top up the mixture as it becomes absorbed by the foliage. As this happens the foliage will change colour from its natural colour to varying shades of brown. This is quite normal and once all the foliage has changed colour it can be taken out of the liquid and stored for use either by carefully packing in tissue paper in a box or by hanging upside down in a cool, dark place.

If the stems are left too long in the solution, the surface of the leaves will become sticky, and if too much foliage is put into a jar, fungal moulds can attack the leaves during preservation.

The change of colour to brown is inevitable with this method but far from looking dead, the foliage assumes some wonderful autumnal shades of mahogany, chestnut and copper browns. As well as branches of foliage, individual leaves can be preserved in this way, providing only the tip of the leaf stalk is put in the liquid and the leaf itself is kept upright during the preserving.

Suitable foliage	
Ruscus	*Mahonia aquifolium*
Eucalyptus	Euonymus
Ligustrum ovalifolium	Bracken
Holly	
Beech, copper and green	

Suitable individual leaves	
Magnolia grandiflora	Epimedium
Mahonia	Aspidistra
Ficus elastica (rubber plant)	

ARTIFICIAL FLOWERS AND FOLIAGE

Silk or fabric, paper or plastic flowers and foliage provide a highly practical and attractive alternative to fresh displays in situations where the real thing is unsuitable. The reasons can be many, from a bride who suffers from hay fever, making fresh flowers unsuitable, to overheated hotel rooms or restaurants where fresh flowers would not survive for more than a few days. For certain types of contract work silk flowers and plants are the only choice for a successful display. The previous reluctance to use artificial flowers and plants has gradually disappeared thanks to the excellent quality and wide range of materials now available. Artificial flowers are now completely acceptable for use not only as a means of decoration in public buildings and the workplace but also in the home, in conservatories, as gifts and for weddings.

Not only are the more familiar commercial flowers and plants produced but also many

Silk arrangement

popular garden flowers such as antirrhinums, delphiniums and sweet peas; shrubs like forsythia, prunus and hydrangea; and tropical blooms such as lotus, strelitzia and anthurium. There is a whole range of flowers and leaves which resemble dried flowers. All these are so lifelike that it is almost impossible to tell them from the real thing. This is especially true of some of the larger tropical plants, used to great effect in shopping malls and leisure centres, in which silk leaves and flowers are attached to real stems, trunks and branches, giving a lifelike effect.

Fabric flowers are becoming increasingly popular for wedding floristry, with the advantage to the bride of keeping her bouquet intact after the wedding. All items of wedding floristry from corsages to large shower bouquets adapt well to being made with artificial materials. Indeed, it is sometimes easier to interpret a chosen colour scheme using silk rather than fresh flowers. The tones and shades of colour available enable the florist to combine colour effectively and with confidence, knowing that the right colour, however difficult, is always available and not subject to seasonal availability as is sometimes the case with fresh flowers. Another great advantage to the florist is that silk bouquets can be made well in advance, therefore avoiding the usual last-minute rush to complete orders on the morning of the wedding day to ensure the flowers are as fresh as possible for the ceremony (see colour section).

With any floristry work involving silk flowers, the same principles of design should be applied as for fresh flowers. There is a tendency to use more silk flowers in a design than when using fresh materials, and this results in an overpacked heavy piece of work. Most silk flowers are made with a few leaves attached to the stem but these are not always suitable to include in a bouquet or arrangement. The range of artificial leaves and foliage has increased in recent years to provide an excellent range and choice. It is well worth the extra cost of using some specially made silk foliage such as ivy trails, fern fronds or maranta leaves to add distinction and realism.

Silk arrangement

Alternatively, the use of long-lasting evergreen foliages such as ruskus, viburnum, laurel or bay arranged in a container with water provides an excellent base for displaying good-quality artificial flowers. Lilies, tulips, hydrangeas or hippaestrum are all good choices. This combination gives an even more realistic effect.

CHAPTER 12

Interior Landscaping

POT PLANTS

Pot plants, both flowering and foliage, play a large part in the florist's business. Although supermarkets, garden centres and garages sell a vast range of plants at very competitive prices, the florist may find that customers like to purchase seasonal flowering plants on a regular basis. It is a good idea to stock a range of these along with a varied selection of the more unusual plants that are not generally available.

To attract attention, the plants should be interestingly displayed in groups in baskets, large planters or attractive pots. Never buy flowering plants which are past their best.

Basic Plant Care

1. Ensure the plants have plenty of light but avoid direct sunlight.
2. Water regularly according to the plant's needs.
3. Feed plants with recommended plant food.
4. Avoid draughts.
5. Keep the foliage clean and free of dust.
6. Check on a daily basis for damage to leaves and any dead flowers which should be removed.
7. Flowering plants will need to be rotated more quickly and sold when in peak condition.

All pot plants sold should be supplied with a care card (this is *very* important), and they should be wrapped as shown on page 168.

Always have a good supply of compost, crocks and moss to be able to make up planted displays at short notice. Displays for peak periods need to be planned and made up in advance.

Most Popular Flowering Varieties for Peak Periods

St Valentine's Day

Miniature roses

Mothering Sunday

Bulb plants	Miniature roses
Narcissi	African violets
Hyacinths	Orchids
Primulas	Azaleas

Easter

Lily plants	Chrysanthemums
Hydrangeas	Bulb plants
African violets	

Summer

Geraniums	Begonias
Petunias	Campanula
Calendula	

Autumn

Pansies	Wallflowers
Ivies	

Christmas

Azaleas	African violets
Cyclamen	Orchids
Chrysanthemums	Poinsettias

Guide to Pot Plants

Common Name	Colour	Availability
	White	
Primula	*Primula obconica*	Jan–Jun
Cyclamen	Cyclamen	Sept–April
Wax begonia	*Begonia semperflorens*	AYR
African violet	Saintpaulia	AYR
White sails	*Spathiphyllum* 'Clevelandii'	AYR
Stephanotis	*Stephanotis floribunda*	AYR
Jasmine	*Jasminum auriculata*	Jan–May
Gloxinia	Gloxinia	AYR
	Yellow	
Yellow maple	*Abutilon × hybridum*	April–Sept
Chrysanthemum	Chrysanthemum	AYR
Begonia	*Begonia semperflorens*	AYR
Black-eyed Susan	*Thunbergia alata*	Summer
Tom thumb	*Kalanchoe blossfeldiana*	AYR
	Orange	
Chrysanthemum	Chrysanthemum	AYR
Begonia	*Begonia semperflorens*	AYR
Chinese hibiscus	*Hibiscus rosa-sinensis*	Summer
Bead plant	*Nertera granadensis*	AYR

Common Name	Colour	Availability
	Red	
Scarlet star	*Guzmania lingulata*	AYR
Red maple	*Abutilon hybridum*	April–Sept
Azalea	Azalea	AYR
Cyclamen	Cyclamen	Sept–April
	Pink	
African violet	Saintpaulia	AYR
Flamingo flower	*Anthurium andraeanum*	AYR
Busy lizzie	*Impatiens walleriana*	AYR
Azalea	Azalea	AYR
Urn plant	*Aechmea fasciata*	AYR
	Purples & Blues	
Italian bellflower	*Campanula isophylla*	Late summer
African violet	Saintpaulia	AYR
German violet	*Exacum affine*	May–Nov
Hydrangea	Hydrangea	Spring–autumn

Shapes and Sizes

Shape	Plant	Size: Small	Med.	Large
Upright	*Pilea cadierei*	✓		
	Abutilon	✓		
	Ficus elastica		✓	✓
	Dracaena sanderiana		✓	✓
	Dieffenbachia 'Exotica'		✓	✓
	Cordyline terminalis		✓	✓
	Aspidistra elatior		✓	✓
	Strelitzia reginae		✓	✓
	Aglaonema crispum			
Spiky-leaved upright	*Sanseviera trifasciata*		✓	✓
	Dracaena marginata		✓	✓
	Yucca elephantipes		✓	✓
	Cocos nucifera			
Arching	*Spathiphyllum*		✓	✓
	Pellaea rotundifolia	✓		
	Philodendron bipinnatifidum			✓
	Nephrolepis exaltata		✓	
	Ficus benjamina		✓	✓
	Chamaedorea elegans		✓	
Rosetted	*Aechmea fasciata*			
	Vriesia splendens		✓	
	Tillandsia cyanea		✓	
	Asplenium nidus		✓	
	Ananas comosus		✓	
	Guzmania lingulata		✓	
	Cryptanthus bivittatus	✓		
	Saintpaulia	✓		
	Streptocarpus		✓	
	Sinningia speciosa		✓	
Bushy	*Begonia elatior*		✓	
	Coleus blumei	✓	✓	
	Impatiens	✓		
	Hibiscus rosa-sinensis		✓	
	Pelargonium		✓	
	Senecio cruentus		✓	
	Euphorbia pulcherrima		✓	
	Rhododendron simsii		✓	
	Cyclamen persicum		✓	

Shape	Plant	Size: Small	Med.	Large
Bushy	*Peperomia caperata*	✓	✓	
	Chrysanthemum morifolium		✓	
	Primula obconica		✓	
	Achimenes grandiflora		✓	
Large-leaved bushy	*Fatsia japonica*			✓
	Caladium × hortulanum		✓	✓
	Aphelandra squarrosa		✓	
	Begonia rex		✓	✓
Small-leaved bushy	*Adiantum raddianum*			
	Pteris cretica			
Climbing	*Hedera* (all varieties)	✓	✓	✓
	Cissus rhombifolia		✓	✓
	Stephanotis floribunda		✓	
	Passiflora caerulea		✓	
	Cissus antarctica		✓	✓
	Jasminum polyanthum		✓	✓
	Plumbago auriculata		✓	✓
Large-leaved climber	*Philodendron* 'Burgundy'			✓
	Syngonium podophyllum		✓	✓
	Monstera deliciosa		✓	✓
Trailing	*Philodendron scandens*		✓	✓
	Zebrina pendula		✓	
	Hoya bella		✓	
	Tradescantia albiflora		✓	
	Columnea × banksii		✓	
	Scindapsus pictus		✓	
	Tolmiea menziesii		✓	
	Chlorophytum comosum		✓	
	Hedera	✓	✓	✓
Creeping	*Soleirolia soleirolii*	✓	✓	
	Selaginella martensii	✓		
	Nertera granadensis	✓		
	Fittonia verschaffeltii	✓	✓	
	Ficus pumila	✓	✓	
	Begonia Tiger	✓	✓	

INTERIOR DESIGN

Plants are now very popular as an aspect of the interior design of a building, and the florist often gets requests for containers planted with indoor plants to complement the interior of an office building, hotel reception area or entrances to a public building.

It is essential to do a site visit to ascertain what will be best suited to the area requiring decoration and to decide which plants are compatible with the surrounding conditions. There are a number of points to consider when looking at a site:

- Lighting
- Temperature
- Draughts
- Flow of people

Many kinds of containers and planters are available:

- Traditional urns and decorated square planters in stoneware
- Terracotta in many varied shapes
- Coloured ceramic
- Fibreglass, round and square
- Basketware with liners
- Wooden planters

They are available in many different shapes and sizes and may be used individually or grouped together. Remember that all containers in a group should be of the same type, i.e. all terracotta or ceramic. Grouped displays work very well in both large and small areas, depending on the size of the planters.

The customer usually likes to be involved in the choice of containers and will be happy to purchase a range of containers on your advice.

Unusual containers may be used if the customer wishes. In a restaurant an antique birdcage planted with scindapsus, ivy or *Ficus pumila* might look very good hanging from the ceiling, or a large Victorian washbowl filled with plants of one type placed on a side table can have tremendous impact.

It is important to remember that the plants need to be in the correct proportion to the size of the container and that there should be enough room for the roots to be able to grow.

The container should be carefully considered. Try to match or complement its colour, texture and style with the plants and their surroundings.

If the area to be planted is traditional, perhaps a Victorian building, then the choice should be glazed ceramic planters or traditional urns. On the other hand, if the area is ultra-modern with lots of glass and chrome, then glass or fibreglass planters would be more suitable. Terracotta or basketware could be used in a less formal setting.

The type of grouping will depend on the space available and the varieties of plants to be used. A selection of planters in the same shape and material but in different sizes planted with the same variety of plant in different sizes can look very impressive.

The same principles of design apply to creating a planted display as to a flower arrangement. It needs to be visually attractive and in proportion to its surroundings. Points to consider include height of plants, texture of leaves and any flowers, leaf shape, colour and compatibility of plants with each other.

A large display can be based on plants up to 3 metres high with underplanting of smaller plants and trailing plants added to give depth.

Seasonal flowering plants can be added if there is a contract for maintenance. These need to be regularly maintained and changed.

Colourful foliage plants can be used to reflect the colour or the decor. Leaf shape also adds to interest; try to choose a combination of shapes and textures. A combination of yuccas underplanted with maidenhair fern would give an interesting contrast of texture and shape. Some plants are not compatible with others in terms of care and this should be borne in mind. African violets, for example, should be watered at the base, as they do not like to be sprayed, whereas ferns need to be sprayed because they absorb a lot of moisture through their leaves.

A written quotation should be sent for approval after the possibilities have been discussed with the customer. It is a good idea to have a weekly maintenance contract. This means that the plants will be watered, fed and cleared regularly. Arrangements for replacing plants should also be costed into the maintenance contract.

PLANTED BOWLS

Planted bowls are always a popular choice with the customer and are very acceptable as a gift. They last longer than an arrangement of flowers, and they are also viewed as being better value for money.

The principles of design which contribute to a good flower arrangement apply equally to the construction and choice of material for a planted bowl.

Height is needed to balance the necessarily deep container. If there is no suitably tall plant, then a piece of bark or driftwood can be used to give the required height. Trailing plants flowing over the rim of the container reduce the size and break any hard lines.

The planted bowl can be made up with flowering and foliage plants or just foliage plants. Variety in leaf form and texture creates interest: e.g. a bold-leafed *Begonia rex* looks well against the delicate foliage of a maidenhair fern and variegated leaves offset green shiny ones.

Seasonal flowering plants like daffodils, hyacinths or spring plants are suitable for Easter or Mothering Sunday and poinsettias for Christmas. Accessories such as Christmas ribbon or baubles or Easter chicks may be used to give a seasonal flavour.

Materials

- Bowl, basket or customer's own container. It should be waterproof, large enough to take several plants and deep enough for the root ball of the largest plant to be at least 2.5 cm below the rim of the container to allow for watering.

Planted bowl

- Broken crocks, leica or gravel. This will provide drainage and keep the container from becoming waterlogged.
- Small pieces of charcoal. This helps to stop bacteria forming and keeps the water from becoming stale and harming the roots of the plants.
- A good potting compost which is sterilised and contains the three essential plant nutrients: nitrogen, phosphate and potash. It is a good idea to add peat to the soil when removing the plants from their pots as this allows for the roots to settle.
- Pot plants. Choose ones which are compatible with each other. Saintpaulias, which should always be watered from below, are often used with plants which can only be watered from the top and so do not survive for long.

  It is a good idea to have a selection of tall plants, trailing plants and round plants. A good planting for a medium-sized bowl would be Kentia palm, *Asplenium nidus*, *Peperomia caperata*, *Adiantum raddianum* and *Hedera helix* 'Glacier'. These all have green foliage but are chosen for the different hues, textures and leaf shapes which create interest. The *Asplenium nidus* could be replaced with a seasonal flowering plant.
- Moss, sphagnum or bun moss, wood chip or leica, to cover any loose soil.
- Ribbon, if required, providing it is in keeping with the plants, e.g. hessian ribbon.

Ensure that all the plants are in perfect condition with no damaged leaves. If the leaves are dirty, wipe them with damp cotton wool. Make sure the root ball is moist.

Set the plants in their pots out on the workbench and arrange them into a design to ensure that the effect will be pleasing when placed in the bowl.

Line the bottom of the container with the drainage material. Cover the crocks with a fine layer of soil. Sprinkle some pieces of charcoal onto the soil.

Gently knock the plants out of their pots and arrange as planned in the container. Add more soil, filling in any gaps, and press down gently but firmly. Cover any bare areas of soil with moss, bark, leica or stones.

Decorate with suitable accessories, seasonal novelties or ribbons as required. Make sure the container is clean and add a care card.

Pot-et-fleur

POT-ET-FLEUR

This is a planted bowl which consists of foliage plants with the addition of cut flowers. It is made in exactly the same way as a planted bowl except that when the plants are placed into the container, a small container with either water or foam in it is also added.

The flowers are then arranged in the small container, with usually only one type of flower being used. Colour is important: for example, if pink flowers such as lilies are used, it is a good idea to select at least one foliage plant of similar colour, such as a *Begonia rex*.

When the flowers die they can be removed but the design should still appear complete and pleasing to the eye. The choice of cut flower should be in suitable proportion to the plants. Large lilies would not look right with small plants; neither would freesias look right with large plants.

The cut flowers in a pot-et-fleur usually provide a focal area. If too many flowers are used they can detract from the design and give a muddled appearance.

DISH GARDENS

This is a planted arrangement in the form of a miniature garden. It looks most effective when made using miniature spring bulbs mixed in with foliage plants. Part of the design should include miniature pathways of stones or bark and there should be areas of moss and gravel.

The planting techniques are the same as for a planted bowl. The design is made in a meat dish or shallow container which has some depth in the centre. The edge of the container is shallow and only allows for small plants with very small root balls. Ideal plants would be cryptanthus, club moss and small lichens or succulents. The plants in the centre should be taller to give some height and create a pleasing landscape effect in the design.

Care should be taken to place the plants so that those requiring less water are grouped away from those which require more water.

TERRARIA AND BOTTLE GARDENS

Both terraria and bottle gardens are made of glass, and when plants are placed inside there is a very humid environment as the moisture given off by the plants runs down the inside of the glass back into the soil.

The choice of plants must be limited to small, slow-growing ones. It is a good idea to avoid flowering plants as they quickly fade. A selection of interesting variegated plants looks very attractive.

The container must be very clean before anything is put inside as bacteria will build up very quickly.

Materials

Funnel made of stiff paper
Kitchen fork and spoon and an empty cotton reel taped on to canes to give extra length so as to reach the bottom of the bottle or terrarium
Small piece of sponge

Suitable plants

Cryptanthus	Club moss
Maidenhair fern	*Pteris cretica*
Fittonia (various)	Mind-your-own-business
Eyelash begonia	*Pellaea rotundifolia*
Polka dot plant	Parlour palm

The same principles apply for drainage, charcoal and soil as for the planted bowl. The funnel is used to put the soil in, and the materials are carefully positioned with the fork and spoon. The plants should be placed in an attractive group with space between each one to allow for growth. Any areas of bare soil can be covered with moss. The cotton reel is used to firm down the plants once they are in the required position. The sponge is used to clean soil off the inside of the glass. Some interest can be added with pebbles or small pieces of rock.

CHAPTER 13

Presentation and Packaging

Packaging is a vitally important area of the florist's work. It does not have to be expensive to look good. The simplest form tastefully done can be just as pleasing as something which has expensive ribbons and paper but is poorly presented and untidy (see colour section).

MATERIALS USED IN PACKAGING

Flat paper, *Roll paper* — shop name, address, telephone number and relay organisation should be printed clearly on it

Cellocoup — cellophane; available in different qualities, plain or decorated

Crepe paper — coloured and metallic available

Tissue paper — plain white and coloured

Ribbon — many different kinds

- *Polypropylene* (waterproof) — can be split and curled; available in many colours
- *Satin ribbon* (not waterproof) — cannot be split; available in different widths and many colours; can be plain or decorated
- *Paper ribbon* (not waterproof) — available in different widths and many colours; appears to be wrinkled; ideal for a natural look
- *Heavy brocade ribbon*(not waterproof) — very expensive; looks stunning on the right gift
- *Moiré taffeta ribbon* (not waterproof) — also very expensive but very special
- *Velvet ribbon* (not waterproof) — gives a sense of luxury and looks good with fruit and Christmas designs
- *Hessian ribbon* (some kinds are waterproof) — ideal for basket designs and natural colours

Cord and braid — can be used in place of ribbon for tying bouquets

Raffia — used for tying packages, also as a decorative medium, especially with terracotta

Message or gift cards and envelopes — a good range should be well displayed so that the customer can choose the card most appropriate for the occasion

Sticky labels — small labels, bearing shop name, address and telephone/fax number

Staplers, scissors, Sellotape — all are a must

Single flower box — available in gold, silver, white and green. Suitable for a single rose or other flower

Acetate cylinder — a cheaper version of the single box but can take more than one flower and can look very attractive

Boxes for cut flowers — one of the best methods of packaging cut flowers, as they are completely protected, but it does make the overall price more expensive

Flower food — should be added to all cut flower presentations

Care card — a general care card is available for most popular flowers, but a specific card should be supplied for flowers such as roses, lilies and freesias. Pot plants usually have a care card label on them when purchased from the wholesaler

MAKING BOWS

There are a number of different methods of making a bow but the quickest and easiest for packaging is to use polypropylene ribbon, which can be split to any width required.

1. Tear some narrow strips about 60 cm in length and put to one side. These will be used for tying the bow.
2. Wind the ribbon round in a loop approximately 18 cm long. Do this four times.

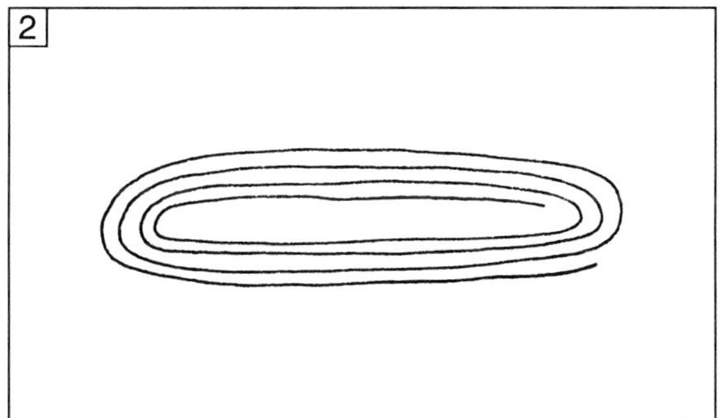

3. Tie the loop tightly in the centre with a narrow strip. Pull out the loops to form the bow.

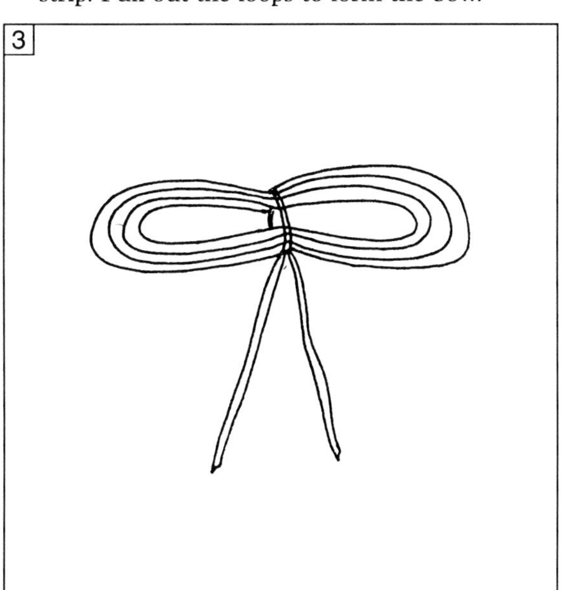

Tip

It is impossible to cut even strips of polypropylene ribbon. Tearing gives much better results.

4. The long tails left from the strips will be used to attach the bow to the bouquet.

Another method of making a bow is to use reel wire.

1. Bind round the ribbon.

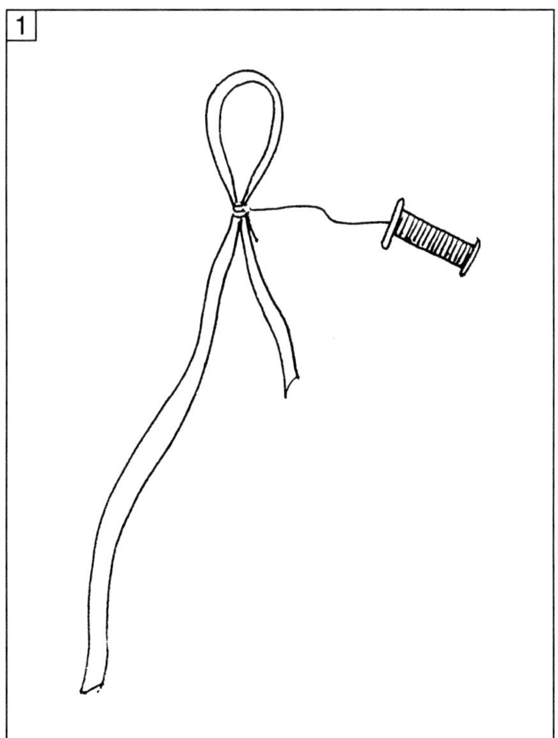

2. As each loop is made the wire is wound round, keeping it at one binding point.

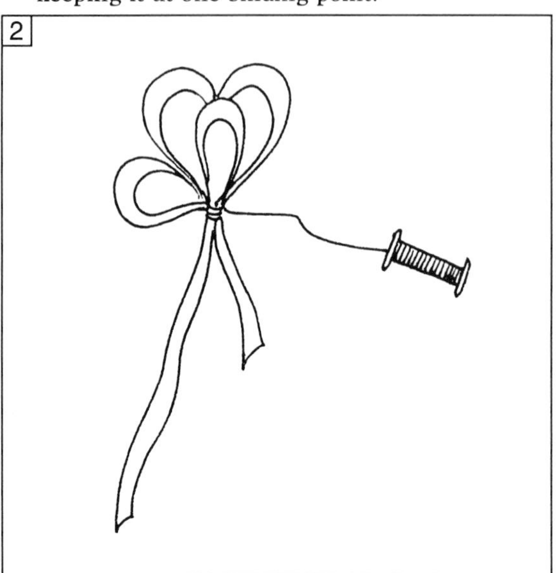

3. Continue adding loops until there are enough to create an attractive bow.

MESSAGE AND CARE CARDS

All materials which have been packaged for collection or delivery should bear a message card inside an envelope which has been clearly written and secured to the design so that it is clearly visible to both the delivery driver and the recipient.

Care cards and cut flower food should also be attached to every order that leaves the shop.

WRAPPING METHODS

All flowers and plants should be wrapped before leaving the shop. This is done to protect the materials from the elements and to ensure they are not damaged in transit. This will also advertise the business, as the wrapping paper should bear the name of the shop. Flowers can be gift wrapped to make them that bit more special. The customer is very drawn to attractive packaging. Flowers are considered a luxury and should always be displayed attractively, whether they are a small bunch of spray carnations or a large bouquet of roses.

Tip

Select wrapping paper which is complementary to the corporate image.

The Cone Wrap

This is the simplest form of packaging and is the method used for all cut flower or plant sales over the counter. Paper and cellocoup can be dispensed from a roll or used as flat pieces.

Method

1. Select a piece of paper large enough to wrap the flowers or plant in.

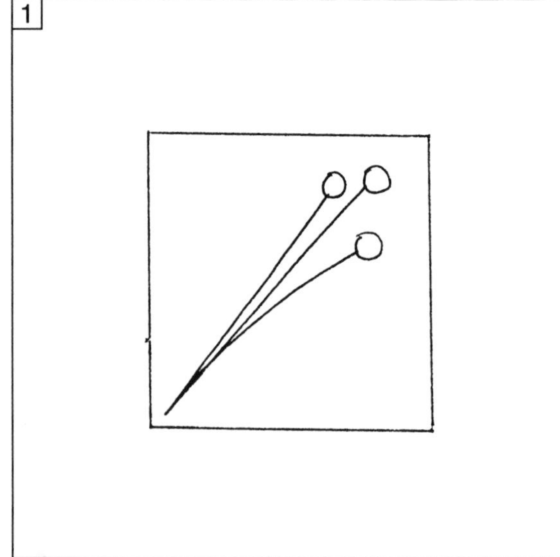

2. Place the flower, or plant, diagonally across the square of paper and fold both sides over to form a cone. Sellotape to secure. The top may be folded over to protect the flowers.

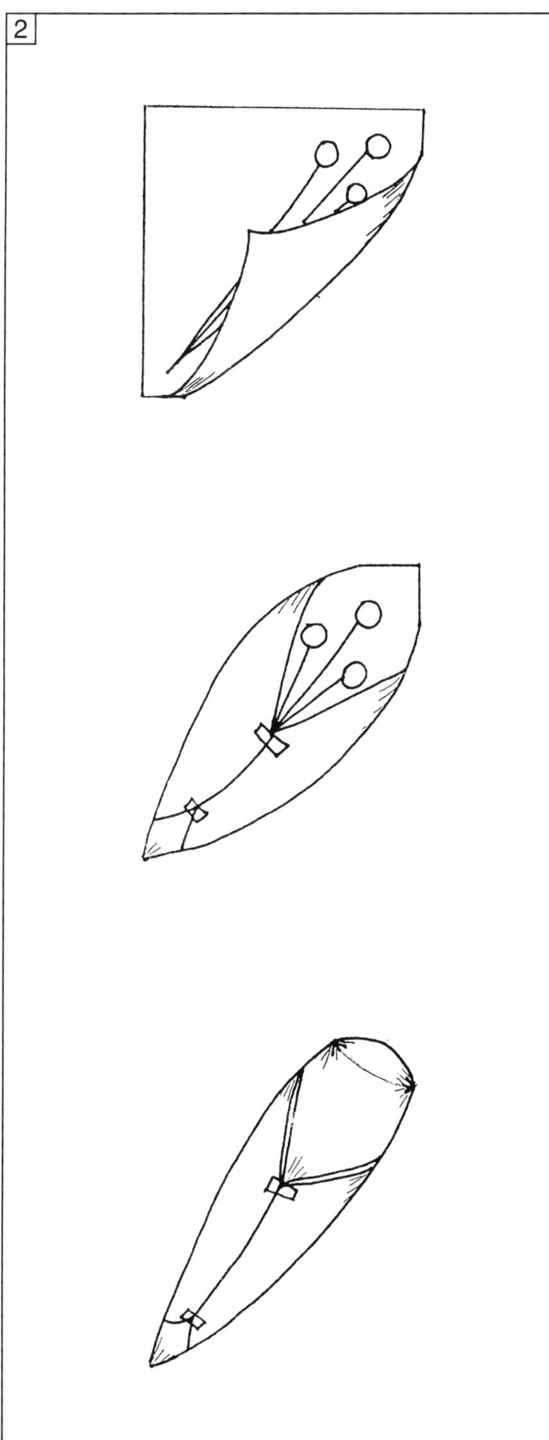

If the flowers are a gift, the wrap can be tied with ribbon or raffia, or braid and a bow added. This is an ideal way of gift wrapping a few roses or a small number of special flowers.

Wrapping a Flat Bouquet

Few florists nowadays buy ready-made bags for a flat bouquet, as it is cheaper, easier and quicker to make their own to the size required with readily available cellophane. Cellophane also looks much nicer than ready-made bags with a paper backing.

Method

1. Take a sufficient length of cellophane to cover front and back of the flowers and fold in half. Lay the paper on the bench with the fold to the left. Fold the top and staple neatly.

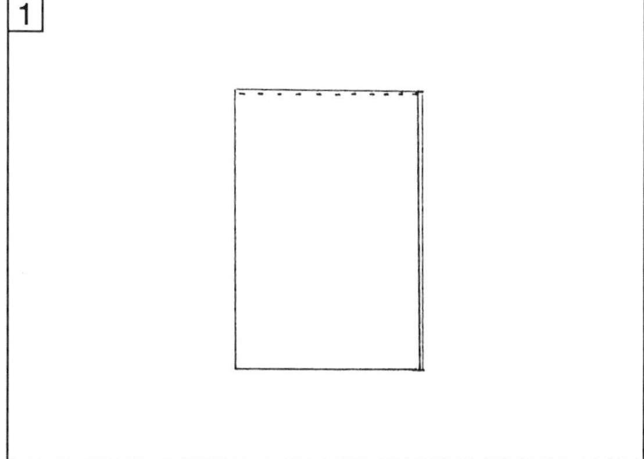

2. Lift the top layer and fold over. The flowers and foliage which have been selected should be arranged attractively in the bag. Remember not to squash the flowers at the top. There should be space between each flower so that it can be seen. Never place one flower on top of another.

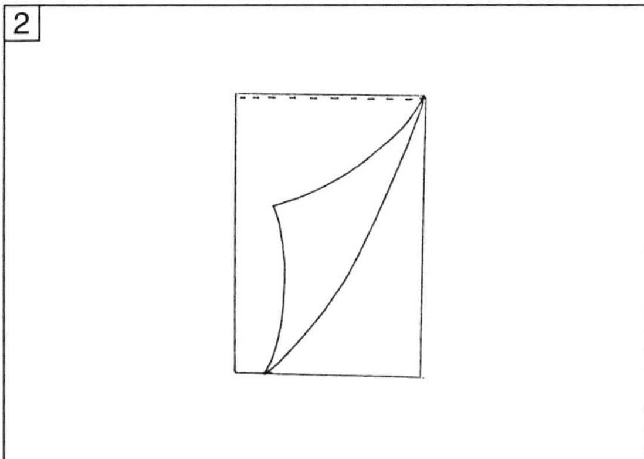

3. The customer has paid for the stems as well as the flowers, so the stems should not be cut but left long and protruding from the bottom. Some people like to cover the stems to retain their moisture. After a pleasing arrangement has been made, tie the flowers together to form a bunch. Bring the top piece of cellophane over the flowers and fold neatly and staple down the side.

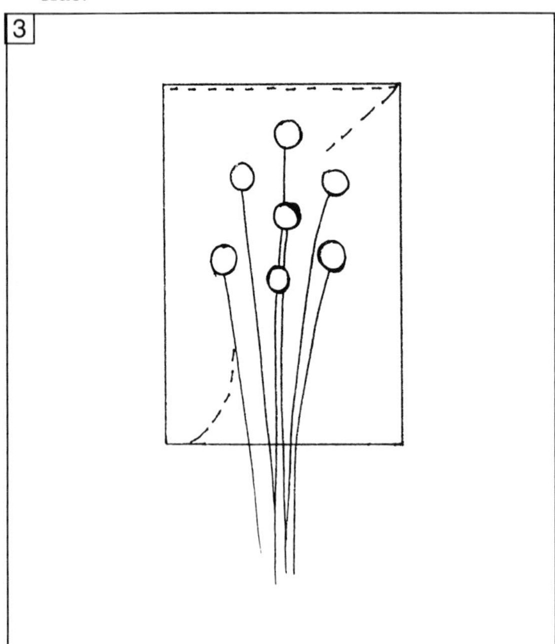

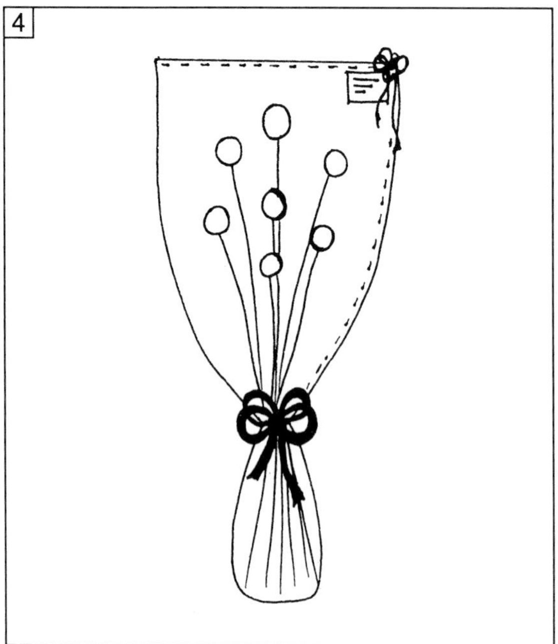

4. Two-thirds down the length of the bouquet, gather the cellophane at the tying point and tie with a narrow piece of ribbon. Cover the stems neatly with another piece of cellophane to protect the stems and reduce dehydration. Secure the bow at the tying point and add the flower food and care card with sellotape beneath it.

The gift card should be written clearly and attached with a pin to the top left- or right-hand corner of the bouquet. A small bow matching the large bow may be added to the gift card. It is important to select ribbon which is complementary to the colour of the flowers and ensure it is in proportion to the size of the bouquet.

Wrapping a Tied Assembly

Hand-tied bouquets are becoming more and more popular, especially when aqua packed. The customer has only to take the packaging off and place the bouquet in a vase without further attention. There are various ways of packing this style of bouquet, the simplest form being to use two squares of cellophane (below) large enough to come up the sides of the bouquet to form a collar around the design (see colour section).

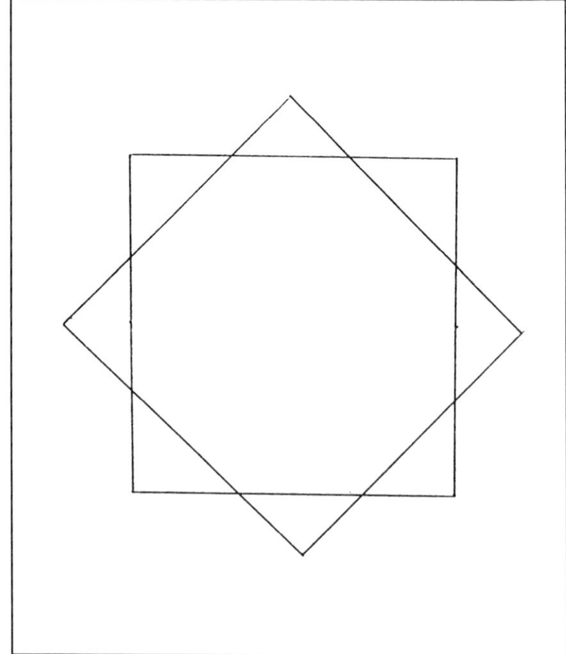

Place the all-round tied in the centre of the cellophane, which is then folded up around the bouquet and tied with string at the tying point.

Pull the cellophane out to form a frill around the bouquet. The tying point should be very firm.

Attach the flower food and care card to the tying point with sellotape. A bow can then be tied in the same place. Put the message card onto a pick and push into the bouquet, ensuring it is clearly visible.

To aqua pack, water is added by carefully pouring into the centre of the bouquet. The water line should not come above the tying point, as it would then spill.

This method of packing is ideal during peak periods because it enables the florist to make up bouquets in advance. It is also a good method of having ready-made bouquets in the shop for impulse purchases. Anything from a small bouquet of violets to a large bouquet of lilies may be presented in this way.

Ready-made circles of cellophane are available in different colours, and using two of these looks most effective. Cut a hole in one circle and place around the bouquet, as shown below. Fold up the second circle around the stems; then tie and add the bow, care card and flower food. This can look very effective if the colour harmony is good.

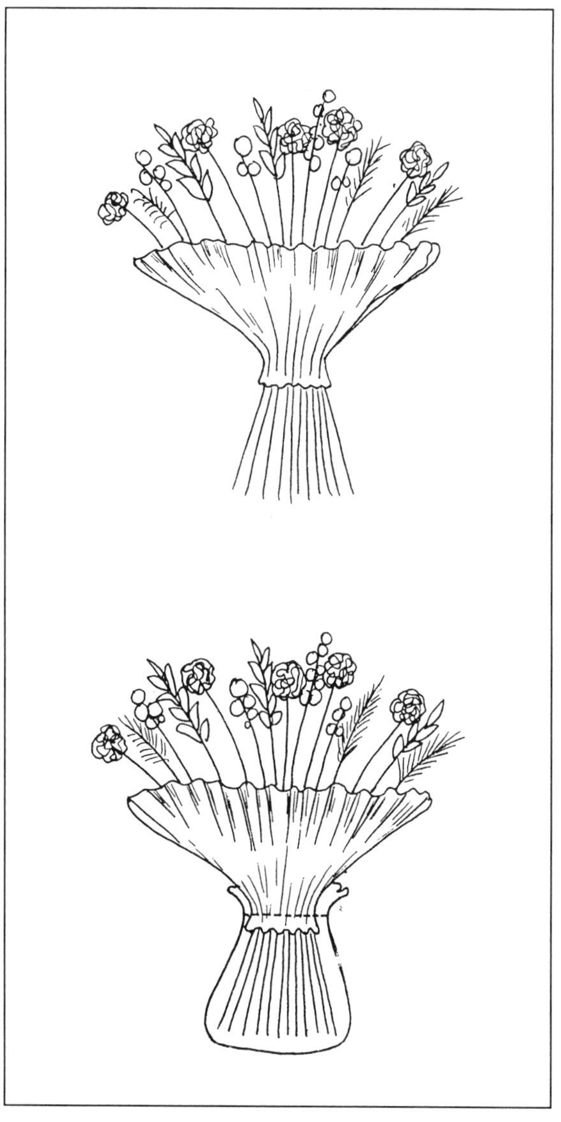

If the top of the hand-tied is to be covered, place a square of cellophane on top of the bouquet, bringing the sides down and tying with string at the tying point. Care should be taken not to pull the cellophane too tightly and hence squash the flowers.

A hand-tied bouquet can also be wrapped in the cone wrap method with cellophane and a bow. To make it more attractive a small bow attached at the top with a long tail linked to the main bow looks very effective.

Wrapping a Pot Plant

Once the plant has been selected, ensure the plant is not damaged and clean the pot with a cloth. Remove the price, as for all gift wrapped items. Take some tissue paper and form a loose sausage to wrap round the base of the plant. This stops the soil from falling out and protects the stem. At this stage a toning bow may be added to the plant. Cut a piece of paper which is large enough to cover the plant on all sides. Place the plant pot on its side diagonally across the square. Fold both sides of the paper as well as the bottom over the plant and secure with sellotape.

Stand the plant up and bring over the top of the paper, securing it with either sellotape or a shop sticker. A bow may then be added with the message card and care card on the top left- or right-hand corner (see colour section).

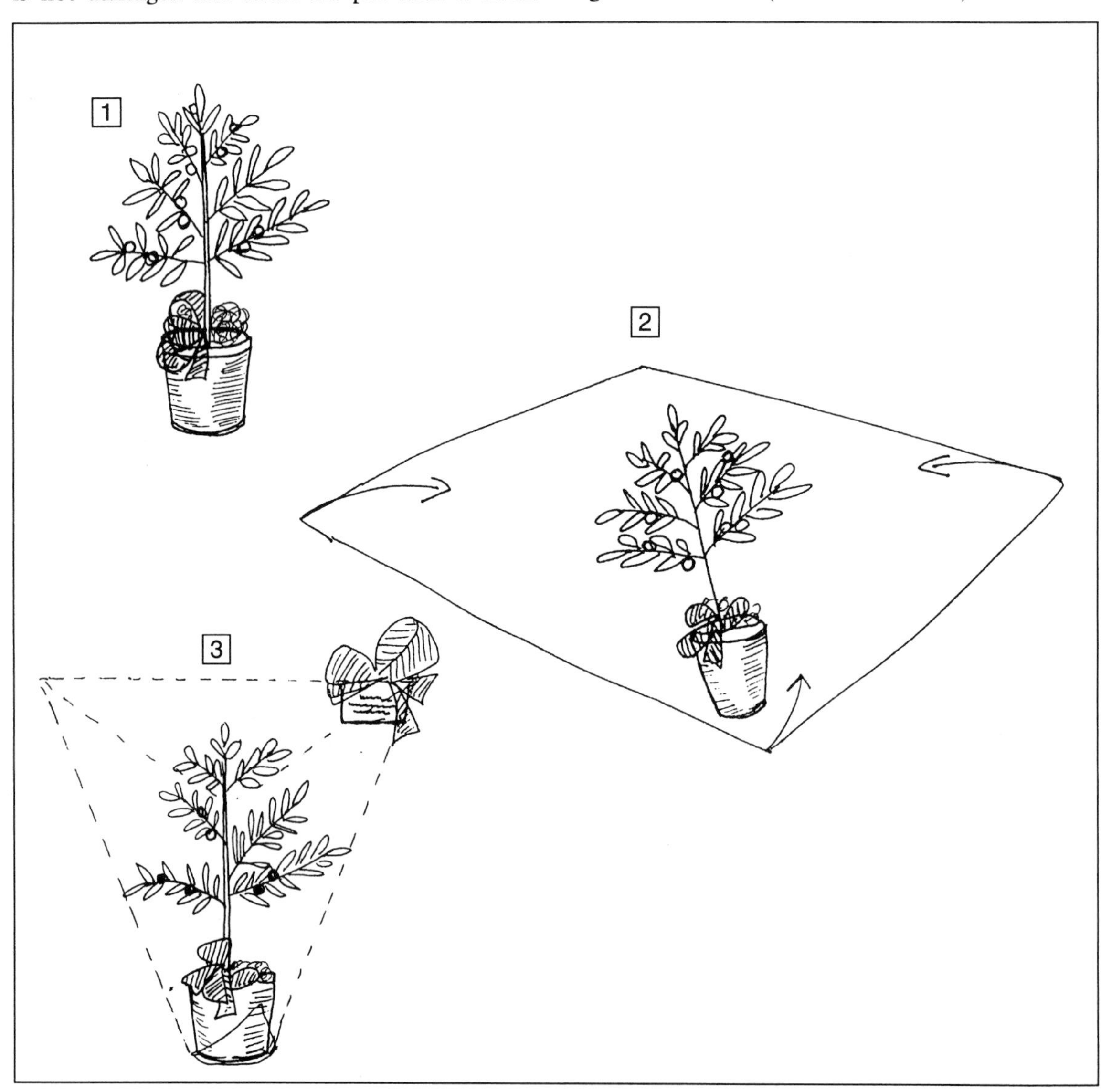

Wrapping a Single Flower

In a box

Many different boxes are available for the florist and most are similar in design. Inside the box there is usually a liner which can be taken out. A cellophane window on the box protects the flower completely but enables it to be seen.

A single flower should be in perfect condition. It is usually a red rose or carnation but other flowers may be used. The flower should be measured against the length of the box to ensure it will fit. The flower stem is placed into a small bottle containing water which has a rubber cap with a hole in it through which the stem is inserted. A piece of fern may be added at this point.

Lay the flower and bottle onto the liner and with a piece of very narrow ribbon tie through the holes in the liner to secure the flower. The liner can then be placed into the box. The bottle should stay in place at the bottom of the box. Some boxes have a piece of card at the bottom shaped to hold the bottle in place.

When the flower has been placed into the box the top flap is secured with sellotape. The box can then be decorated with a ribbon bow and the message card and care card attached with sellotape.

In an acetate cylinder

This is a slightly cheaper way of presenting a single flower. The cylinder is completely clear and the flower can be seen at all angles.

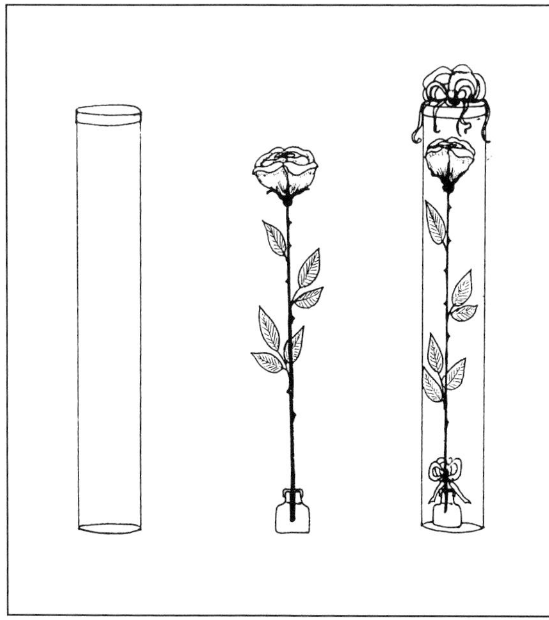

Having made sure that the flower is a suitable length for the cylinder, place it into a small plastic tube with a rubber cap which has been filled with water. A bow may be tied to the stem. Place the flower in the cylinder and secure the lid with sellotape.

The cylinder can be decorated with a suitable ribbon by either attaching a bow to the lid or winding ribbon around the cylinder from top to bottom.

Boxed Cut Flowers

This is one of the nicest ways of presenting cut flowers as a gift, but it is more expensive than the cellophane gift wrap.

Boxes are available in different sizes. Sometimes there is a liner with holes, which enable the flowers to be tied with ribbon. If there is no liner, then the flowers can be tied together when placed in the box.

Make sure the correct-sized box is chosen to accommodate the stem length, as stems should never be cut to fit the packaging. The packaging should be suitable for the stem length. Arrange the materials in layers so that the flower heads are easily seen.

Flower food and a care card should be placed inside the box beside the stems. The lid is then secured with sellotape and the message card attached to the end of the box. A bow should be attached on the top right- or left-hand corner.

This is a good way of packing flowers at peak period trading times, when the delivery van is very full, as the boxes can be stored one on top of the other on a shelf. The driver can easily see the names and addresses on the cards on the ends of the boxes.

Another way of packing flowers in a box is to line the box with tissue paper toning in colour with the flowers. Alternatively, if, for example, the box is gold and longiflorum lilies or a dozen roses have been ordered, gold tissue paper can be scrunched and laid between the flower heads. This looks very chic and expensive, but costs very little.

Wrapping a Planted Bowl

The bowl must be absolutely clean with no bits of soil dropping off. A gold or silver cake board or a board covered in attractive paper or fabric can be used as a base, which makes the planted bowl more easily transportable. This is placed on a large piece of cellocoup, which is drawn up over the plants and tied with a ribbon bow with the tails split and curled. The care card and greetings card are sellotaped to the cellocoup at a point which can be easily seen.

Preparing a Box for Wedding Bouquets

All wedding work should be packed very carefully and also attractively. The bottom of a flower box turned upside down and with holes cut for the bouquet handles makes a secure holder. It should be covered in plain paper (very busy patterned paper detracts from the flowers); gold or silver looks very nice. Usually two or three boxes are required if there are bridesmaids' bouquets, headdresses and buttonholes. Cellocoup should then be placed over the designs and secured with sellotape. Great care should be taken not to squash the flowers. Good-quality cellocoup should stand on its own above the flowers.

Another method of presenting wedding work is to cover the box lid inside and out with paper, then scrunch up tissue paper and make a bed with it inside the box. The handle of the bouquet can be wrapped loosely with more tissue. A plain piece of tissue should be laid over the scrunched tissue and the bouquet will nestle on the tissue. Headdresses, buttonholes and corsages should then be placed around the bouquets. Cellophane should be placed over the box and secured with sellotape. A bow

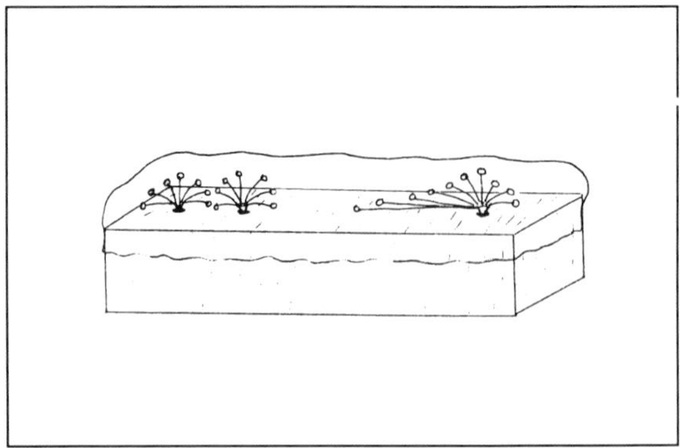

matching those used in the bouquet work is added to a corner of the box.

An envelope with the bride's name and address should be secured on the side of the box. A nice touch is to put in a greetings card with a message wishing the bride a happy day.

Individual corsages or buttonholes can be placed in small acetate boxes decorated with ribbon. These are available in various sizes.

Packing a Funeral Tribute for a Car Journey

Sometimes a customer wishes to take a funeral tribute by car to the funeral. A paper-covered box of the correct size for the tribute should be selected. The tribute should be placed on scrunched-up tissue paper with a piece of tissue over it.

CHAPTER 14

Presentation for the Flower Shop

A corporate image is very important nowadays. People like to identify with smart presentation.

Choose a colour scheme which runs throughout the shop, from the colour of the paintwork through to paper used for wrapping packages. The colour choice should be fairly neutral so that it does not detract from the products on display. All the various colours of the materials in a flower shop can appear very muddled and confusing to the eye unless thought and care are given to the display. Products should be grouped together by colour and type.

The colour scheme of a corporate image should be used for the logo on stationery, shop paper, business cards, uniform and any promotional stationery such as leaflets. The logo should appear on the van, which should also reflect the shop's image. Wrapping paper should be printed with the shop logo, and remember to have the relevant details – e.g. shop name, address, telephone/fax number – clearly visible to the customer. A supply of stickers with the same details is invaluable as these can be attached to any kind of product from a box of flowers to a card on a funeral piece. Cards and envelopes should be printed with the shop details.

Shop staff should wear uniforms, which should also coordinate with the general colour scheme. Name badges are a good idea so that the customer can identify the member of staff. Staff should be clean and tidy. Smoking and drinking or eating food should not be allowed in the shop at any time.

Tip

Select wrapping paper which is complementary to the corporate image.

The shop front should also reflect the logo and colour scheme. The shop fittings should have a commonality: if pine furniture is used, then shelving should also be pine, just as glass and chrome, if used, should be repeated throughout the shop.

Containers for cut flowers should all be of the same material – glass, aluminium or plastic. It is unnecessary nowadays to use buckets for shop displays, as some very attractive cheap containers are available. If you have a mixture of containers you might invest in some baskets of different sizes and put the odd containers inside them. This could also be done using terracotta pots of different sizes. It is worth the investment to give a pleasing display at all times.

Flower shops look very attractive with plants and flowers displayed outside if possible. Stick to one colour harmony at a time as this will have more impact and customer appeal.

The window should be attractive at all times and should be changed frequently. Peak periods should obviously be promoted at the relevant times. There is a tendency to overcrowd the window with a wide range of products but just one large item which is well lit can be equally effective. A large vase of fresh foliage and flowers will last quite a long time and looks very good.

The law requires that everything in the shop should be priced. It is a good idea to have a display board clearly listing the prices and varieties of cut flowers. Each container of flowers should also have the price as well as the flower name displayed on a pick. Customers don't like to admit that they do not know one flower from another.

The cut flower and plant displays should be checked daily for water and any wilting flowers or dead leaves removed.

Cut flowers should be displayed in colour groups. This has more selling impact and encourages the customer to buy more.

Always have made-up items of work on display

in the shop to attract impulse purchases: hand-tied arrangements of varying sizes in aqua pack, gift arrangements, planted bowls or any work which has been made for an exhibition or competition.

Any diplomas and certificates which belong to the staff should be displayed. You should be proud to show your achievements.

The shop should be kept clean and tidy, and the floor washed daily. Windows can be a problem. They should be cleaned on a regular basis and checked daily for condensation.

The entrance to the shop should be clear. It is tempting to put buckets of flowers around the entrance but it should be free for easy access and movement.

Change the displays within the shop on a regular basis so that when regular customers come in they think the products are new.

PROMOTION OF THE BUSINESS

Advertising is one of the main ways of promoting the business but be selective as it is a very costly exercise. Yellow Pages and Thompson directories are two musts as a lot of orders are taken by telephone on credit cards.

Local press and radio can perhaps be used prior to and during peak periods. Flyers in newspapers offering a discount for a limited period of time have a good impact on sales. It is a good idea to write to large companies offering good terms to gain contract work, or to offer a service for promotional work, exhibitions, etc. Displaying a piece of work at a relatively low cost with leaflets and business cards in local hotels, hairdressers and banks will also attract new custom.

Giving lectures, demonstrations and talks can generate interest and new business. You also become known for your knowledge and understanding of the industry you represent.

Discount offers to local flower clubs and churches attracts custom and encourages more people to come into the shop on a regular basis.

The atmosphere in the shop reflects your business style and there is no better advertisement or promotion than that of a smiling face, welcoming the customer, together with good presentation and professional knowledge of the product. Remember that the customer is always right and word of mouth and personal recommendation are the very best form of promotion and advertising.

All promotional material such as display boards, signs, etc. should be made professionally and be clearly printed in the business's colours. Home-made signs around the shop look very untidy. Promotional leaflets and posters displayed around the shop and particularly in the shop window should be avoided at all costs as they look untidy and messy and distract from the displays in the shop.

Appendices

SUNDRIES

Aqua-pack Method of gift packaging hand-tied bouquets or gift flowers in water, in either cellophane or a vase. Also a commercial packing method for the wholesale market whereby flowers are boxed in a small amount of water.

Auto-corso Piece of wet foam in a plastic cage with suction pads; used to attach flowers to cars or any other shiny flat surface.

Bouquet holder Plastic holder with dry or wet foam in the top used to make bouquets.

Dolly bag Small plastic pot with a frill for wedding designs.

Dry foam Dry foam which cannot be soaked.

Fix Used to secure frog or any other sundry requiring fixing. Similar to plasticine but slightly sticky.

Frog Small plastic base about the size of a 2p piece with four spikes like a pin holder; used to secure foam in a container.

Iglu Wet foam in a plastic cage in the shape of an igloo. Used for cake top arrangements, pew ends, etc.

Mini-deco Small piece of foam in a plastic cage with adhesive pad; used mostly for gift arrangements.

O-bowl Cheap plastic dish commonly used in making table arrangements or small designs.

Pick A plastic pick which is inserted into a design to hold the message and care cards.

Pot tape Sticky tape used to secure foam in containers.

Spray tray A rectangular flat plastic dish used in making funeral sprays, table arrangements, window designs.

Stay wire Wire used to strengthen material or on which material is made up for use.

Tape Plastic or crepe tape which stretches when gently pulled and sticks to itself; used to cover wires and stems.

Tubes Plastic tubes on long stems to make larger designs in pedestal work.

Wet foam Foam which is sold dry but can be soaked.

Wire netting Plain or plastic-covered netting used to make mossed designs or for covering foam.

Wires See table on page 00.

GLOSSARY OF TERMS USED BY THE FLORIST

Balance, actual and visual A design constructed so that it will literally not fall over and, by grouping and colour weighting, also looks stable.

Basing Completely covering a base of foam, moss, etc., with a carpet of flowers, foliage, etc. Used particularly in funeral work.

Binding point The point at which a bouquet, corsage or hand-tied assembly is bound, usually at the focal point, which also may be the widest point of the design.

Bonding Placing plant material close together so as to give continuous and even coverage of a surface.

Cluster A small arrangement, also called a spray, used on some funeral tributes.

Distinction The unusual use of plant material which is eye-catching.

Economy The economic use of materials to achieve maximum effect.

False stem A wire stem that has replaced the natural stem.

Feathering Wiring petals from a flower into little bundles; three or more petals are used individually or made into units.

Focal area The point to which the eye is first drawn, usually a choice flower which is the largest in the design and the point from which all the stems appear to radiate.

Formal bouquet A bouquet which is wired for support and control on false stems.

Funeral tribute Term used for any kind of funeral design.

Harmony Unity and oneness of the overall appearance of a design.

Impact In floristry terms another word for striking.

Informal bouquet Where the stems of the bouquet are wired only if necessary for support and the natural stems are tied together.

Leg mounts, single and double Wire mounts twisted around a stem base as a false leg or legs. They should be covered with tape for wedding work.

Limited flower arrangement or bouquet A design based on flowers of only one type and a limited amount of foliage.

Massing Another term for basing.

Mechanics Materials such as wire, foam, pins, etc. used in constructing a design.

Natural unit A single flower on a natural stem; also material wired together to form a small bunch.

Pipping Wiring florets individually as single flowers or to make into units.

Plant material Any materials which are natural, either fresh or dried.

Proportion Dimensions and quantities in a proper scale with each other and the surroundings.

Recession The positioning of larger plant material at a lower level in the design to give depth.

Repetition The repeated use of one type of plant material in a design; can also be referred to as grouping.

Return end The area below the focal point. A design is usually in the proportion of two-thirds to one-third, the one-third being the return end.

Spray A branch of small flowers or foliage (spray of heather); a small wired or tied arrangement used on Bibles or prayerbooks in wedding work and on some funeral tributes (also called a cluster when used thus); a type of funeral tribute.

Transition The gradual movement from larger, more developed material, well recessed in the centre of a design, to smaller buds on the outside.

Unit A single stem formed from binding several pieces of material together. There are three types: branching, ribbed and natural.

Workmanship The neatness of finish in wiring, making sure all mechanics such as pot tape or foam are concealed.

MOSSES AND THEIR USES

Remember that all moss is protected in the UK and may not be taken from its natural habitat without a licence, and one can be obtained from the Forestry Commission.

Sphagnum Moss

Sphagnum moss is used for covering wire frames in funeral work if foam is unavailable or if a shape is required which is not made in a foam base. All florists should know how to work with moss.

The moss should be fresh and showing some green. It is usually purchased in plastic sacks in which it is packed down. It should be prepared by 'teasing', which means pulling apart, and then cleaned of any debris such as cones, pieces of wood, worms, etc. It should be sprayed lightly to moisten if it is dry. If it is too wet, it is difficult to work with and the piece of work is very heavy and cumbersome. If it is too dry, it is difficult to push wires into and there is no moisture for the flower or foliage.

Mossing a Frame

- Attach 0.56 mm reel wire or string to the wire frame.
- Lay pieces of moss on the frame and bind in place. Follow the shape of the frame exactly.
- If a bump for a cluster is required, make a ball of moss and attach with the string or wire.
- Tie off the string or wire.
- Trim off any excess to give a smooth appearance.

Sphagnum moss may also be used to make artificial topiary trees or to cover baskets. It is very popular for unusual designer work based on shapes created with wire netting, which is then covered with the moss.

Reindeer or Lichen Moss

As the name suggests, this forms part of the reindeer's diet and is imported mostly from Norway. The natural colour is light grey. It is also available dyed in many colours. It is purchased dry-packed in large boxes or in its natural state (slightly spongy) in plastic bags. If it is dry-packed, it should be reconstituted in water by soaking for about a half-hour. It is then squeezed to get rid of the excess water. The bottom 'roots' should be cleaned off and only the top part used. Reindeer moss has various uses:

- To serve as a base for a funeral tribute
- To provide a different texture in continental design

- To cover mechanics, i.e. foam in flower arrangements
- To cover soil in planted designs

Bun or Sheet Moss

This moss is purchased in small boxes and harvested in the UK, mainly from the New Forest. It should be bright green and have a velvety texture and smell fresh. Imported bun moss is also available. It can be kept for some time if it is sprayed regularly and laid out so that the light can get to it. It should be kept cool. Freeze-dried bun moss is suitable for dried work and is very useful for window display. Bun moss is used for:

- Covering soil in planted bowls
- Basing on funeral tributes
- Continental flower arrangements
- Creating an unusual texture in designer work

Spanish Moss

This moss looks a bit like long, grey strands of wool. It is purchased either fresh or dried and it can be dyed. This moss may be used for:

- Large display work
- Interpretative and continental design
- Modern bridal work

WEDDING ANNIVERSARIES

All florists should be aware of the different wedding anniversaries and what they stand for. An anniversary is a very popular reason for sending flowers and sometimes it requires some imagination on the part of the florist. When taking an order for anniversary flowers find out which one it is and advise the customer accordingly, suggesting any suitable gifts as accessories.

Number	*Symbol*	*Colour*
1	Paper	Any colour
2	Cotton	White
3	Leather	Orange-brown
4	Fruit and flowers	Mixed
5	Wood	Natural colours
6	Sugar	White and pink
7	Wool	Mixed
8	Bronze	Oranges/golds
9	Copper	Oranges/golds
10	Tin	White/black/gold
11	Steel	White/black/gold
12	Silk and linen	Pastels/white
13	Lace	White
14	Ivory	Cream
15	Crystal	White
20	China	Mixed
25	Silver	White
30	Pearl	Pinks/creams
35	Coral	Peach/cream
40	Ruby	Dark red
45	Sapphire	Blues
50	Golden	Yellow/gold
55	Emerald	Greens
60	Diamond	White
70	Platinum	White

PEAK PERIODS AND SPECIAL DAYS

Day	*Date*	*Traditional colours and ideas*
St Valentine's	14 February	Red roses, carnations, single boxed roses, hearts, teddy bears. A day when flowers are sent to loved ones, anonymously by secret admirers.
St David's Day	1 March	Celebrated by the Welsh. Daffodils, leeks. Single daffodils, baskets of daffodils, continental design including leeks.
St Patrick's Day	17 March	Celebrated in Ireland. Shamrock buttonholes.
Mothering Sunday	4th Sunday in Lent	Small posies, planted bowls, hand-tied bouquets. Wide range of mixed flowers, pastel colours.
Easter Sunday	First Sunday after the first full moon after 21 March	Traditionally white or yellow flowers. Arum lilies for churches, Easter rabbits, chicks, planted bowls, spring arrangements.
Whitsun	6 weeks after Easter	Red and white flowers in churches.
St George's Day	23 April	Red rose buttonholes traditionally worn.
Father's Day	3rd Sunday in June	Gift arrangements with wine or gardening tools, golf balls, strong colours.

(*continued*)

Jewish New Year	Always in September	Bright colours, gift flowers.
Harvest Festival	Sept–early October	Autumn colours, flowers, fruit, vegetables, corn.
Halloween	31 October	Dramatic colours: red, orange, black.
Guy Fawkes	5 November	Dramatic colours: red, yellow, bright pink, blue.
Remembrance Day	Sunday nearest to 11 November	Memorial tributes, laurel wreaths/chaplets, red poppies, regimental colours.
St Andrew's Day	30 November	The thistle is traditional, also tartan ribbons.
Advent	The 4 Sundays before Christmas	Advent rings with four candles, traditional Christmas colours.
Christmas	25 December and the 2–3 week period preceding it	Red, green, gold, white, silver; other colours also requested. Door wreaths, table designs with candles. Holly, mistletoe, ivy. Cyclamen, poinsettias, azaleas, orchids. Large demand for accessories such as baubles, candles, cones, fruit, nuts.

It should be noted that weddings come at any time of the year but traditionally the peak season is from April–July/August, May and June being the most popular time. This often coincides with staff holidays so it is a good idea to have relief staff available to help cover this work.

It is very important to be aware of the traditional days around the world as these will affect the availability of flowers worldwide and will also generate business in the relay sector.

Candles

Candles can provide a decorative element within floristry whether it be for weddings, parties, promotional events, seasonal occasions or within the home.

The range and choice of candles available is enormous. Church candles are extremely popular due to their long-lasting burning time. They also create a dramatic visual effect within certain designs. The colours and shapes of candles are extensive and include metallics, textured finishes and perfumed wax. This range enables the florist to create many different effects.

Always use the best quality candles available, not only is this important from a visual aspect but also from a health and safety point of view. Cheap or inferior candles will burn away quickly and drip wax more readily. The burning time/lasting quality should always be considered in relation to the type of event for which they are required. Wholesalers have a whole range of candles in stock.

Index